THE KINTA YEARS

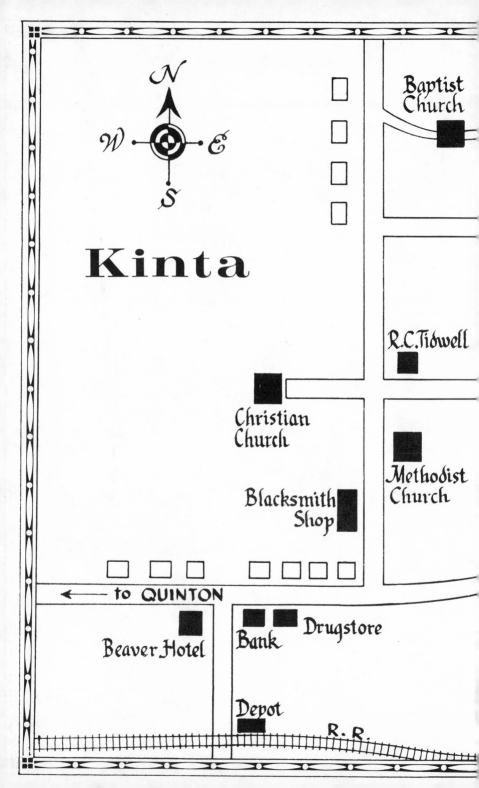

Wesley Rabon

PRAIRIE

Our House

Moore House

Dr. Johnson

Sam England

Dick Rabon Luke Allen

Tirey

Schoolhouse

Green McCurtain

TO LEQUIRE →

THE KINTA YEARS

JANICE HOLT GILES

illustrated
with photographs

HOUGHTON MIFFLIN COMPANY BOSTON

1973

To

THE HOLTS AND THE MOORES

and

THE KINTA YEARS

First Printing   w

ISBN: 0-395-14011-0
Library of Congress Catalog Card Number: 72-9016
Printed in the United States of America

*

AUTHOR'S NOTE

*

I OWE AN IMMENSE DEBT of gratitude to Corinne Moore Rabon and her husband, Otway Rabon, and to Inez Moore Von Derau, for willingness to help in reviving and reinforcing the old memories of the Kinta years. They were also of invaluable help in the history of the McCurtain family and each provided me with good pictures.

I am grateful to my aunt Florence McGraw McRaven for much of the maternal family history. Although I did a lot of research myself, the early years in Arkansas are pretty well documented in her privately printed book *Swift Current*. My grandmother McGraw's diaries were also invaluable.

For the history of the Choctaw Nation I relied heavily upon *The Rise and Fall of the Choctaw Republic* by Angie Debo. I thank her for her gracious permission to use those facts. The University of Oklahoma Press, Box 88, Norman, Oklahoma, holds the copyright on this book, and I thank them also for permission to rely upon Miss Debo's book.

Within the family, my sister, Mary Holt Sullivan, and my brother, John A. Holt, Jr., were always encouraging and helpful. The reproduction of all the old photographs was done by my brother-in-law, Kenneth Giles, and he accomplished miracles with the old, faded prints. The excellent and clear

modern pictures were made by my grandson Mike Hancock
on a trip we made together, which neither of us will ever forget because of the cold and the snow. Mike did a good job
and I am very grateful to him.

J. H. G.

CONTENTS

*

*

ILLUSTRATIONS

following page 210

THE KINTA YEARS

THE CURTAIN RISES

✳

"WHAT'S YOUR NAME?" the other child said.

"My name is Janice Holt," I said.

My remembered life begins at this moment. I had lived four years and a few months. There are some vague, unsorted earlier memories, mostly of smells, sounds, emotions, and blurred snatches of pictures — a paling fence, the white of a little boy's shirt, dust under my feet; as much feeling and smell as sight, dry autumn leaves; again as much feeling and smell as sight, a big fish, told about more than remembered. All mostly prompted by stories told by my parents of things done, said, events in which I had participated. Also prompted by photographs, especially the big fish — especially the paling fence.

But this, now, was mine. Nobody was there but the other child and me. "What's your name?" she said.

And I, myself, a person, an individual, replied and identified myself.

The first clear, unaided, unprompted memory of my life is therefore the identification of myself. Who I was. In all the world, the entire universe, the galaxy, the species, the race, there was a me — Janice Holt. There was a person, a recognizable and identifiable self.

I had a skin, white, easy to see white on my hands and feet and legs. It could bruise, be cut, be scratched, feel hot and cold, hurt and make me cry. It felt heat, now, hot sun on my head, hot wind on my face, hot earth under my feet.

I could smell. Dust whipped up by the hot wind. And a pungent, acrid odor of dogfennel weeds. I could taste — hot on my lips, and dust, and the salt of my own sweat.

I could see, with eyes which did not yet tell me the truth, if eyes ever do tell the truth. They saw all adults as very tall, and older than they really were. They saw all chairs and tables as very big, all buildings as enormous, a dog as big as a cow, a cow as big as a dragon. Everything was tall and over my head, too big. Distances were great, too far away. Only another child was the right size. I could see this other child now, about my height, looking at me with her own large, dark eyes.

I had ears and could distinguish sounds and sort them out and make sense of them. I could hear her question. I had a tongue that could tell and the word with which to tell, who I was.

I was an entity, a living human being, separate and distinct from every other human being, like but unfathomably different. I was an individual, not yet knowing of the pain or the glory of being an individual, of being supremely and uniquely me — nor did I yet know anything of the great and bleak loneliness of being an individual.

I was myself, and I so identified myself. My name is Janice Holt.

*

It was an August morning. It was hot. Sweating, searing, brain-baking, blazing, brassy hot. Any August morning in eastern Oklahoma is always hot.

My family had moved fifty miles from one little town to another little town. From Howe, Oklahoma, to Kinta, Oklahoma. From Leflore County to Haskell County. We had moved because my father was to be the new principal of the Kinta school. This was a day and time when all men teachers were called professor. My father was Professor John Holt.

He had made several trips back and forth between Howe and Kinta. On one of them he had rented a house for us. He had returned then to crate our furniture to be shipped by rail freight and to bring my mother, my sister and me to Kinta. We had arrived on the morning train, in late August, so as to be in good time for the school term which was to begin early in September.

I do not remember any of that. I have heard it told. I do not remember arriving in the town, but I know it was on the Fort Smith & Western, the short-line railroad which ran from Fort Smith, Arkansas, through Spiro, Oklahoma, Bokoshe, McCurtain, Lequire, Kinta, Quinton, Indianola, Dustin and points farther west into the coal fields where it made connection with a longer line and the state capital.

At Kinta the railroad tracks ran south of the town by some several yards. There was a small red (or was it mustard-colored?) station which was called the depot. A walk, either of concrete or boards, led up to the town. Beaver Creek ran along at the foot of a low ridge beyond the tracks, and a dusty road wound from the town across the tracks, across the creek and up the ridge.

I do not remember how we got from the railroad station to the new house, but the Beaver Hotel sent a hack to meet all trains — two in the morning, one going east and one going west, and two in the evening, one going east and one going west. I have heard it told that my father hired the hotel hack because it was so hot and my mother was not well. She was pregnant with my brother, who would be born in January.

I do not remember the drive from the station to the new house, but the hotel hack would have followed the dusty road north to the main street of the town, which differed from the road only in that it was a little wider. It, too, was a dusty road. There were no paved streets in town, nor for that matter in any other small towns. Only cities had paved streets. The main street may have been oiled to keep down the dust. If it was, I have forgotten.

At the main street the hack would have turned east, to the right, traveled the two blocks of the business section, then turned north again, left, jogged past the brand-new red brick Kinta schoolhouse with the white Corinthian columns across the front, trotted the team one more block to the house Professor John Holt had rented for his family.

I do not remember my first sight of the house he had rented for us, but because we lived in it for six years, I know it was a neat little house, a frame house painted white with red trim around the windows and doors. That it was built with two rooms across the front, and two rooms in an ell at the rear. That a porch extended across the front and that a back porch filled the corner of the ell. It was a relatively new house. I believe only one other family had occupied it before we came to live in it. It was in good condition. That is, the paper on the walls was not torn or faded. The floors did not sag, nor were they splintery. None of the window-panes were broken and the windows all worked; that is, they could be raised and lowered. I do not know who owned the house. It was ours, so long as my father paid the rent regularly the first of every month.

I do not remember arriving at the house nor what was done

immediately. Nor do I remember why or when I wandered out of the house to explore the yard. Like all children four years old, I must have been curious. Doubtless my parents' conversation did not interest me, I must have grown restless and bored. For whatever reason, permitted or stolen away, I did wander outside alone. I have no recollection of where I went or what I did or of how long it took me.

Memory begins, my life begins, in a corner of the yard, behind the house. A pen had been fenced off in one corner. I do not recall finding it, but within moments it would be forever fixed in my mind. The boards of the pen were rough-sawed, weathered, were nailed horizontally around the pen, with narrow cracks between. The pen must have been too high for me to see over and I must have been dissatisfied with what I could see between the cracks, for shortly I wedged my toes into the cracks and using them as a ladder climbed the fence to peer over the top plank. Being four years old, naturally I had to see what was in the pen, I had to examine it closely and well.

From the moment my head was high enough to see over the top board, I remember. I have forgotten nothing. I remember everything else that happened that morning as clearly as if it had happened yesterday.

It is as if the smooth, unetched, unmemoried mind of the child had been waiting for this moment for time, earth-time, living-time, to begin. As if the director of the drama that is life on this earth had been waiting in the wings for some cue, for the appropriate moment, to pull the curtains, shove the little actor onto the stage, saying, "Now!" As if the child had become ready to play its role, act out its part, say its lines. As if the smooth, memoryless chunk of gray matter under the skull, which was able only to remember long enough to obey

— come here, go there, do this, do that — suddenly began, at this moment, to do whatever it does when it etches memory forever. Electrical circuit endlessly circling the brain, or infinitely small tracings on some part of the brain, something began to work, and the small actor was able to remember the action and the scene and the lines for the rest of her life.

As my head rose above the top rail of the fence, as I steadied my hands and my feet on the rough-sawed boards and lifted my head to peer over, directly across from me another head was rising, rising, rising. First a pink hair ribbon, on the head with black, straight, long hair. Then the face. It was an unsmiling face. Rather sober, earnest, searching, a slight frown puckered between the strong eyebrows. The skin of the face was a little darker than mine. The mouth was steady and firm. The eyes were very, very large and very, very black. They met mine with absolute directness, straight and unwavering, steady, no blinking, no shifting, no embarrassment. Steady and, of course, curious.

I was to learn that this was the way she looked at the world — directly, unwaveringly, unflinchingly, asking no quarter, no favors, steadily and boldly confronting.

I was startled. She was not. My heart beat fast for a moment, then settled back into its steady pace. It was only another little girl, about my size. We stared at each other a long moment, neither of us saying a word. Then as if by mutual consent both of us climbed back down the fence and sidled around the corner of the pen for a direct confrontation.

We were like two strange dogs meeting, stopping in our paths, hackles a little raised and uncertain yet, eyes probing, noses sniffing, going through the preliminaries of getting acquainted, of making sure there was nothing unfriendly here.

She wore a pink dress of some soft cool fabric — to match her hair ribbon. I had on the green and plaid gingham which I had worn for the train. Trains were cindery and dirty in those days before double-sealed windows and air conditioning and one dressed to show the least signs of dishevelment.

Her hair hung long and loose almost to her waist. Mine would have hung as long, unloosed, but it was done up in two braids, looped and tied at the neck with ribbons. Two ribbons, one on either side of my head. The ribbons were red.

We looked each other over and then she took the initiative and said, "What's your name?"

And I found my tongue and told her.

There was a pause while she absorbed the name. "Janice" was an unusual name at that time. Then it was my turn. "What's *your* name?"

"Corinne Moore. I live over there," and she pointed across the road toward another white frame house, a larger house than ours, with a lush grassy lawn and trees and a white picket fence around it.

I absorbed the larger house and knew instantly that it was an important house in the town and that her family was an important family. This was not a reasoned thing. I simply knew it, by the size of the house, by the care it had been given. It was a home, not a rented house. People who didn't move around, as we did, had these larger homes. They stayed in one place and cared for their homes. Whatever the town, they had importance in the caste system of small towns.

I could not have known this through experience. I had probably absorbed it from overhearing my parents' conversations. However, I knew it, I did know it — that Corinne Moore lived in a home, had probably been born in it, might probably never leave it, and that she was thus a little different from me, who came from gypsies and was destined to move about forever.

"How old are you?" she asked then.

"Four years old."

"I'm five," she said, establishing immediately a superiority over me. "Have you got any brothers and sisters?"

"I've got a little sister."

"What's her name?"

"Mary Catherine Holt. We call her Mary C."

"How old is she?"

"Two years old."

"I've got a sister *and* a brother," she said.

"What are their names?"

"Inez and Green. Inez is three years old and Green is just a baby."

Corinne, Inez and Green McCurtain Moore (to give him his full name). There were strange names to me. I pondered them and knew I should never forget them.

This was as far as we could go for the moment. We turned around and peered into the pen through the cracks. There was nothing in it, save the hard-packed, sun-baked dirt floor and a few dogfennel weeds in one corner. As we turned away Corinne said, "It was a rabbit pen."

I nodded, satisfied. The mystery was solved. Whoever had lived here before us had kept rabbits. This was where they had kept them.

We had now used up the pen. By mutual but unspoken consent, we put it behind us and started around the house. The path narrowed at the end of the back porch, squeezed there between the porch and a small, windowless building.

It was built of the same rough-sawed weathered boards, but they were vertical — board and batten — and it was roofed with hand-riven shingles. We stopped and opened the door. "It's a smokehouse," Corinne said.

We did not go inside, but stood in the door and gazed. It was dark inside and dirt-floored. There was a strong smell of meat, salt, woodsmoke and ashes. Hooks were driven in the roof rafters from which to hang the meat while it was being smoked and cured. Shelves had been built around the sides to hold the cured meat — the shoulders, hams and sides of bacon. The smokehouse deserved only a few moments of our time and we wandered on.

Nearby was the well, unhoused, simply a tile casing coming up from the bowels of the earth with a wooden lid fitted into it. Two small logs had been driven into the earth with a strong two-by-four nailed across their tops. This supported a wheel through which a rope was threaded, the rope was attached to a long well bucket, later known to me as a pump because of its valve action. The bucket was lowered into the well, water pressure pushed the valve upward in the bucket and when the bucket was full it sank and by the sudden, heavy weight one knew it was time to begin hauling it up.

Beside the well was a watering trough. It was a simple affair of two wide pieces of planking nailed together and caulked to prevent leakage. It stood on sawbuck legs and leaked anyway. It was full of water, lukewarm on this hot day, and the wet inner sides of the trough were green with moss. I touched it and it was slick, a little slimy. Not a very nice feeling and I quickly wiped my hands on my skirt.

There was no green lush lawn of grass in the yard. It was bare and baked hard by the sun. A few tufts of grass grew here and there and, as in the rabbit pen, dogfennel and sticker weeds grew in the corners. There were no trees. It was evidently unprofitable for renters to seed a lawn or to plant trees. They never knew how long they were going to stay.

The yard was fenced around with the same rough-sawed, weathered boards as the rabbit pen, laid horizontally, with wide cracks between. Some child had pushed a wide plank in the crack between two boards and made a seesaw. Corinne Moore and I tried the seesaw and soon had used that up, too. One just goes up and down, up and down, and about ten minutes is the attention span of four- and five-year-olds for going up and down.

Behind the yard, and also fenced, was a barn lot, a barn, a corncrib, a chicken house and the outside toilet which we always called the "closet." This was a day when few houses had clothes closets. Clothing was kept in wardrobes which were tall, impressively carved pieces of furniture made especially for hanging clothing in. If a family had no wardrobes, clothing was simply hung behind curtains on nails on the walls.

We explored the barn, a dim, roomy place full of old straw and hay, full of bits and pieces of this and that, parts of an old harness, leather straps, pieces of rusty metal, a broken plow, odd pieces of things and stuff, some old bottles and fruit jars, a stone crock, boards and nails and an old saw, even a broken hammer head. Laid over it all was the smell of cows and horses, that strong odor of manure and ammonia and leather and oil and sweat, which is repulsive to some people, but which is the life-smell, the earth-smell, to others and is good and right and satisfying. A barn was obviously a heavenly place. There was no end to the pleasures and opportunities it offered.

"Do you have a cow?" Corinne asked.

"No, but we're going to have one," I said, "and a horse and chickens, too."

Corinne nodded. In those days, in that kind of town, in all small American towns, a cow, a horse or a team of horses or mules, chickens, were necessities of life. Everybody had them. Presumably we had had them earlier but they had been sold, or disposed of, rather than move them fifty miles. There was no other way to have eggs and milk and butter, which were necessary to life. Such things were not sold in stores, could not be bought, unless one had an accommodating neighbor and it was best to depend on nobody else. Best to have one's own cow and chickens. And a horse, or team, provided the only means of transportation. One took the train for a long journey, but locally one rode a horse, or rode in a buggy or wagon. Henry Ford's Model T had not yet reached Kinta, or any other towns in such rural areas.

When the two little girls came out of the barn, my father was at the well drawing a bucket of water. "Is that your papa?" Corinne asked.

"No," I said, "that's my daddy. My papa lives in Altus, Arkansas."

Confusing? Perhaps. To Corinne, papa was her father. To me, daddy was my father. Papa was my mother's father, my grandfather. It needed some explaining and got it. Corinne understood finally. "He," she said, watching my father go back in the house, "is the new professor."

Everything explored, everything named to me, its uses identified, there was nothing left to do but wander toward the house, linger about the back porch, look at its floor, explore a crack or two, then wander inside.

The house was bare and strange. Our furniture had arrived

before us but was still in crates, now rapidly being pried free. My father was wielding a crowbar deftly. The two younger sisters, Inez and Mary C., were playing in a corner of what would be the dining room. They were occupied with nails and loose boards from the crates. Corinne's baby brother was tied in a chair, contented to watch the confusion all around him with big, round, black eyes.

Corinne's mother and my mother were in the kitchen, unpacking china from barrels of straw, setting it on shelves. My father had already put up the big black kitchen range and on it sat two warm fruit pies Lena McCurtain Moore had brought over to welcome her new neighbor. She and my mother, Lucy McGraw Holt, were of about the same height and slimness. They looked tall to me, but neither was above five feet four. They looked old to me, but Lucy McGraw Holt was twenty-six years old and Lena Moore was twenty-seven.

They were fair and dark. My mother had a thin white skin, light brown hair touched with red, and very blue eyes. Lena Moore was part Choctaw. Her skin was olive, her eyes were dark and her hair was black. Both women wore their hair long, piled in a loose knot on top their heads. Their dresses swept the floor and both wore aprons. Mrs. Moore unpacked the barrels, handing the china to my mother who put it on the shelves above a kitchen table. They talked together as they worked and laughed occasionally. Probably Lena Moore had quickly observed my mother's pregnant condition and had taken upon herself the bending and stooping of unpacking.

Corinne and I wandered through the house, she telling me about the rooms. This is the parlor. This is the bedroom. This is the dining room and the kitchen spoke for itself.

Our bedroom would hold two double beds, one for our parents and one for Mary C. and me. The rooms were fairly large, much larger than rooms in the average home today. Our parlor, or sitting room as my mother sensibly called it, would be useful only in the summer for there was no way to heat it. It had no flue or fireplace.

In the winter the dining room became our all-purpose room, the only room besides the kitchen that was heated in the long, cold winters. A big coal-burning stove stood in one corner, with isinglass doors through which one could see the fire. This stove did not come with the house. It was ours, but even in August my father had already put it where it belonged. Our heating stove was never taken down in the summers. It stood cold but still a friendly companion in the corner of the dining room the year round.

In our wandering through the house I spied the telephone on the dining-room wall. It was not yet connected, but it would be. I *think* our number was 26.

The mothers called us to the kitchen. They had cut the pies and we gathered about the long kitchen table. The round oak dining table, taken apart to be crated and shipped, had not yet been put together. Lena Moore must have brought milk, also, because in my memory I see us clustered about the table, eating warm fruit pies and drinking cold milk. The pies were either apple or peach. There my memory fails me, and there the memory ends. One long scene from a play begun, or one long scene from a movie being filmed, re-run through my memory.

It was the beginning, the opening scene. It might have begun earlier, in Howe, in that town of coal mines. But it did not. It might have begun in Altus, in the home of my McGraw grandparents, but it did not. It might have begun in Charleston, in the home of my Holt grandparents, but it did not. The drama, myself an actor in it, began in Kinta, Oklahoma.

It began in auspicious happiness, in the aura of friendship and neighborly welcome, neighborly helpfulness thrown around it, myself knowing and knowing myself to be happy, to be excited and gay, myself knowing for the first time the bubble in the throat which meant happiness. Myself, sentient, responsive, remembering. Myself unknowing the pain, the joy, the grief, the gladness, the unutterable loneliness, the drabness, the dullness, the sometimes piercing happiness, the energy and drive and health and ambitions, the living, daily, repetitively, of life and whatever it brought. Myself unknowing that by and large the bubble in the throat was to prevail, that when Janice Holt was conceived, Fate was kind to her, unbelievably kind when one thinks not only of Professor John Holt and Lucy McGraw Holt, but of all the parents behind parents behind parents and all the genes of all the generations possible to draw on for those peculiar genes which made Janice Holt. Which gave her good health, vitality, humor, resiliency, a capacity for joy, a reasonably good mind, the ability to learn and a forgiving disposition.

It began in Kinta, in happiness and friendliness, it has continued mostly in happiness and friendliness, and it will end in some last gleam of mind, hopefully in clarity of mind, in a rattle of breath and slowing heartbeat when the director of the drama once again says, "Now," and the curtain goes down.

2

THE DRAMA BEGINS

*

THE DRAMA behind Janice Holt had been going on in America for generations and all the genes of those generations were mixed in her. Who were they, those people who bequeathed life, and all her weaknesses, abilities, strengths, capacities and incapacities to this small child?

On the maternal side the family line is fairly well documented, mostly because my mother's eldest sister, Florence McGraw McRaven, wanted to become a member of the Daughters of the American Revolution. This organization requires such unimpeachable documentation on one's ancestry that it would be difficult to doubt my aunt's research on the family.

This maternal branch of the family tree begins with an Englishman named Saxon who came to South Carolina in the latter part of the seventeenth century. He settled in the Piedmont country there and became a rather prosperous cotton and tobacco planter.

By the middle of the eighteenth century a cluster of families had settled land in this northwestern part of South Carolina and although there was no name to the community, Greenville County was formed eventually and in 1777 the county town was given the name of Pleasantville. It was changed to Greenville in 1797.

The children of these families married among their neighbors for the most part. One of the families who lived adjacent to the Saxons was that of John Rodgers. Another family was that of William P. Ware.

There were several generations of Saxon sons, but it is not until a daughter, Sarah, married a son of John Rodgers, that we begin to near the immediate family line. The eldest son of John and Sarah Saxon Rodgers was given the imposing name of James Saxon Rodgers. He was to become the great-great-grandfather of this small child named Janice Holt.

Another near neighbor was William P. Ware, who had served with General George Washington at Valley Forge that hard winter of 1777–78. In the neighborhood he was known thereafter by his military title, Colonel Ware. He had a very large family and among his younger daughters was a beautiful girl named Emily. At a very young age James Saxon Rodgers and Emily Ware were married. He was not yet twenty-one and she was barely seventeen.

James Saxon Rodgers must have been a true South Carolina firebrand, for he had no more than married his beautiful Emily Ware than he left her to join General Andrew Jackson's Brigade and fight in the War of 1812, from which he emerged a colonel. He was a good planter and a good businessman and he prospered. The plantation was vast and he owned around one hundred slaves. The home was large and gracious.

Precisely when James Saxon Rodgers acquired land in northern Mississippi is not known, but it was after the removal of the Choctaws. A good many South Carolina planters invested in Mississippi land between 1840 and the Civil War. The land James Saxon Rodgers bought lay near the small community of Byhalia, in Marshall County, some twenty-five or thirty miles southeast of Memphis, Tennessee. Marshall

County adjoined Lafayette County whose county seat was Oxford, which William Faulkner was later to make famous.

Colonel Rodgers and his wife, Emily Ware Rodgers, had twelve children. One of the eldest, born in 1828, was named for her mother, Emily.

When she was eighteen years old there came courting her a young twenty-two-year-old man by the name of Josephus Cook Babb. Family tradition has it that he was brilliant, dashing and handsome, that he had a classical education and that he taught a small private school in Greenville.

Josephus Cook Babb and Emily Rodgers were married, in her home, on May 28, 1846. Shortly thereafter the decision was made by Colonel James Saxon Rodgers to remove to his land in Mississippi. It was also decided that the young Babbs should move there with them. By 1850 the Rodgerses and the young Babbs were living near Byhalia.

J. C. Babb and his wife had six children, five daughters and one son. The second eldest daughter, born in 1854, was Catherine Babb. She was my grandmother.

After she was herself a grandmother, Catherine sometimes told her grandchildren about the old days in Mississippi before the war and how gracious the life was then. She told about how cool and big and comfortable the homes were and how there were servants for every chore. A Southern woman's life was to manage her big household, of family, slaves, visitors, but she never had to lift a finger to do any of the actual work herself. She gave the orders, doled out the daily rations, assigned tasks, dosed the sick and was the comfort and haven of her children without ever having the precise care of them.

Catherine held no brief for slavery, but she staunchly insisted that the slaves belonging to her grandfather and to her own parents were well treated, they were catered to, they were spoiled, pampered and petted and were, actually, the masters of the situation. As a cotton planter, with a large property, James Saxon Rodgers was dependent on his slaves for his prosperity. He was dependent on their work, on their whims, on their health and on their well-being. His slaves were not overworked, they were well fed, their health was watched, and they were adequately clothed and housed. Nor did he hold with selling them. My grandmother did not remember a slave ever being sold. He also allowed them to marry as they pleased and on several occasions bought a Negro girl for one of the hands who had taken a fancy to her and wanted to marry her.

Grandmother used to tell about Christmas in those days — how on Christmas morning the slaves all lined up and appeared at the back door of the big house, bowing and scraping. "Chris'mus Gif'!" each chanted, a big grin stretching from ear to ear as his turn came to receive his Christmas gift. It was usually a new shirt, or dress if it was a woman, some extra provisions, and always some whisky for making the traditional Christmas eggnog.

Christmas lasted as long as the Yule log burned, which meant there was no work. To make certain the log would not burn away too fast, the Negroes cut as big a log as would fit in the fireplace of the big house and they cut it from a big green tree. Then for several weeks it was soaked in water. On Christmas Eve it was taken out of its water bath and hauled to the big house, laid as a backlog in the huge master fireplace, and the Christmas fire was built in front of it. Sometimes a Yule log did not fall into ashes for two weeks. Colonel Rodgers abided by the custom and no Negro worked until the big log was nothing but a pile of cold gray ashes.

Grandmother told us about all the visiting that went on back and forth between the members of the family. They thought nothing of spending two or three days on a visit and they were forever turning up at each other's homes for dinner, which was eaten at two o'clock in the afternoon. They also did an immense amount of calling on their neighbors. And the parties! She told us about her mother's ballgowns, satin, silk, brocade, all made with voluminous skirts which went over the enormous hoops women wore in that day, and her mother's beautiful, delicate little satin slippers for dancing. There must have been a party or ball every week.

I never tired of hearing these stories. My grandmother's mother sounded better than Cinderella to me, for Cinderella's ball lasted only one evening and ended at midnight. My great-grandmother's balls went on and on forever. They didn't. They ended with the war, but I refused to think of the war and the end.

"The summer our kinfolks came from South Carolina and visited all summer with us," Grandmother said, "there was a ball nearly every night. People outdid themselves entertaining for our kinfolks. Oh, my mother's gowns were so beautiful. There was a gray satin with little jet beads on the yoke. There was a heavy white brocade with seed pearls all around the bodice. There was a heavenly blue one, clouds and clouds of gossamer silk with panniers of velvet set in front and back. She was so pretty when she was dressed for a party. And she always came for us to see her after she had dressed. She was a beautiful dancer and we did not doubt that she was always the belle of the ball. She was little and she was slim and graceful, very light on her feet. That she was also a married woman and a mother we ignored. To us she was a spirit and a flame and the most beautiful woman in the world."

For years the image of this little, slender, graceful great-grandmother of mine was as clear and defined for me as if

I had seen her photograph. When I finally did see a photograph of her it made me feel ill. It was taken just a couple of years before she died, but she was only fifty-two. She had on a widow's black bonnet, a shapeless black dress, and she looked as shriveled and shrunken and as withered as a dried apple. I comforted myself with the thought, "Well, she was sick and she was old." Because at sixteen, fifty-two did seem incredibly old. But I had no more daydreams about a little, slender, graceful great-grandmother.

Grandmother told us about her father's gardens. They were vegetable gardens, but they were arranged in squares with graveled walks between the squares bordered with flowers. All the old-fashioned annuals were planted each year, as well as peas, beans, tomatoes, squash, beets, cucumbers, onions and potatoes. The Negroes raked the walks every day as well as keeping the rows of vegetables free of weeds. Grandmother remembered the children were allowed to walk through the gardens, but were never allowed to play in them for fear of disturbing the raked gravel walks. They were allowed to cut flowers for the house and occasionally to gather the vegetables. But his gardens were an enormous pride to Josephus Babb and he oversaw the planting and tending of every seed whether flower or vegetable.

Grandmother told us about how brilliant her father's mind was. How he was bookish and often could be found reading when he should have been working. She acquired her love of Charles Dickens from her father, who named a daughter Lucie Manette for a Dickens character. Grandmother later had a full set of Dickens in her own home. She was constantly quoting him and constantly trying to persuade us to read him. I began with *David Copperfield* and loved it, then went on to *Bleak House* and that was enough of Dickens for me until I discovered *The Pickwick Papers* long after I was grown.

Young Babb farmed his land, but he must have been an inept planter, and then his holdings were small compared to the really big plantations. He did land surveying and taught a school in Byhalia to help eke out a living. The marriage was not overly happy. Young Babb had a fondness for drink, which his wife objected to strenuously and apparently nagged him about. In a day when all men drank pretty heavily, I should say that in all probability J. C. Babb drank to excess and could not carry his liquor like a gentleman.

Young Babb kept a diary in the year 1857. Over and over he chides himself for this weakness of over-drinking. But on May 28, 1857, there is a revealing statement. "Eleven years ago this night I was married. *Alas!*"

The four daughters and one son were born to Josephus and Emily Rodgers Babb at regular intervals of about two years, from 1852 to 1860. There is an interval of six years before the youngest child, another daughter, was born in 1866. J. C. Babb was serving with the Confederate army during four of those years.

In 1861 the old South Carolina firebrand, James Saxon Rodgers, now seventy-one years old, had mustered all his sons, brothers, sons-in-law and neighbors to form what passed for his own company. He led them personally to Byhalia to offer their services and most of them did serve together in the cavalry, although a few were dispersed into the Rifles, what was then the infantry of the Confederate army. Some of the cavalrymen were finally incorporated into General Nathan Bedford Forrest's brigade.

The years the men were away fighting were very lean years for James Saxon Rodgers' family and the families of all the men who were serving what to them was *their* country, their country's cause and flag. The Rodgers, Saxon and Babb lands were fought over many times.

The Yankee soldiers would swarm all over the place, take all the food from the smokehouse and the cellar, shoot the chickens and the calves and the hogs and leave with them across their saddles. The families soon learned that at the first grapevine message "The Yanks are coming!" they must dig holes and bury both food and valuables, and camouflage the spots with piles of brush. The mules and one cow, which eventually were all the Rodgerses had left, would be tied in a thicket far away from the house.

During the conflict the slaves slowly disappeared, stealing away, as dark as the night, in the darkness of night. They believed implicitly that the Yankees who had set them free would take care of them. The time came when only a few faithful house servants were left. The beautiful Rodgers house was burned, although the Babb house, in the village of Byhalia itself, was not. The time also came when no household had salt or coffee. They dug up the earthen floors of the smokehouses, where the salt had dropped from the meat hung to cure in hickory smoke, and they extracted the salt from the dirt by boiling it down.

For coffee they parched dried okra seeds, put them through the coffee grinder and had a dark beverage that looked, but did not taste, like coffee. Sugar became a thing forgotten. Molasses took its place. It was a nightmare time of want and privation and the slow poison of defeat, which Catherine Babb never forgot.

When I read William Faulkner's book *The Unvanquished*, I understood better what my own great-grandmother had gone through, for after James Saxon Rodgers' home was burned my great-grandmother had to live, as did Faulkner's staunch women, in the slave quarters.

In time my grandmother could talk about it all without bitterness, but it did something to her deep in her soul. The fear of privation and want never left her. Money and provisions were always important to her. Though she yearned to live graciously, and in time did live graciously again, she was always very thrifty, even stingy, with money. She kept a full and accurate account of every penny she earned, every penny her husband gave her, and she also kept an account of how every penny was spent and moaned when prices seemed high to her.

J. C. Babb came home from the war and resumed his work of farming a little, land surveying and teaching. As has been said, he fathered one more daughter, then he died in November of 1866 at the age of forty-two. He was never well after the war, having been wounded several times. One of the wounds, a chest wound, had been nearly fatal. It was probably this weakness in his chest that caused him to die so young of pneumonia.

He had personally conducted the education of his elder daughters until he went off to the war. After his death Catherine Babb was sent to the Byhalia Female Institute by the members of her father's Masonic Lodge. Like her father she had an excellent mind and she cherished this opportunity for more formal education and made a splendid record.

Only one thing embarrassed Catherine Babb during her school years at Byhalia Female Institute. Her school dresses were made of her mother's old silk and brocade ballgowns. Catherine was ashamed to wear them among the other girls, whose fathers, having taken the oath of loyalty, could now afford new calico dresses. Catherine's mother, a widow, could not afford new calico.

*

While Catherine Babb was growing up in Byhalia, a young man four years older was also growing up not far away. His name was Daniel Murdock McGraw.

His grandparents had emigrated from Ireland to the United States in the early part of the nineteenth century and settled in Pennsylvania. There a son named William Pinkney Mc-Graw was born in 1822.

Probably because an older sister married a man who took her to northern Mississippi to live in Tate County, near the village of Coldwater, William Pinkney McGraw moved to Mississippi, where he met a young widow, Elizabeth Woolverton Hanks, who had lived as a child on the road the Choctaws took across northern Mississippi when they went to their new homeland in the west.

Elizabeth Woolverton Hanks was four years older than William Pinkney McGraw, having been born in 1818. Nothing is known of her antecedents. She married a young man named Hanks when she was fourteen years old, and by him had two sons, Joshua in 1834 and Julius in 1836. Her husband died when Julius was still a baby. She was a tiny woman, red-haired, less than five feet tall and never weighed more than eighty-five pounds in her life. But she was healthy and stout-hearted. She asked no favors and worked her small farm and took care of her two young sons.

On December 10, 1840, she married William Pinkney Mc-Graw. She was twenty-two and he was eighteen.

William Pinkney McGraw left his wife and growing family to take part in the Mexican War of 1846. He served in the field artillery branch of the army and was involved in the Battle of Chapultepec, where he loaded the guns of a battery commanded by a young lieutenant who was later to become one of the most famous men of his time. His name was Lieutenant Thomas F. Jackson. In 1861, at the first battle of Bull Run, he earned the name by which he became known forever after, Stonewall Jackson.

Unscratched, William P. McGraw returned to his farm to continue his legitimate business of growing cotton and corn and fathering children.

He had seven children of his own, six daughters and one son. With Joshua and Julius Hanks, there were nine children in the family. Daniel Murdock McGraw was born on January 22, 1850, the middle child of the McGraw seven.

William Pinkney McGraw was a large man with a positive, dominating manner. He did not, however, dominate Elizabeth McGraw. She was not red-haired for nothing. Quick-tempered, she held her own with her husband.

She must have had extraordinarily good health and energy. With the help of her daughters she spun the thread from wool and cotton raised on the farm, wove the cloth on a hand loom, and sewed by hand most of the clothing worn by the family. She spun and wove bed linen and coverlets and blankets. She pieced quilts out of leftovers and carded the cotton batts with which to pad them, then quilted them. She spun the yarn and knitted the socks and stockings for her family. She did all her own housework and cooking and did the family wash with soap she herself made. The McGraws were not in the same category as the Rodgerses and Babbs. They had no slaves.

Elizabeth McGraw found time to attend church and to visit her neighbors. There was usually a gentle horse for her to ride. When her husband was at the house she did not bother to lead the horse to the mounting block. Her husband picked her up like a child and set her in her sidesaddle.

She knitted constantly. Family tradition has it that if she visited a neighbor or friend and walked, she carried her ball of yarn in her apron pocket and knitted as she walked, knitted all during the visit, knitted as she walked home.

William Pinkney McGraw liked good whisky and loved fine horses. Once when he was slightly the worse for wear, he had his young son, Daniel, riding to show off his horses to some friends who were visiting. Obediently young Daniel put the horses through their gaits, took the fences and ditches, risking breaking his own young neck. Elizabeth McGraw watched from the porch where she sat knitting. Finally when Daniel dismounted while another horse was saddled she called to him to come to the porch. She said, then, "Dan, when you start riding again you *keep going* and don't you come back here until your Pa's sober."

Young Dan obeyed his mother and did not return until late that night. His father was in bed. Nothing was said about it the following morning when he awoke, sober.

In 1861 young Daniel McGraw, aged eleven years, had to become the man of the family. His father and his two half-brothers went to war. William Pinkney McGraw served all four years of the Civil War with Company E, 3rd Mississippi Cavalry, in the Confederate army.

Joshua Hanks did not return from the war. He died of a fever while in service.

In 1865, feeling desperate over the plight of the Confederacy, Daniel McGraw ran away to Byhalia and enlisted in the army. He was fifteen years old. His mother, however, had the enlistment annulled and he returned home, a somewhat chastened young rebel.

Unlike the Babbs' and Rodgerses', over in the next county, the McGraw farm was not a vast cotton plantation. It was an ordinary small family holding of some 150 acres, much of it in woods and timber. When William Pinkney McGraw was at home the farm yielded a comfortable living, but that was all. With him off to the wars, and with only Daniel and what day help she could occasionally hire, Elizabeth McGraw was hard put to hold the place together. She did much of the rough work herself.

It was ravaged by the Yankee soldiers time and again, as the Babb and Rodgers places were, and Elizabeth learned to be as clever at hiding her food stores, livestock, family treasures, as did the women of the Babb and Rodgers families.

Once, with not enough time to hide it in a better place, she hid the family silver on a ledge in the well and suffered agonies of anxiety when the Yankee soldiers riding into the yard proved friendly and only wanted to water their horses and themselves. If the lowered bucket, which was lowered many times, had brushed against the wooden chest it would have sent the chest to the bottom of the well and the clatter and clamor would certainly have made the soldiers alert. They would have fished the chest out and perhaps been tempted to take the silver and to loot the rest of the place. She was lucky that day. The soldiers watered their horses, drank deeply themselves, looked the barn lot over for a stray chicken or two (the family had put them in coops which always stood ready in a plum thicket) and rode off without burning or looting.

The worst time for all Mississippians came after the Battle

of Shiloh when the entire state was invaded by Grant's army as he prepared for the siege of Vicksburg. The men literally lived off the land and while the ravaging was not constant it was frequent and, like the Babb and Rodgers families, Elizabeth McGraw and her young son and her daughters lived in daily anxiety and in daily determination not to be caught unawares and left with nothing but the ashes of a home and the ravaged land.

So well did Elizabeth McGraw manage that when William P. McGraw returned from the war he found two mules, a cow, a flock of chickens, his house in good order and a crop of corn which young Daniel and his mother and older sisters had put in. The corn was growing and thriving.

The little eighty-five-pound woman was never daunted by adversity. Instead she seemed to thrive on it. Difficulties were only something to be overcome. Threats were to be met by cunning. Lack of the usual foods only turned her mind to substitutes. And she somehow managed not only to continue to raise her foodstuffs but to keep them once they were raised.

It may be because she was so tiny that the men of the Northern armies usually passed her by with only minor thievery. Or it may be that she learned to hold her tongue when dealing with these men, did not give way to the contempt or pain or grief she felt. She was so clever that it is not beyond imagination that she learned to bargain with them — they might have the meal that was on the table, or she might have been willing to gather a meal and cook it for them, in return for her garden's being left unspoiled.

However she managed, she did manage and her husband came home at the end of four years to a home still standing, to a family still fed and clothed, to a fenceless farm but one still producing.

AND CONTINUES

✳

DANIEL MURDOCK MCGRAW and Catherine Babb grew up within a few miles of each other but did not meet until the summer of 1871, when they met at a party given at the home of mutual friends. Catherine Babb was sixteen and Dan McGraw was twenty-one. They were smitten at first sight, the courtship flourished and they were married on his twenty-second birthday, January 22, 1872. Catherine had become seventeen on September 16, the fall before.

They were married in the parlor of Catherine's home in Byhalia, but for the first six months of their married life they lived with Daniel's parents, while Dan set to work to make a crop on some rented land and Catherine taught the district school.

Dan and Catherine tried hard during those difficult days of the Reconstruction period. But the babies came fast — by the time they had been married five years, they had three children, Percy Pinkney, Frederick Josephus and Florence Emily. And the times were just too hard. When they finally got down to corn bread and blackstrap molasses for supper one night, Dan felt desperate.

He had heard of homestead lands in western Arkansas. He thought about it a long time and finally came to the conclu-

sion that he would take up some land there and see what he
could do.

His father thought he was out of his mind. "Away over
there in Arkansas?" he said. "Why there's nothing over there
but wild animals and cutthroats. Get in the swamps and
you'll die of malaria. Get in the mountains and you'll starve
to death."

But Dan persisted in his crazy idea. "A man will be free
of the North there," he said, "and we're going to starve here
for sure, for I can't swallow any more of these humiliations."

Early in 1878 he went to Memphis, crossed the Mississippi
on a ferry and then took the train for Ozark, Arkansas. Ozark
was a pretty little town in the foothills of the Ozark Mountains. Dan McGraw fell in love with what he found there,
and he never returned to Mississippi to live.

Ozark was about forty miles northeast of Fort Smith, Arkansas, a small town even in those days. It fronted on the
Arkansas River; and the Boston Mountains, the Arkansas
Ozarks, were at its back. Dan went up north of Ozark into
the homestead lands, which were in the foothills of the mountains, near the small community of Cass. Here he carefully
looked over the land and filed a homestead claim on a small
parcel. Then he sent for Catherine, who made the long journey across Arkansas by a cindery, bucking, halting train, with
three small children.

In the meantime Dan had built a one-room log cabin. It
had one window, covered with deerhide, and a door, also covered with deerhide, and Catherine cooked on the fire in the
fireplace. When Catherine first arrived the cabin still had
a dirt floor but shortly Dan had a puncheon floor laid.

Dan cleared and improved his homestead according to the
legal requirements. He had a fine garden that summer and

a good crop of corn. The family ate well of green beans, squash, cabbage and corn and Dan also provided venison and fish in plenteous supply. The deer were so plentiful that he rarely had to go farther than his own barn lot to find one. A mountain stream flowed directly back of the cabin and the little boys caught fish almost every day.

Once he had his own work caught up, Dan hired out as a farm laborer. There *did* have to be some cash. He worked ten hours every day, hoeing corn and chopping cotton, for fifty cents day, walking four miles to work and four miles home again at the end of the day.

Catherine, although she was now pregnant with her fourth child, took pupils to teach in her home. She had ten pupils, children of neighbors, and she charged one dollar per month for instructing them.

Florence remembers that Ozark Mountain cabin as being a cozy, comfortable, though crowded little home. The furnishings were almost all homemade. She slept in a trundle bed which Dan McGraw made and which rolled under a big bed in the daytime.

In time Dan built a lean-to kitchen on the back of the cabin, of rough, hand-sawed, unplaned lumber. It never had any floor except the hard-packed earth. But Catherine knew how to keep it wet down and tamped so that eventually it became as hard as cement and as easy to keep dust-free.

Small wild animals invaded this kitchen. One night Dan heard noises and found a possum trying to get into the food cupboard. Excited, he grabbed the first weapon he could lay his hands on to kill the varmit. It was Catherine's only iron skillet. He fetched the animal such a lick that he broke the handle off the skillet. But possum was good eating and he made a fine meal at dinner the next day.

Early one morning in August, the fourth child was born. She was named Mary Lenore, but was destined to be called Mamie all her life.

Florence (whom we called Aunt Sister) remembers they heard a panther screaming during the night before Mamie was born, sounding for all the world like a woman in agony. She never forgot the anguished sound of a panther's cry. Wolves were also frequent visitors around the cabin and on cold winter nights set up a regular chorus of howls. But inside the cabin nobody was really afraid. Papa and Mama were there, the fire was bright and warm, there were brothers and the baby sister to play with, to sleep with, to feel near to.

And Mama's voice, singing, could be heard all day and as she rocked the baby to sleep at night. Catherine McGraw sang as she worked, perhaps not even conscious that she was singing. It was as natural for her to sing as it was for her to breathe. She sang as she cooked, as she washed the dishes, as she did the laundry, the ironing, and my grandfather vowed that she sang to ease the pains during childbirth. I believe it. For just as her hands were rarely idle, her voice was rarely silent. She had to be very ill, or very sad and depressed before she stopped singing. It is a memory I have of her, too. She sang mostly hymns. She knew all the stanzas of every song she sang, and she frequently repeated them several times before going on to another song. She had no patience with the usual church habit of skipping the third stanza. "It was written, wasn't it?" she would say, "so it was written to be sung. If we don't have time to sing all four, or five, or six stanzas of a song, then we'd better find the time."

Aunt Sister remembers the first Christmas in the Ozark Mountain cabin. She remembers the excitement of waking, of wondering if Santa Claus had actually found their house in the middle of all the mountains, and so small a house, at that, compared to the mountains. She remembers tumbling out of bed before Papa got the fire in the fireplace going well, of shivering with both cold and excitement as she found her stocking. And what heavenly joy to find in it, not a new rag doll, such as Catherine made for her and made beautifully, but a real doll with a china head. True, the eyes were a painted blue, the lovely yellow hair was painted on, but her body was a fine white leather stuffed with sawdust and her rosy cheeks and painted hair and eyes were flawlessly beautiful to Florence.

I know how she felt, because I found a china-headed doll in my stocking our first Christmas in Kinta. She, too, had a fine white kid body, yellow painted hair, blue painted eyes and rosy cheeks. I named her Gretchen (Mama must have suggested the name for I would never have thought of it) and she was my dear friend and companion all during the earliest years of my childhood.

Gretchen lasted well into my teens, her yellow hair just as bright as if she were new, her eyes just as blue, her cheeks just as pink, in spite of having her face washed thousands of times. I'm not sure what finally happened to her, but I *think* I gave her to the small daughter of a neighbor after we moved to Fort Smith.

4

EARLY ARKANSAS DAYS

*

DAN AND CATHERINE McGRAW lived on their homestead three years. Then a neighbor and friend was elected sheriff of Franklin County and he asked Dan McGraw to be his deputy. So the homestead was closed and allowed to lapse. The young McGraws, with their four children, moved to Ozark in 1882.

Florence, or Sister, was old enough to remember the move, all the McGraw possessions piled in one wagon, the children and Catherine on top. Florence also noticed that the road was very rough and that on the roughest places her mother got out of the wagon and walked. She did not know why, but Catherine, at twenty-six, was pregnant with her fifth child and the time was near for the birth.

This fifth child was born on October 6, 1882, only a month or two after Dan and Catherine moved to Ozark. She was named Lucy Elizabeth, and she was to become my mother. Until she ran out of them Catherine used a family name for at least one of the names of each of her children. There was the Pinkney for Dan's father in the eldest son's name. There was Josephus for her own father in the second son's name. There was her sister Emily's name in the eldest daughter's name. Mary Leonore, called Mamie, had the Mary for one of

Dan's sisters. And Lucy bore the name of Catherine's sister, Lucy, as well as Dan's mother, Elizabeth.

In June of 1883, Catherine McGraw was called home to Byhalia. Her mother was dying. She took the three daughters with her but left the sons at home with Dan. Her mother died shortly after Catherine arrived in Byhalia.

In those days grief was not silent, contained and controlled. As the minister preached the funeral sermon he spoke of how much a mother unselfishly did for her children and how little children did for a mother in return. "Suddenly," he said, "it is too late. When this service is over you will go home and she will not be there. You will listen for her voice but her voice is forever stilled." He continued in this vein, piling guilt after guilt onto the shoulders of the bereaved children until all at once a daughter, Lucy, screamed in her anguish. Aunt Sister still remembers that piercing scream and her Aunt Lucy's fainting fit, how frightened she suddenly was and how sorry she felt for Aunt Lucy.

Catherine visited her married sisters, her Rodgers aunts and uncles and cousins extensively. A visit so far from home, and so expensive for the young McGraws, had to be made the most of. Nothing less than a month could possibly have been considered a visit.

In the fall of 1884, Catherine was expecting her sixth child. Grover Cleveland was closing his campaign for the Presidency and Catherine's oldest son, Percy, known as Brother, was very excited about the campaign and much impressed with the Democratic candidate. Grover Cleveland was the first Democratic candidate since Buchanan's administration to have even a chance to be elected. Needless to say, Dan McGraw and his entire family were ardent Democrats. In those days the South was solidly Democratic.

At twelve, Brother was already working and earning. He had gotten himself a job after school and on Saturdays, as printer's devil on the weekly paper, the *Ozark Democrat*. As a wild partisan of Grover Cleveland, Brother pled that the new baby, if a boy, should be named for Grover Cleveland — if Cleveland were elected.

Humoring her eldest son, and thinking Cleveland didn't have much of a chance, Catherine agreed to wait until after the election to name the baby, which was a boy born on October 1. She kept her promise, but hedged just a little bit on it. Cleveland was elected when the baby was slightly more than a month old. Catherine felt it was a little silly to name a baby after a President, so she persuaded Brother to be satisfied with only the President's first name, Grover.

He was five days short of being two years younger than Lucy. The two became as inseparable as if they had been twins and in time Lucy and Grover became known in the family as the two little imps of Satan. When there was mischief they were usually at the bottom of it. When there was rebellion, they were the leaders. When there was vandalism, impudence, downright disobedience, sauciness, arguments, Lucy and Grover got the blame. Sometimes it was justified. Most times perhaps. But they had such a bad name for being behind most of the trouble that they got much blame that belonged elsewhere and they probably got some undeserved punishment.

Lucy became as much boy as Grover. She could climb any kind of tree, ride any horse she could clamber up on, shoot a rifle better than any of her brothers, swim, row a boat, steal watermelons, torment a cat, jump and run as well as any boy.

In turn, Grover picked up some feminine traits from Lucy. Much to Dan McGraw's disgust, Grover loved dolls so much that, a big boy at four, he cried for one of his own. Catherine finally bought him one, over Dan's objections. "To think," Dan said, "I'd ever see the day a son of mine would want to play with a doll! I'm ashamed of him!"

"I'm not," Catherine said, staunchly, "I'd far rather see him play with dolls with Lucy, quietly and gently, than with a gun."

Catherine was a pacifist, far ahead of her time. She had been reared in the strictly traditional Methodist church of Byhalia. After she and Dan had been married a few years, however, she attended a "Campbellite" camp meeting, was converted to the idea of total immersion as the only true baptism, and to all of Alexander Campbell's other teachings. She therefore "went forward" and was properly "saved," baptized in a little muddy creek near her home by the envangelist and was thenceforth a dedicated, hard-working and faithful member of the Christian Church. It could almost be said that her every thought was governed by her efforts to be a good Christian, and to lead others to Christ.

She made something of a nuisance of herself with Dan and her children and her neighbors. She had a passion for the church, for doing good works, and for trying to lead others into the church. She took personally the command to take the gospel to all nations and she did her not very small best on all occasions. She, personally, was responsible for the building of the Christian Church in Altus. Literally she browbeat the members into building it and, as she was responsible for its building, she personally ran it. And she was never happier than when, by nagging from the time they got up until time to leave, she managed to get all her brood to church on Sunday morning.

She never quit hoping she could get Dan to go, too. This

she did not accomplish until most of the children were grown. She never persuaded him to offer grace at meals in the home (which she did, devoutly, instead), nor could she nag him into holding evening prayers with the children. "I see no reason for special prayers," Dan said sensibly. "If a man lives as blameless and good a daily life as he possibly can, his life itself is a constant prayer."

Catherine's children took after their father when it came to joining or attending the church, once they were old enough to be beyond their mother's commands. Few of them turned out to be unquestioning members of orthodox churches, although all of them were eventually deeply religious in their own eccentric and individual ways.

Perhaps Catherine nagged too much, brought the church and Christianity into the home too constantly. The McGraw children were all bull-headed individualists. If for no other reason, they would have rebelled against attending and joining Catherine's church because she so obviously desired it and so constantly nagged and preached at them to "save their souls" by confessing their sins, being baptized and then never missing Sunday School or church. They were too intelligent, too free-thinking and, it has to be said, too eccentric, to be orthodox in anything, much less something as personal, as profound, as private, as their own religious views.

*

The McGraws lived in Ozark for three years and then moved again to Altus, a small town some five miles east of Ozark.

The public school system had not yet begun in Arkansas in the 1880s. The only schools were small subscription schools, the usual school term being about three months between crops when the children were not needed in the fields.

But a Methodist preacher, the Reverend I. L. Burrow, had come over into Arkansas from Tennessee, in a pioneer and missionary spirit, looking for a likely place to build a boarding school. He wanted to offer educational opportunities in an area where they were meager, some place on the frontier. Brother Burrow, as he became known, must also have had a lot of the adventurer in him to choose western Arkansas.

The place Brother Burrow chose for his school was the small community of Altus. It was the highest point between Little Rock and the Ozark Mountains. He built his boarding school there in 1875, calling it the Central Collegiate Institute. He chose and bought ten lush acres on a lovely hill overlooking the little village and on it he built a three-story red brick building with a seven-story bell tower. It was a beautiful location and he built the traditional square structure to house the classrooms and the administrative offices. From old pictures of both, I judge the Central Collegiate Institute building closely resembled Old Main at the University of Arkansas, and while both buildings were plain, traditional structures, they had a grace and beauty in their red brick, white-trimmed, ivy-covered plainness. They were sturdy, solid, four-square and central-towered, conventional and unassuming, functional and simple.

Although Brother Burrow called his school the Central Collegiate Institute, he actually took pupils in all grades from beginners to the equivalent of about the tenth grade. The Mc-Guffey Readers, Webster's old *Blue-Backed Speller*, *First Steps in Geography* were used in the lower grades. The upper grades were taught the rudiments of science, had an excellent mathematics department, good departments in English and history, and offered four years of Latin and four years of German (Lucy McGraw had all four years of both these languages). Music was emphasized with studies in voice, and the piano and violin were taught. The school had an excellent choir which often gave concerts and it also had an orchestra — or rather a small band. Naturally Bible was taught and was compulsory for all students.

By 1885 the school had a good start with many young people from Arkansas and the Indian Territory spending nine months out of the year as boarding pupils. A boys' dormitory, and a girls', had been built on the campus. They were big, white, rambling structures, framed and painted, which were run on the principle of boardinghouses with a married couple in charge of each. Brother Burrow felt that a married couple gave the boardinghouses the feeling of home to the students, the husband taking the place of the father, the wife becoming a sort of mother to them. It was also a very practical arrangement. A man could be the disciplinarian and do most of the upkeep of the houses and he could also raise an immense garden. The woman could supervise the cleaning, cooking and physical care of the students. There was no infirmary so she also became a nurse when a pupil fell ill and tended him, or her, in his room in the boardinghouse.

That year, 1885, Brother Burrow called on Dan and Catherine McGraw in their crowded, rented house in Ozark and asked them to move to Altus, live on the ten-acre campus and run the girls' boardinghouse.

They were especially interested because such a move afforded an opportunity for their own children to attend the school and get a better education than the meager subscrip-

tion schools offered. After giving it much thought they accepted Brother Burrow's offer and made the move.

The town of Altus had an interesting history, but I did not
learn about it until after I was grown. In the mid-nineteenth
century an emigration society was formed in Giessen, Ger-
many, which planned to found in the United States an essentially German state — for all those to whom conditions at
home had become unbearable. Generally their objection was
to compulsory military conscription. In no sense was the essentially German state to be a sovereign nation. It would be
a state; it would come under the law of the United States.
But its purpose was to transplant the best of the old German
culture and to preserve it in the new republic across the sea.

Arkansas was selected for the experiment, and in the 1860s
a few families emigrated and took up their residence along
the base of the long mountain. They named their small community Altus, which is the German word for high. They
brought cuttings from their vines with them and established
their vineyards and wineries.

Further emigration languished, I would suppose from lack
of funds, and nothing really came of the goal of establishing
an essentially German state in Arkansas. The German families who founded the small town of Altus remained, however,
and being thrifty and hard-working they flourished and the
town slowly attracted other people to establish businesses
there.

While Catherine and Dan McGraw had German-Catholic
neighbors of whom they were very fond and with whom they
were consistently friendly, Catherine did not truly approve of
either Germans or Catholics. Germans were really foreigners
and Catholicism was popery, it was the religion against which

Protestantism had rebelled. Here, as in her Mississippi South-
ernism, Catherine remained an "unreconstructed rebel." She
did not ever quite understand how any intelligent person
could believe in Catholicism.

In addition to her complaint that Germans were essentially foreigners, her other complaint against them was at least
more rational if equally narrow. Catherine McGraw was one
of the original joiners of the WCTU. She organized the
chapter in Altus, and Frances Willard, the organizer and head
of the Woman's Christian Temperance Union, was her ideal.
Catherine, who never for one moment forgot that her own
father had been what her mother and perhaps the town of
Byhalia called a drunkard, and who believed all her life that
her own mental powers had been impaired by his alcoholism
at her conception, was fated to be an impassioned WCTU-er.
She wore the little enameled white ribbon pin every hour of
the day. It was pinned on the breast of whatever dress she
put on when she got up in the morning, it was transferred to
any garment she changed to during the day. I never saw her
without that small pin on her dress and it was there on the
black satin dress with white collar which she had made for
her Golden Wedding Anniversary in 1922, and it was there
on that same black satin dress as she lay in her magnificent
bronze casket in November of 1926. It was buried with her.
Even in the grave I think she would have been lost without it.

Catherine kept a diary which was very full from 1898 to
1902. It has frequent criticisms of the Germans and their
wineries. To Catherine they were a good, hard-working, decent people, if only they wouldn't raise grapes and turn them
into wine. For this she condemned them, all of them, out
of hand. There were no exceptions in her book. They were
Catholics, which was one strike against them, and all of them

were connected in some way with the making of wine. Either they raised the grapes, or they owned the wineries and they and their families worked at the making of wine. For Catherine, this put them beyond the pale.

Florence was made to suffer grievously because of this narrow prejudice of both Catherine and Dan. When she was eighteen, she fell in love, deeply and truly in love, with a German youth, young Jacob Post, and they became engaged. But when she told Dan and Catherine they were horrified. Their feeling of horror was as real and as deep and as true as young Florence's love. Jacob Post was a fine young man, decent, sturdy, financially well-off, handsome, with a good singing voice and an artist's interest in music. He was also studying medicine with the intention of becoming a family doctor in Altus.

The truth was that young Jacob Post was a good catch for any Altus girl, coming as he did from a solidly successful family who had been in Arkansas far longer than Dan and Catherine McGraw and was one of the settled pioneer families of Altus.

However, not only was he the son of a German wine-maker, Jacob Post was a devout Catholic. Florence herself would have been willing to become a Catholic perhaps, but she knew this would hurt her father and mother beyond bearing. Jacob met her halfway by refusing to permit the sacrifice. It was only necessary, he told her, for them to be married by the priest and for her to vow that any children should be brought up in the Catholic Church.

The idea of Catholic grandchildren appalled Dan and Catherine almost as much as the idea of Florence becoming a Catholic. They began a program of strenuous and highly vocal disapproval. Florence was made to feel that she had become sinful, that she lacked respect and love for her parents, that she was ungrateful, that she was somehow lacking in the graces of a cultured young lady, which they had striven so hard to give her. "This," they constantly reminded her, "is how you repay all the years of loving devotion. By disobedience and by disrespect of your parents."

Her parents finally wore their daughter out with their constant nagging. Let me say here that my grandmother was one of the world's best naggers, in the nicest way. She was never hateful, high-tempered, ugly with her nagging. But she was very effective because she literally never quit. Her little darts went flying through the air and they pierced you as she laughed or joked or even as she sang. Even the hymns she sang as she worked were frequently chosen for their propaganda value. When you were with Catherine McGraw you were usually much aware of what she wanted you to do — whether it was come home by ten o'clock from an evening out, if you happened to be spending a week with her, or joining the church, if you were still holding out, or not to get married too young.

Nice, sweet, endearing, good, clever, smart, highly intelligent, grand sense of humor, witty and full of fun, Catherine McGraw was nevertheless one of the world's worst and most successful naggers. After all her children were grown, married and living widely scattered all over the United States, she nagged at them to "come home" for a visit. She nagged at them to write oftener. She wrote the poems which nagged by stressing her loneliness for them. And when, adults as they were with families of their own, her nagging could no longer succeed, she did not admit defeat. She just nagged Dan into driving all over the United States so she could "visit the children."

I feel no guilt in so describing Catherine McGraw. I recognize the same nice nagging propensities in myself. When I want something very badly, or when I disapprove of something very strongly, my family hears about it pretty steadily. I don't think I do as much of it as Catherine, but like her, I usually get my way.

*

When Brother Burrow approached Dan and Catherine McGraw with the proposition of moving to Altus and taking over the girls' boardinghouse, the small town had grown to have a population of around four hundred and fifty.

The move from Ozark was made in the fall of 1885, into a big rambling house that had seventeen rooms, with two girls to every room, except the kitchen, dining room and the Mc-Graw family bedrooms. Dan McGraw did all the managing, the buying, and he raised much of the food that was served to the girls.

The problems were many. Sometimes the cook quit, without notice, and Catherine and her older daughters had to take over all the cooking and washing up for twenty-five girls, do all the housework. The girls were all ages and from all kinds of homes. Some were spoiled, disagreeable and disobedient, some were thoughtful, pleasant and easy to work with. Paired in rooms, and responsible for the care of their rooms, an older girl was usually placed with a younger one, in the hope she could teach her to be careful of her belongings and neat with them and the room. Occasionally, however, it would be the younger girl who had such supervision to do.

And there was always the problems of boys and girls on the same campus. Teen-age boys and girls *will* notice each other, will slip away to some secret place to talk together, will neglect their studies and write notes to each other. Once a fifteen-year-old girl eloped with a boy not much older. Dan McGraw went after them, intercepted them before the marriage could take place and expelled them both.

But here in the big boardinghouse, in the midst of all their problems and responsibilities, Dan and Catherine's seventh child was born in 1886. She was named Annie (for Sister Annie, naturally) Ophelia. She was called Phele all her life.

*

One school term was all that Dan and Catherine could take of the boardinghouse. Then Dan ran for the office of county surveyor of Franklin County and was elected. He moved his sizable family off the college campus into a rambling old rented house and provided himself with the proper equipment to survey land.

At some time in his life he had learned something about surveying, but he probably learned most by actually doing the job. He rode horseback over all the county, carrying his instruments in leather saddlebags, his long Jacob's staff across the saddle in front of him. He was so accurate a surveyor that for many years after he was finished with the office he was called back by people who would not accept a survey unless it carried McGraw lines, and a McGraw line never failed to stand up in court when there were disputes over where a boundary line ran.

Catherine continued to help out financially by teaching small district schools between babies.

By the time he was fifteen years old, the eldest son, Brother, was publishing a weekly newspaper, the *Altus Albion*. I think I can see Catherine's fine hand in the name of that little newspaper. Albion was England. The paper, while not obviously a strike against the German population, was primarily aimed at the native American and English-speaking population.

Brother had been working off and on since he was twelve years old and somehow had acquired enough cash to buy an old hand press and some type. Catherine McGraw wrote much of the material for the little weekly. She used a combination of local news items and the lead stories from the city newspapers, but it was also heavily loaded with religious material, some lifted from religious periodicals.

The little paper endured for three years and then died of financial starvation. Brother, however, had found his calling. When he closed down the *Altus Albion*, he went to Helena, Arkansas, as a printer for a newspaper there.

He must have remained at Helena several years because he married there, coming home to Altus to claim his childhood sweetheart, Pearl Lawson.

Sister, who had worked a while in the post office, grew weary of that work and went to stay with Brother and Pearl. There, at Helena, an admirer several years older than she, who had watched her grow up and had off and on tried to court her, caught up with her in this muddle of her life and persuaded her to marry him. He was John McRaven and he probably was the only son-in-law Dan and Catherine ever had of whom they almost wholly approved, for he was the son of Harvey McRaven, a neighbor from the northern Mississippi days and he and Dan had grown up boyhood friends.

Catherine had been delighted when Brother married Pearl Lawson, for the beautiful girl had grown up with the McGraw children and Catherine thought of her almost as another daughter. She was later to provide the first scandal in the family when she left Brother, got a divorce and married again.

She was rarely mentioned in the family after that and I only learned about the scandal when Uncle Brother himself married again.

In June of 1888, Dan and Catherine's eighth child was born. This was Tom Dan, named for Catherine's brother, Thomas Babb, and for Dan McGraw. One wonders a little that she waited so long to name one of her boys after her husband, for she was devoted to him. Perhaps it was he who objected to having a Junior in the family.

In June of 1890, the ninth child was born. Her name was Sallie Roberta, *not* Sarah.

In 1893 there were twin sons, Paul and David. These were obviously biblical names. Paul died five days after birth and David lived only eighteen months.

A daughter, who was given the name of Agnes, was born in 1895, but she lived only a few hours. Catherine was now forty-one and obviously the years of her healthy childbearing were nearing their end.

*

It was in the 1890s that the Western Coal and Mining Company of St. Louis began operations about one mile south of Altus, down in the valley. Soon a mining town had grown up around the mining operations. The new town acquired a post office and became Denning.

Dan McGraw went to work for the coal company, first as a checker of building materials, then he became weigh master, then "top boss," then assistant superintendent, and finally he was made superintendent of all the Western's operations in the area.

Life became a little easier for the McGraws, although as late as 1893 Catherine was still teaching. In that year she was principal of the Altus school in the newly established public school system.

The last baby, a daughter given the name of Babb, was born in June of 1897.

What a lively record that old account-book diary of Catherine's reveals. What a vital household it was! With eight children at home, ranging in age from Fred, who was twenty-four, to the baby, Babb, the home fairly burst its seams with explosive vitality and energy.

The older, married children were forever coming and going also. Sister had been the first of the children to graduate from the college, whose name had been changed to Hiram and Lydia College.

Mr. Burrow was not a very good administrator and he had financial difficulties with his Central Collegiate Institute. In time the Methodist Conference took it over, changed its name, and moved it to Conway, Arkansas. Altus was left with a lovely ten-acre campus and the buildings, but no school. The community felt this loss so keenly that it went to work, in fact that entire section of the state went to work and financial backing was found to open the school again, with Mr. Burrow, naturally, as president. He named the new school Hiram and Lydia in honor of his parents.

Sister had been the first of the McGraw children to graduate from Hiram and Lydia in June of 1898. She received a beautiful real parchment diploma granting her the degree of M.E.L. — Master of English Literature. Mr. Burrow did not lack imagination with his degrees! General accreditation was probably not a fact yet and each so-called college granted whatever degrees it liked. But my own mother's work at Hiram and Lydia was given full college accreditation when, years later, she began work on her A.B. degree.

Mamie, the second eldest daughter, now eighteen, was studying music in Fort Smith and later in Memphis. She became an accomplished pianist.

Fred tried his hand at various things, even going over into the Indian Territory in one effort. Catherine disapproved of this heartily and with her usual candor said so. To no avail. Fred was of age and could come and go as he pleased. He did go, but he stayed only a few weeks and when he returned it was to find his niche with the coal company, as bookkeeper.

Lucy, now sixteen, was attending the college and studying music. The smaller children were all in the newly established public school system.

Lucy, however, did not graduate from Hiram and Lydia with her class. Suddenly she had a most unsuitable suitor. I have no idea who he was or why he was considered so unsuitable. She would never talk about this episode in her life. All I know of it is what was in Catherine's diary and it was very discreet. She only says that Lucy had been saved from a great disaster and that she had been sent to spend the summer with the Mississippi relatives. Apparently the idea was that time and absence would take care of the affair. And evidently it worked. Nothing more is heard of the unsuitable suitor.

When she returned home, however, Lucy did not return to the college. A job was found for her in the post office. Lucy was always one of the most refractory of the McGraw children, giving her parents more anxiety than most of the others. She was high-tempered, she was not neat (Catherine considered her lazy because she had to be made to do her part of the enormous amount of housework), and she was far too popular with boys to suit her parents. She was actually guilty of sly disobedience when she set her head to do something she badly wanted to do. Sometimes she got by with it, but more often than not there was a neighbor, or Mamie or Fred, if they happened to be at home, to tell Catherine that Lucy had sat by a boy at a band concert and had actually *held hands with him!*

None of the children stayed away from home very long, not even after they were married. They returned for long visits. The family was very close-knit, abounding in high spirits, all of them bright, intelligent, inclined to be indivdualists, creative, high-strung, gifted with wit and quick laughter. Both Mamie and Lucy had been given music. Lucy played well, but Mamie played far better. She also played the guitar and mandolin. Fred played the violin, sort of, and all of them sang. Evening after evening they and their friends gathered in the parlor, Mamie or Lucy at the old upright piano, and played and sang.

In August of 1899, Catherine took Babb, who was just past one year old, and went to Fort Smith to stay with Sister. Shortly after she returned home Dan was seriously injured in an ambush. There had been some trouble at both the Denning mines. The men, or at least some of them, were disgruntled over working conditions and pay. Dan McGraw had no authority to do anything about the complaints except to pass them on to the home office in St. Louis. His job was simply to oversee the work and to implement company policies. Nothing was done about the men's complaints and since there was as yet no miners' union the men had no alternative except to quit their jobs or continue to work under conditions they thought unfair.

The men were paid each week — in *gold.* It seems strange to think that no longer ago than 1899 gold was the accepted form of currency. Each week Dan went to the bank and

withdrew the gold with which to pay the men. On payday
he was always late coming home, but on that night he did
not come home at all, that is not of his own accord. He was
waylaid by a group of the miners, masked to conceal their
identities, and the gold of the payroll was taken from him.
He himself was beaten up and when found was still uncon-
scious. One wound, on his forehead, just over his left eye,
was so severe that a silver plate had to be inserted. Of course
he was taken to the hospital in Fort Smith where he slowly
recovered. But he wore that silver plate and there was a slight
indentation over that eye for the rest of his life.

This was not the first time Dan McGraw had been wounded
in performing his duty. During the period he was a deputy
sheriff he had been sent, alone, to bring in a man who had
evidently gone mad. He had barricaded himself in his log
cabin in the mountains and he would allow no one to come
near his home. He shot at everybody who tried to approach
him.

Dan knew the man personally, nevertheless he approached
the house cautiously, taking cover behind trees as he came
near to the cabin. Finally he was near enough the house to
call out to the man that he meant him no harm, that he had
simply come to help him, to take him to town to a doctor.
The answer was a shot.

Safely hidden behind a tree Dan continued to try to talk
to the man. He could see the barrel of the man's gun in a
chink between the logs of the cabin. Suddenly the gun barrel
was withdrawn, and thinking he had finally made some impression on the man, Dan left the shelter of the big tree trunk
to run to another big tree within a few yards of the house.
In that brief moment the man fired again. He had simply
moved to another position. Fortunately he was using bird

shot as ammunition and while Dan's face and upper chest were filled with the tiny pellets he was not killed. Wisely he decided this was a job that required more than one man and he retired to his horse and rode back to Ozark. It took the doctor hours to pick out all the shot and Dan's face was slightly pitted on the forehead and upper cheeks for the remainder of his life.

5

MR. JOHN HOLT

✳

ON NOVEMBER 6, 1899, Catherine McGraw recorded, matter-of-factly, in her diary, "Mr. John Holt came to board with us last Thursday the 2nd. He commences school at Greenwood Schoolhouse today."

What had happened was that Fred, still living at home, though now paying board himself, had persuaded his parents to take this particular boarder. He had met the young man who had just contracted to teach the Greenwood School, some two miles outside Altus. Fred McGraw liked John Holt, but there was more to it than that. Fred liked to fiddle but was no great shakes at it. In John Holt he found a real fiddler and he wanted him handy to join in the evening music in the home.

A little reluctantly, for a boarder was the last thing in the world the McGraws needed in their overcrowded home, the parents agreed. Furthermore, a teacher was held above reproach in Catherine's eyes and Fred vouched for the fact that he came from a good family in Charleston, a larger town than Altus, and some fifteen miles across the Arkansas River. So a bed was put up for him in Fred's room and John Holt came to live with the McGraws.

He was twenty-eight years old in 1899, tall, slender, inclined to be a dandy in the matter of clothes, with a roguish twinkle in his hazel eyes and a nice sense of humor. He also had one of the most beautiful tenor voices the McGraws had ever heard.

He added much to the musical evenings, no fiddlers' tune being too much for his fast fingers; when he struck up "Soldier's Joy," "The Devil's Hornpipe," the "Irish Washerwoman," the "Eighth of January," or "Sallie Stuck a Needle in Her Heel, by Joe," Fred would have to give up the fast pace, follow along with chords as Mamie was doing on the piano. Nobody could keep up with those flying fingers.

When Mamie, or Lucy, and John Holt played a polka or waltz, Catherine McGraw would sometimes lift her skirts slightly above the ankle and dance around the room until she would drop in a chair, out of breath and laughing. She was only five feet one inch tall, but she had grown very heavy, weighing around 170 pounds. She walked lightly and she danced lightly, as so many heavy people do, but she easily became breathless.

John Holt had a brand-new buggy and a fast horse named Blazer. It was two miles to the Greenwood schoolhouse and the horse was so fast that Mr. Holt only allowed himself seven minutes to get there. Tom Dan, who was twelve years old at the time, recalls the scene every morning. John Holt would hitch the horse to the buggy, then stand beside the buggy, reins in his hand. Blazer would be standing with his back slightly humped and muscles tensed for a quick getaway. John Holt would step into the buggy. The instant he was up, the horse was off like a shot, accelerating to twenty miles an hour in nothing flat, rounding the corner on two wheels at McGraw Lane and the Roseville road, up over the hill and out of sight all in about fifteen seconds.

*

Not much is known about the Holt family. Unfortunately none of the women ever wanted to become a member of the Daughters of the American Revolution apparently and there is only family tradition. My grandfather Holt told me, when I was a little girl, that the original Holt in America emigrated to Virginia from England sometime in the early eighteenth century, and that his son fought in the Revolutionary War with troops of the Virginia Line.

My grandfather's branch of the family then moved to North Carolina, and early in the nineteenth century, my great-grandfather Martin Holt, moved farther west to Shelby County, Tennessee. His farm is now in the suburbs of Memphis. His wife had been Mildred Barnes. Nothing at all is known of her antecedents. It is not even known how many children Martin and Mildred Holt had, but in 1845 a son was born, who was to be my grandfather. He was given the name James Knox Polk Holt. James Knox Polk was then President of the United States and apparently it was a fashion to name children after Presidents in those days.

The family shortly moved to northern Mississippi, to Tate County in the vicinity of Coldwater. They were known to Daniel McGraw's parents there, but they were not close neighbors.

Martin Holt died young and in a few years his widow married Jack Tolleson. Some time after the marriage Jack Tolleson's brother, David, lost his wife. His little girl, Mary, came to live with the Jack Tollesons.

The Tollesons were part Indian. Where they came from originally, when they went to Mississippi, is not known. Family tradition has it that the Indian blood was Cherokee, and that the Tollesons had lived for a time in eastern Tennessee near the Cherokee towns. There is no proof whatever of this, however, and it may well be that the Indian blood in the family is Choctaw, picked up in northern Mississippi where there were no Cherokees. Mary Tolleson was supposed to have been about one-eighth Indian. She was quite dark-skinned, with large brown-black eyes and very black hair until it went gray.

Jim Holt, as he was always called, married this young Tolleson girl when he came home from the war, and they had ten children, coming at two- and three-year intervals. The oldest child was a daughter, Elizabeth, always called Lizzie. She married William Darr and was the mother of our cousin, Verna, whom we were taught to call Aunt Verna because she was so much older than the rest of us. Lizzie died young of tuberculosis.

In 1868, David Harrison Holt was born. For some reason he was always called Judge, probably because of a serious turn of mind and a tendency to solitariness which excluded him from close friendships. He never married and lived at home with his parents until the home was broken up by the death of my grandfather.

John Holt was the third child, born on January 10, 1871. There followed James Thomas Holt in 1873, who was the opposite of Judge and was a merry, gay, happy-go-lucky boy and man. He too died young of tuberculosis.

George Holt was born in 1876 and, in 1878, Charles Holt followed.

There is a tragedy connected with these two boys who were inseparable companions. When George was seventeen and Charles was fifteen they were out squirrel hunting together. They separated, as men do when hunting. Suddenly George thought he saw a squirrel a short distance away from him. Having no idea where Charles was, he shot at the squirrel, but what he hit was Charles' head, and his brother was instantly killed. Nobody in the family blamed George, but it must have cast a pall over the entire family for a time, and I doubt if, in his deepest heart, George ever got over it. It was simply the carelessness of youth. Today, men hunting together wear something bright to distinguish themselves — a red cap, or a red shirt or jacket, but in those days there were too few clothes anyway and men simply went hunting in whatever farm clothing they had on.

Mary Belle Holt was born in April of 1881. We always called her Aunt Belle. She married the son of the only doctor in Charleston, Ed Northum, and they had three sons. She, too, died of tuberculosis in, I think, her fifties.

Another daughter, inexplicably named Willie Mae, was born in 1885. She married Elisha Cannon of Dustin, Indian Territory. She met him while visiting a sister who lived in Dustin. He died in 1918 and Aunt Billie, as we called her, went back to northern Mississippi to live with a younger sister and there married again. She had no children by either marriage.

Emma Lee Holt was born in 1888, and it was she who lived in Dustin and whom Aunt Billie was visiting when she met her first husband. Emma Holt was teaching in Dustin and had met and married there a young man named Clifford Hartzell. He came of a quite well-to-do family of Memphis, with large holdings of land in northern Mississippi. Evidently, however, he was trying it on his own in the small coal town of Dustin when Emma met and married him. Shortly they moved to northern Mississippi, near Batesville, and Clifford took over the management of the family lands there. He inherited them, in time. They had six children and the Hartzell cousins were the joy of our lives.

The last child, a daughter, Grace, was born in 1892. She was eight years younger than her own niece, Verna Darr.

Jack Tolleson moved his family to western Arkansas shortly after the Civil War. The family settled in the small community of Charleston, about twenty-five miles southeast of Fort Smith. The choice of Arkansas seems to have been motivated by young James K. P. Holt, who had fought almost the entire four years of the war with an Arkansas regiment. When his own outfit was practically wiped out, he had attached himself to Hindman's Sixth Arkansas Regiment and fought with it at the Battle of Pea Ridge, at Shiloh, and until the end of the war. He had been sixteen years old when he enlisted. He was wounded at the Battle of Pea Ridge but not badly enough to be mustered out. When he returned home in 1865, Mary Tolleson had grown up. She was now sixteen years old and very beautiful. She and Jim Holt were married shortly after his return.

They made their home in Charleston where Jim Holt was always a farmer and small cotton planter. It is said that he prospered for a time but was ruined by his propensity for going security for any and all of his friends, particularly if they were, as he was, Confederate veterans.

*

John Holt, the third child, never knew anything but a farm life, but by the hardest of efforts he managed to get an education beyond the meager schooling offered in Charleston. By alternately working and going to school he finally gained a diploma, in 1898, from the Arkansas Industrial College at Fayetteville, the forerunner of the University of Arkansas. He was determined to teach and the Greenwood School near Altus was his first school. But this is why he was twenty-eight years old before he could begin teaching. His schooling had been gotten in the hardest way possible.

During the first year he boarded with the McGraws in Altus there is only an occasional mention of him in Catherine's diary, usually in connection with the musical evenings in the parlor. But in 1900 the diary begins to chronicle that Mr. Holt and Lucy went to a musical at the college, or went to theatricals at the college, or went driving, or sat in the parlor on Sunday evening and talked. Between school terms when he went home to Charleston, the diary records several times when he drove over to visit the McGraws, specifically Lucy.

By the spring of 1901 the diary begins to show alarm at the frequency with which Lucy and Mr. Holt drove out together, and the first signs of opposition. "Lucy and Mr. Holt went with several others over to Paris and Subiaco today. Too long a drive, I thought."

It *was* a long drive. Like Charleston, Paris and Subiaco were on the other side of the river and even farther away than Charleston. It must have been ten or eleven o'clock before the young people got home. It has to be remembered, however, that they were with a group.

Mr. Holt's school term was over the last of April and he went home. But on May 4, 1901, Catherine's diary records: "Mr. Holt came over and he *brought Lucy a ring!* O, dear! The only encouraging thought about it is that she has discarded two or three others so *this* may not be the one she wants either."

Lucy had been born in October so that the opal was her birthstone. Her ring was a beautiful opal with a tiny diamond on either side of it.

What her opposition to Mr. Holt was she does not say, nor to the best of my knowledge did she ever say, and if my mother ever knew she never mentioned it. Catherine may have thought since Mr. Holt was eleven years older than Lucy, he was too old for her eighteen-year-old daughter. But to tell the truth Dan and Catherine McGraw were just a little bit snobbish. They did not mean to be, I'm sure, and there was never a better neighbor or friend than Catherine McGraw. But they had come from Mississippi, from an old established culture, into a raw and new frontier land, and the mores of the old culture clung to them. Subconsciously perhaps they felt that with their background they were just a little superior to the people they found in the new land. For whatever reason, only three of their children married to suit them. There was much reservation about the men and women all the others married. In time, however, they came to love most of them.

On the twenty-fifth of August, 1901, Dan McGraw was called to his old home in Mississippi where his father was dying. On the thirty-first of August, Catherine's diary bristles with exclamation points. "Today Lucy and Mr. Holt were married! She had told us they would marry the last of September and I was having her some nice dresses made. But she disappointed us all! *He* walked in suddenly yesterday morning and wanted *permission* to marry her 'in a few minutes!' Brother Burrow was even then in the house over in Mr. Holt's room! Well, of course I was powerless, though Mamie and I said everything we could to persuade them to wait at least until Papa came home — but no! Well, I did *not* consent to their marriage but couldn't help myself and pray God to help them!"

What got into those two to make them suddenly decide to change their plans and marry immediately? Well, they had had a quarrel and Lucy had given John Holt back his ring. There was one day of stiff-necked stubbornness, then the quarrel had been tearfully patched up and suddenly they could not wait until the end of September to be married. They would be married immediately, right now!

None of this was explained to the family, however, and to Catherine and the older children it was puzzling and inexplicable. Privately Catherine thought the sudden wedding plans were made to avoid an eruption from Dan McGraw. He was in Mississippi at the time and by the time he returned the wedding would be over and the marriage a *fait accompli*. Dan's opposition to anything of which he disapproved was formidable, but faced with something irrevocable he could be depended upon to make the best of it. He had stormed and raged considerably when Mr. Holt had given Lucy her ring, but Lucy had stood up to him bravely and worn the ring in spite of him. The quarrel had much to do with the change in wedding plans, but I would guess that Catherine was more than half right. Lucy certainly would have dreaded the unpleasantness with her father.

Lucy McGraw and John Holt were married on Saturday evening in the parlor of the family home, Brother Burrow officiating. At least Catherine could approve of their choice of a minister. Lucy wore a white silk mull dress dotted with pale blue tufts, with a high collar of stiff net tied about her throat. The wedding picture shows her chestnut brown hair piled loosely on top of her head and she is softly and happily beautiful.

I don't think my grandmother ever quite forgave them. At any rate she never called my father anything but Mr. Holt. This may have been simply the habit she had gotten into, but not once did I ever hear her call him John, and I was grown and had been married several years, had a young daughter of my own when my grandmother died. My father was still Mr. Holt to her.

The newlyweds left immediately for Charleston to visit a few days with John Holt's parents. Then they went to Ozark to rent a house and get it ready for occupation. John Holt had a contract to teach in the Ozark school and they meant to live there.

They only lived there one year, but Catherine's diary is full of Lucy's coming and goings. With John in the schoolroom all day and only a tiny house to occupy her, Lucy was often homesick for the big house and the big family she had left. Two or three times a week she drove over to spend the day "at home."

At the end of the term, the next spring, John Holt's superintendent went to the Choctaw Nation in the Indian Territory to teach. The Department of the Interior, under whose care the Indian nations came, had taken over the Choctaw schools and had set up a public school system. John Holt's superintendent was one of the first teachers to be brought into the Choctaw Nation, under its new school system, and he immediately wanted John Holt to come, also.

That summer of 1902, John and Lucy Holt thought long and hard about whether to go to the Indian Territory. The position offered was at Dow, in the old Moshlatubbee District of the Choctaw Nation and it was in the heart of the coal-mining area. Lucy and John would feel pretty much at home in a mining town, it was not more than seventy-five miles from Arkansas and only six miles from the growing small city of McAlester. The pay was better than in Arkansas and they convinced themselves the opportunities for John's advancement would be better. It was also very hard for John to turn down his old superintendent whom he had much liked and admired. They decided to go. Thus John Holt became a teacher under the new public school system in the Choctaw Nation the second year it was in effect.

The decision was again against the wishes of Lucy's parents, who echoed their own parents' concern when they left Mississippi and went to live in western Arkansas. But if Catherine and Dan McGraw heard any echo of their parents' warnings, "It's a wild and lawless country. If you don't starve to death, you'll be killed by outlaws or wild animals!" they gave no sign of it and they used almost these identical words in their efforts to try to persuade the young couple who now wanted to set out on their own.

I don't know how long they lived at Dow. Presumably two years, for they had time to make friends and to have some happy and gay times with them. The closest of these friends were John and Annabelle Snodgrass. The tie between these friends was so close that it lasted an entire lifetime, although they never again lived in the same town. We were taught to call them Uncle John and Aunt Annabelle and to tell the truth I think we were fonder of them than we were of many of our own blood aunts and uncles. They visited us oftener and we visited them at least once a year.

Lucy was pregnant when they went to Dow to live and Annabelle and John Snodgrass had a six-month-old son, Robert. He was to be their only child. The men were good companions, enjoying the same things to the same extent — baseball, fishing and hunting. My father had played baseball with the Charleston team. Tall, slender, fast-moving, he was equally good at shortstop or second base. But John Snodgrass was a phenomenally good catcher. He was built like Yogi Berra — short, very broad-shouldered and with an unbelievably good throwing arm. He was so good that he was scouted and offered a Major League contract.

John Snodgrass always got at least two weeks of vacation. He was the manager of the company store for the mines at Dow. By paying a substitute he could stretch this to a month.

John Holt, of course, always had the entire summer, unless it was a year when he had to go to summer school to keep his teaching certificate up to date. The men, and occasionally the two grandfathers, went on long hunting and fishing trips back into the Kiamichi and Winding Stair Mountains, both parts of the immense Ouachita Range. Finally the women put their feet down and insisted on being taken, too, even with children. There was big game in those mountains in those days, deer, elk, wild turkey, even bear. I do not remember those earliest month-long camping trips, but I do remember many of the shorter ones later.

These two young couples also shared a love of dancing and one of the things I heard my parents talk about many times was the opportunity to go into South McAlester to dances. A dance pavilion had been built right on the shore of Dow Lake. Once when they wanted to go to Dow Lake to a dance, their decision, with other young friends, was made too late to take the little dinky train into town. Not to be outdone, they borrowed the railroad foreman's handcar and six of these young married people rode the handcar to the dance. Six miles of pumping that heavy handcar must have left the men fairly breathless for the dance, or perhaps they had time to get their breath back before they reached the dance. One can see them all, young and gay and absolutely undaunted.

In Dow, Lucy and John Holt lived in a little three-room boxy house which she made gay with blue-checked gingham curtains and for which John had provided most of the furniture himself, made from wooden crates. He was by nature a "handy man." There was very little in the way of making things, repairing them, inventing conveniences, he could not do. And the little home was made as comfortable and attractive as, between the two of them, it could be made.

Lucy almost lost her life in this little house when her baby was born in January of 1903. The baby itself, a boy, was still-born.

Catherine McGraw had come to be with her daughter during her ordeal. When I was older, maybe a teen-ager, I heard the story several times. Lucy had been in labor three full days before the little dead baby was born. And then she had lain almost dead herself for nearly a week. Catherine McGraw and Annabelle Snodgrass did everything they could for her, but Catherine, at least, despaired of her life and she bitterly blamed the doctor. "But what else could be expected," she said to her daughter when at last she began to recover, "of such a poor, outlaw country? The next time you come home and let our good Dr. Butts take care of you."

Lucy and John must have moved to Haileyville, in the same school district and not far from Dow, sometime the following year. It was a larger town than Dow and a step up in both pay and status for John. Haileyville was their home when, taking her mother's advice, Lucy went to Altus for the last six weeks of her pregnancy with me and I was thus born in my McGraw grandparents' home.

There is an old yellowed letter in my box of valuable possessions. It is dated March 28, Altus, Arkansas. It is addressed to Professor John A. Holt, Haileyville, Indian Territory. It is a letter written by my Aunt Florence McGraw McRaven (Aunt Sister) to my father announcing my arrival on that Tuesday morning, at about eight o'clock. Apparently Aunt Sister had been visiting in the family home when I arrived, or she came purposely to help prop up Catherine who, remembering that first agonizing birth, was fearful. It turned out to be an easy and normal birth. Although I weighed almost nine pounds, my mother's labor lasted only seven or eight hours.

I am grateful that my aunt, at least, called my father John, for the letter begins, "Dear John," not "Dear Mr. Holt."

The name given the new baby must have startled him. It had been agreed between my parents that should the new baby be a girl she should be named for the two grandmothers, the beautiful name of Mary, for my father's mother, and Catherine, for Lucy's mother. But Lucy had been resting and reading much of the time during the last six weeks before my birth. With no household duties, with solicitous parents and sisters and brothers, there was not much else for her to do.

Among the books she read was the novel *Janice Meredith* by Paul Leicester Ford, which was very popular just at that time. My mother so admired the heroine, whose first name was Janice and whose family name was Meredith, that in a romantic mood and without consulting my father at all, she determined I should bear that name and the family names could be saved for a later little girl, should there be one.

I have always regretted this decision on the part of my mother and begrudged the loss of those beautiful names Mary and Catherine, either of which is lovely, and combined sweet and dear and full of family meaning. But for some reason, probably because the two names were so long, my sister, who inherited the names meant for me, was never called Mary Catherine, or very rarely called that. My father and mother and all my mother's family called her Mary C. My father's family, all the Holts, called her Mary K. I am sure that eventually they learned the Catherine was spelled with a "C" but the Mary K. had been established in that family too long to change.

Much later, when she was about seven or eight years old, my father likened her and me to a team of stubborn old mules Grandpa Holt owned whose names were Bill and Pete. Jok-

ingly and teasingly he began calling us Bill and Pete. The Bill
never stuck to me, probably because I made such a fuss about
it, and I could be pretty noisy when I strenuously objected to
something. But the Pete stuck to Mary C. and in time she
was known in the family, and to all her friends, as Pete, or
Petie. She is still called Petie and to her grandchildren she is
known as Grandma Petie.

But she is Mary C. in this book because that came later.

After about two years in Haileyville, Lucy and John moved
again, to Howe, another mining town, but in a different school
district. John Holt moved on when he had better offers from
other schools.

Mary Catherine was conceived in Howe, but, like me, she
was born in her McGraw grandparents' home. It was but a
summer home, however, in Paris, Arkansas. The mines in
Paris came under the supervision of Dan McGraw. Probably
mostly for the change of scene and the fun of sort of camping
out, Catherine had moved enough furniture and housekeeping
equipment to spend the summer in Paris with Dan.

But camping out or not, Lucy wanted to be with her mother
and in "civilized country" again, with a good doctor, when her
time came, so she went to Paris where her second daughter was
born on July 9, 1907. Like me, she was a Tuesday baby. Lucy
had been a Tuesday baby herself, and it turned out that all
three of her children who lived were Tuesday babies. My own
daughter was a Tuesday baby. But there the Tuesday sequence
ended. Only one of my daughter's three sons was a Tuesday
baby, the middle boy, Mike. Her eldest son was born on Saturday and the youngest was born on Friday.

We lived in Howe two years and then we made the move
to Kinta. To a new town, the first one I remember, to a new
school district, to a new home and to new neighbors.

A MAGICAL DISCOVERY

✳

New town. What was it like?

Well, for one thing it was located dead center in the world. In the universe. Kinta was located precisely and exactly at the middle, right in the solar plexus of the whole, entire world.

I discovered that for myself one day not long after we became residents of the town. I made several other discoveries that same day, dazzling, astonishing, dumbfounding, flabbergasting, staggering discoveries. Within the space of one hour I equaled Galileo, Leonardo da Vinci, Sir Isaac Newton and everybody else who ever studied the sky, the horizons, the curvature of the earth and the law of gravity.

The barn was a constant magnet that summer we moved to Kinta, and until the winter made us prisoners of the house. Enchanting place. On a day when the sun beat down and the heat was searing, when the air itself was lifeless and prostrate with heat, when nothing moved unless the wind moved it and then with torpid exhaustion, the barn was cool. On a day when the sun was like a brass fire in a stark sky, when its glare broke into ten thousand splintered fragments to hurt the eyes, the barn was a healing place, dim and restful and twilit.

In the fall, when the rains began, the barn was a cave, a primordial home. It was hay-nested for snuggling into and curling up in and listening. Rain on the roof, rain leaking through sometimes, rain drowning all other sounds, and a child nested, so full of a strange delight, so full of exalted happiness to be alone, to be so safely, snugly nested while the rain poured and drowned and leaked that shivers of joy raised goose-bumps as she huddled deeper into the hay. Heaven was to be let alone and small and safely nested in a barn on a rainy day.

Not very often let alone, however. Some adult called. The mother's fear of lightning. The father's fear of wind. Where are you? What are you doing out there? Come in the house! Don't you know it's storming? The parent animal's instinct to huddle the young under its own wings.

But my father did not like the leaks in the barn roof, especially after the cow, Brindle, came to occupy it. A cow, then as now, was valuable property. Great care was taken of a cow, almost as much care as was expended on the family. There must be a warm, dry place in the winter. A green place for browsing in the summer. She must be milked twice a day at regular unvarying hours. She must have good mashes and plenty of salt and water. Rubdowns when she had gotten herself wet. A veterinarian when she showed the least sign of being sick.

So my father set out to mend the roof. He worked all one morning replacing rotten shingles, nailing down loose shingles, tarring good but cracked shingles. When he finished he went away, but he forgot and left the ladder propped against the barn.

To me, the barn was enormous, but it must not have been. It must, instead, have been a rather small structure. It was built in the way most barns in that part of the country (in most parts of the country for that matter) were built. It had a center section, with a hall down the middle and stalls and cribs on either side of the hall. Above, in this section, was a shallow hayloft. On either side of the center section a shed was built, lean-to wings with low, sloped roofs. Wagons, buggies, farm implements were kept in these sheds. Because when we were older, and larger, we could climb up on the nearest shed roof from the fence, the sheds must have not have been much higher than my father's head. It was against the nearest shed the ladder had been left.

It was a struggle to climb the ladder. The rungs were too far apart for short legs. But some four-year-olds can climb like monkeys. Small bodies are agile, short legs will stretch, small arms and hands can cling and pull and haul the weight of the whole body. With much such stretching and pulling and hauling I managed to reach the top of the ladder, to fling myself over the top onto the shed roof.

When I stood upright, the roof sloped so gently it felt almost level under my feet. There was a brief period of running around, dancing about, spreading my arms, feeling like a bird in such high freedom. Then inevitably the steeper roof over the center of the barn presented its challenge. The shed roof was fine, but how much finer it would be up on the rooftree.

Although it was steeper than the shed roof, even the barn roof was gently sloped. A shallow roof not deeply pitched. And my father had nailed some cleats up to the ridgepole to keep his own feet from slipping. The cleats made good hand and foot holds for crawling up. It was far easier to reach the ridgepole than it had been to climb the ladder to the shed roof. Shortly I was on the top and when I had thrown one leg over the ridgepole, I sat up straight to look around.

What I saw took my breath away. Never had I been so high before, and never before had I been able to see so far and so wide. I was on top of the world and the whole world was

spread out all around me. I could see forever in any direction.
Away to the northeast across the prairies. Away to the south
and the mountains. Away to the north and a house that sat
exactly on top a low swell of land. Away to the west, flat for
a long stretch, then heaving into low hills. Kinta was a shallow
saucer, with a wide crack northeast where the prairies spilled
out and ran into the horizon.

The town lay below me, in clusters of buildings, dwarfed by
my great height. One clump of the town looked like building
blocks lopped off and square. This was where the stores were,
all built adjoining. The Methodist church steeple spired up
higher than anything else. The homes of the town clustered
near the square blocks, then tailed off in widening gaps between. Our house was on the edge of town, the prairie opening just behind it.

Having examined the town I noticed that squiggles of roads
came into it from all directions. One came up over the crest of
the low ridge to the west and slid down, winding, into the
town. Another wound like a snake across the prairie, disappeared into gullies which crisscrossed the prairie crazily, then
heaved up out of the gullies and came on, growing wider, toward the town. Someone was riding into town on that road
— a horseman, leaving a rooster-tail of dust in his wake.

Another road came into town from the east, bordering the
railroad tracks. Another one wound down the ridge south of
town, crossed Beaver Creek and the railroad tracks, then bored
straight into town.

In whatever direction I looked there was a road coming into
town. Like the spokes of a wheel, fixed in the round iron rim
of the wheel, they came inward, coming together in the middle, in the hub.

The world was as far as I could see. That was all of it. The whole world. And the spokes of the whole world came into Kinta. Those roads showed it. From the very outside edges of the world, in front of me, on either side, behind me, the roads came to the center. All the spokes, all the roads, came into Kinta. So Kinta was the dead center, the middle, the hub of the world, the hub of the wheel.

What a stupendous discovery I had made! I, my family, the Moores, everybody who lived in Kinta, lived in the very heart of the world! What a special place Kinta was. What a special place to live. How fortunate were the people chosen to live there. How had my father ever learned about it? And how had he managed to get us admitted to it?

The discovery was reinforced a few moments later, became a certainty. It was nearly noon, the sun almost directly overhead. I thought about it first because it beat down with such heat on my head. I noticed the short shadow my body cast on the barn roof and knew the sun was almost directly above me. I thought about how it rose in the east every morning, how it set in the west every evening, traveling all day above us. Observed and noted. Why? Why did it pass directly above us? Logic answered. Because Kinta was not only the hub of the earthly world, it was the hub of the sky, too. Kinta was located directly under the center of the sky. It had to be, for the sun came up in the morning and rose to its greatest height when it was immediately above the town. Thus we were bound to be under the exact middle of the sky.

If I was astonished and exalted to discover that Kinta was at the middle of the known world, I was awed to discover that it was under the center of the sky. This stretched mind to its farthest limits. Mind almost exploded under the impact. The brain, that cluster of matter thrown together to perform usefully, could barely think these thoughts, could barely, meagerly, put them together. How did it work? What made the sun rise, pass directly over us, then set? This was beyond mind. It was too mysterious and inexplicable. Mind could not hold on to these thoughts.

Examining the sky, looking in all directions, one segment at a time, it then became evident that there were no corners to the sky. On every side it came down to the earth, was pinned to the earth, in one long rounding piece. Northward it met the earth behind the low swell of land on which a house sat. Eastward it flowed with the prairie so far as the eye could see, but out where objects disappeared, out beyond where the horse and rider had come, it touched the earth in a clear, even line. Southward the San Bois Mountains humped themselves up, blue in the distance, looking like huge sleeping animals. I made no mistake about it. Everywhere I looked the sky was round and smooth. In all directions it came down to the earth in a clean dividing line. And there were no corners. It did not break into squares. So the world had to be round, too. If the world had corners, the sky must have corners, for at no point did the sky fail to meet the earth. And I made very certain the sky had no corners.

This discovery made me dizzy. Almost sent me tumbling off my perch. It left me breathless. What a strange, enormous, miraculous world it was! Did my father and mother know about all this? Why had they never told me? But perhaps I had stumbled onto something they did not know, although I believed them to be the wisest people on earth, almost all-knowing. To live on a round world was a mystifying thought. It did not occur to me it was round like a ball. It was round like a saucer.

The next discovery was a little fearful. If the sky met the earth all around, then where it touched the earth must be the edges of the world. Beyond those edges there must be nothing. The world began where the sky touched it, but beyond lay . . . what? I could not imagine. If one went far enough out one of the roads, one of the spokes of the world, would one reach the edge, the sheer edge? Did it go straight down? Did it fall off into nothingness? But, no, people came into Kinta on those roads. How could one climb up, as obviously the horse and rider had done, and reach the round, flat top of the world? There was born a great curiosity to go out one of the spokes and see the edge of the world, but at the same time there was a shuddering fear of it. One might so easily fall off. Imagine falling off the world! Where would one land? Could one get back onto it?

It was a momentous morning. So much learned. So much discovered. All of it mind-blowing, enlarging the mind almost beyond comprehension, making even the body seem larger. The final discovery of the morning was ignominious, however.

There came a call. "Janice! Come to dinner!"

In those days, in that place, we had breakfast, dinner and supper. We had never heard of lunch, except picnic lunches and what one took to school. At home the noon meal was dinner and it was the biggest meal of the day. "Come to dinner," Mama said.

My mother never put up with delay. A child called was expected to come immediately. If she had to call twice the child was in trouble. No delay, unless it was caused by a catastrophe, was allowable. I had to scramble down from this barn roof right now, in a hurry, or be late . . . be called again.

I then discovered I could not get down. Newton's law of gravity did not work voluntarily. There were some things stronger than the law of gravity. Fear, for instance. Climbing up I had not once looked down, had only looked up at the next rung of the ladder, or the next cleat on the barn roof. But now, looking down, I was suddenly frozen to that ridgepole. If I turned loose of it for a second I would fall. And the ground was an awfully long way down. I sat there, frozen with fear, paralyzed by fear, unable to move, unable even to take my eyes from the ground so far below me.

I did not yet have the mental equipment to conquer this fear. I could not rationalize it. I could not tell myself not to look at the ground, to look instead at the cleats on the roof, to find a foothold on the nearest one, then to crawl backwards down the roof, the same way I had come up but in reverse. I could only cling to the ridgepole in terror. Even the roof looked much steeper going down than it had coming up. I had to get down, but I did not have the will to begin to do it.

There was only one way to get down. Somebody had to come get me. Some adult, my father, reassuringly grown up and steady and sure, had to come get me. I squalled like a scalded cat, yelled my terror and plight as loud as I could. Screeched, screamed, shouted and shortly cried. Terror let loose lets more terror loose. I was now so scared I was certain I was going to fall anyhow. I could not hold on to the ridgepole tight enough. It would slip away from my clinging hands. And I would roll, tumble, fall, to the ground, so far away, and be killed.

This was so terrifying that I closed my eyes and screamed louder and louder, longer and longer, until my wails were one long sustained scream. With my eyes tightly shut, I did not see my parents come flying out of the house, come tearing into the barn lot, though I know they did. Some sound finally penetrated my terrified mind, reached through the sound of my own screams. "Hush, Janice, hush. Be quiet. Daddy's coming after you. Just hold on tight and be quiet. Daddy will come up and get you."

I made myself stop screaming, but still could not force my eyes open. I would fall if I opened my eyes. I heard my father coming up the ladder, heard him walk across the shed roof. This his voice reached me. "My goodness what a wonderful thing you've done! Climbed all the way to the top of the barn. I'll bet you can see miles and miles from up there. Tell me what it looks like. Open your eyes, hold on to the ridgepole, look and tell me."

Quiet voice, a chuckle, footsteps coming nearer. I opened my eyes, just a slit, blinked through them and opened them wide. "You can see the whole world," I said.

"The whole world? Are you sure?"

He was halfway up the roof now.

"Oh, yes. The whole world. As far as the sky goes."

"Think of that! As far as the sky goes. It is a big, big world, isn't it?"

"The biggest world you ever saw!" I was looking boldly again now, making certain. I could even turn loose of the ridgepole with one hand and wave it about. My mother later said that her heart stopped when I did that.

But my father was very near now. Almost near enough to touch. He took the waving hand in his, finally, and tightened his clasp strongly. "I want to see, too."

He slid down astraddle of the ridgepole behind me, the way he often rode me in the saddle before him on his horse. Both arms went securely around me. He looked all around, quietly. "I believe you're right. It's the biggest world I ever saw."

He did not hurry me. He sat there what seemed a long time, looking, letting me point out things, such as the town, the depot, the Methodist steeple. Then he said, "Well, dinner's ready. Shall we go down?"

There was not the slightest feeling of fear now. Shall we go down, he said, and we did. He slid off the ridgepole first, then helped me off, placed my feet on the first cleat, but kept his hands on my ankles. He made a game of getting down — one cleat, two cleats, three cleats, four cleats and so on. Now. Across the shed roof. Down one rung of the ladder. Down two rungs. Then he handed me into my mother's arms. She hugged me close, then spanked me lightly and held me close again. It was my father who got the rough edge of her tongue that day, for leaving the ladder against the shed.

But I *was* forbidden ever to climb on the barn roof again. Not that I would have. At the moment it was like forbidding a burned child not to burn itself again. Nothing could have tempted me to climb up on that barn roof again. Later, when I was bigger and the barn was smaller, climbing to the barn roof was one of those delicious small sins — like stealing watermelons — that tasted all the sweeter because it was forbidden.

However, even if I had been frightened almost out of my wits, I had also enlarged my horizons, come to a better understanding, even if faulty here and there, of the world around me. And it was of very great import to know we lived in the center of the world.

*

Lying just a little south of middle, athwart the Arkansas-Oklahoma line, is one of the most beautiful mountain ranges in the United States, the Ouachitas (pronounced Washitaw). A peculiarity of this range is that the spine runs east and west. Its bulk lies in Arkansas, south of Fort Smith and extending well toward Little Rock in the center of the state, in a band some one hundred miles wide. Mount Magazine is the highest mountain in the Arkansas range, 2880 feet. When one remembers that this is low-lying land, that the average altitude is between five and eight hundred feet, the height of Mount Magazine is almost sheer and is most impressive.

The Ouachitas extend some fifty miles into eastern Oklahoma, their bulk broken here into separate ranges — the Winding Stair Mountains, the Kiamichi, the Jackforks and the Sans Bois. Rich Mountain, highest point in the Oklahoma range, lofts its long upheaved head 2900 feet above sea level.

The Sans Bois Mountains lie the farthest west, like the paws of a great animal, sliding off gradually into the prairie that flows on westward for fifteen hundred miles, not again meeting anything that even looks like a mountain, or even a very high hill, until it surfs against the majestic chain of the Rockies.

Kinta lay at the western foot of the Sans Bois Mountains. When one looked southeastward from Kinta they were the backdrop against the sky, ancient mountains, gently etched, no sharp angles or saw-toothed peaks, they were eroded into soft humps. They were forever blue, bluer than the sky against which they were engraved. Nearer Kinta they broke down into low ridges, foothills flattening out to join the prairie. One knobby hill, just west of Kinta, broke the low crest-line, thrust up into a peak with a strange flat top. This was Tucker's Knob.

The mountains lay behind Kinta. One never thought that the town fronted the mountains. The town fronted the prairie. Except for hunters and fishermen, for whom the mountains were a paradise, there was little travel into them. The country was too broken and rough. No, the mountains lay *behind* Kinta. The prairie was the front porch of the town.

*

Kinta. It is a Choctaw word which means beaver. The
Chocktaws who gave the village its name pronounced it Keen-
tah. But that was long ago when they first came to the lands
set aside for them in the southeastern section of the Indian
Territory, when Choctaws still spoke their own language almost exclusively. It had become just plain Kinta by the time
we lived there.

The first village was a string of little log houses built along
Beaver (or Keen-tah) Creek. The creek teemed with beavers
and the creek and the village took their name from them. The
village remained Kinta, though its pronunciation was changed,
but the creek was eventually anglicized to Beaver.

As the village grew it slowly spread back away from the
creek, northward. It was the only way it could grow, out toward the flat prairie because immediately beyond the creek the
land rose up onto a long ridge.

When it had taken its final shape the town was only a few
hundred yards north of the creek, the railroad tracks lying
between.

The main street lay not quite true east and west but nearly
so. It angled slightly northeast-southwest, as the mountains
did. The business section was a scant two blocks long. Coming from the depot (we never called it the railroad station)
one turned onto the main street at the bank — the Kinta State
Bank, Mr. Sam England, president. Next to the bank and on
the same side of the street was the drugstore. Mr. Luke Allen
owned the drugstore. He was also chairman of the Board of
Trustees of the Kinta School. My father's contract was signed
by Mr. Luke Allen.

On the left of the corner as one turned onto the main street
was the Beaver Hotel. In those days the town was enterprising,
promising. Among the businesses which advertised in the *Kinta*

Journal, a weekly newspaper, were L & F Hardware; the Roler Mill (flour, meal, also alfalfa and kaifa); Ritter Bros. Dry Goods, shoes, groceries; Short-Ogle Lumber Company; R. C. Tidwell's General Store. The Busy Bee Cafe was owned by a family named Willard. They had a son named Mitchell who was the first boy to make calf's eyes at me — in the first grade.

Mr. Will Jones had an insurance company — Insurance & Farm Loans. W. H. Jones, Ph. 47. Yes, there was a telephone exchange. Mr. Will Jones was to marry my first teacher, Miss Lena Thurman.

Dr. Johnson lived just down the road from us, the last house before the town came to an end and the prairie began, his wife kept a parrot so lice-ridden and raucous that it was obscene. Dr. Johnson's office was in a small white building behind his house. Every day Mrs. Johnson put the parrot's cage outside, much too near the path going to Dr. Johnson's office. When I was sent, as I was occasionally, for quinine or calomel, the two specifics which everybody took for every ailment, I had to pass much too near that parrot to suit me. Although he was in a cage, I was still terrified of him. He screamed outrageously at everybody but Mrs. Johnson. He must have hated all human beings but her.

The most fascinating place in town for every child, and from the number of men who were always hanging about, for the men of the town also, was the blacksmith shop. Fatally for me, it had to be passed going from our house to town. It cost me many a whipping. Almost every time I was sent to town on an errand, for a spool of thread, a card of buttons or hooks and eyes, or whatnot, I was admonished, "Come straight back. Don't linger anywhere."

The only way I could get past the blacksmith shop without stopping was if the blacksmith was idle, which was seldom. I

could never pass without stopping if George Lantz was working. It was such a grand, marvelous, wonderful sight — the
bellows, which sometimes Mr. Lantz allowed a child to work
— the big, hot fire in the forge in one corner of the immense
barnlike building was like a magnet, sparks flying, hot fire roar-
ing. The tongs lifting the hot iron out of the fire, placing the
hot horseshoe on the anvil, then the hammer pounding it. Mr.
Lantz, black with the coal of his forge, leather apron covering
him, would make the anvil ring. It fascinated me to watch his
hammer stroke — down, bounce a little, two or three more
bounces, then up and hard down on the horseshoe again.
Then, the horseshoe shaped, it was lifted with the tongs and
plunged into a sizzling bath in a tub of water. Then the
leather-aproned man bent over the hoof of a horse, fitted the
shoe, pared the hoof (which he assured me did not hurt
the horse any more than cutting one's fingernails) and nailed
on the shoe.

When we moved to Kinta there was only one church, the
Methodist Church. Shortly after we came a Baptist Church
was built almost directly behind our house, and a year or two
later a third church was built, the Christian Church. I strongly
suspect my mother was instrumental in getting this church
built, as her mother was instrumental in getting the one built
in Altus. Having grown up in the Christian Church, my
mother would not have been comfortable in any other.

Every summer there was a revival meeting in each of the
three churches. Our parents loved music and wherever they
lived they formed a core around which either an orchestra or
singing group grew up. In Kinta they were part of a quartet —
John Holt singing tenor, Lucy singing alto — which faithfully
sang during the revivals at all three churches.

A lasting memory, imprinted I think on my tailbone by the

hard benches, are those long revival nights. The music was great fun and there was always a full thirty minutes of a warm-up of it, with special numbers by the quartet. But one paid for the music with dreariness when the evangelist held forth, endlessly it seemed. The bench grew harder and harder, and one was forbidden to wiggle and squirm.

Lucy's eagle eye from the choir saw the slightest restlessness, a frown threatened, and one sighed and tried to sit still. Short legs could not touch the floor and feet went to sleep, or ached, or even swelled from hanging. Only the baby was allowed any privileges. He was not expected to stay awake so long. Nor was he expected to sit perfectly still. He wiggled and squirmed as much as he liked, so long as one kept him quiet, then he drifted off to sleep, his head in my lap. It was always a relief to me when he went to sleep because if he grew fretful and cried, or caused any kind of disturbance, I was in for trouble when we got home.

Babysitters were unheard of in those days. Children went where their parents went. The congregation any revival night had more children in it than adults, the audience at any affair in the town — a tent show, a play, a lecture — was at least fifty percent children. If the mother went, the children went. It was acceptable and nobody stayed home because of small children.

*

Kinta was about fifty miles southwest of Fort Smith, Arkansas. This city, of around 25,000 at that time, was on the Arkansas side of the Arkansas River, which divided it from Oklahoma. Fort Smith was where everybody went to shop for those things the stores in Kinta, or Quinton, the next small town west, could not provide — that is, if they preferred or could afford personal shopping instead of mail order. It was where the daily paper, the *Southwest American*, which came down on the first westbound Fort Smith & Western train in the morning, was published. It was where, if you got sick enough to die, the doctors sent you to the hospital. Very early I came to have an abiding distrust of hospitals. Nobody ever seemed to come back from one alive.

Fort Smith was where, going to Arkansas to visit grandparents, we changed trains. The Iron Mountain (Missouri Pacific) came from St. Louis through Fort Smith, went on to Little Rock and points west. If we were going to the McGraw grandparents, we took the Iron Mountain for Altus, some forty-five miles northeast of Fort Smith.

I loved the Iron Mountain depot. To me it was an immense red brick building, with brick-paved platform. There were lots of benches, several ticket windows, and a gift shop where one could buy little glass baubles filled with cinnamon drops. Mostly they were in the shape of a locomotive. We were nearly always given a nickel with which to buy one of these baubles. And we inevitably, though warned, got smeared with the red, sticky drops. But there was a big ladies' rest room where we could be washed up.

If we were going to the Holt grandparents' we took the Arkansas Central, a short line running from Fort Smith to the coal towns of Paris and Spadra. We took it from the Frisco depot which was directly across the tracks from the Iron Mountain depot, but not nearly so roomy or nice, and of course the Arkansas Central was not nearly as luxurious a train as the Iron Mountain.

The Fort Smith & Western was the lifeline between Kinta and the outside world. People traveled on it. It brought freight. In the summer it brought ice every day. In the winter it brought the coal to be burned to warm our homes. Twice a week the year round, it brought bakery bread. Occasionally it brought fresh meat, oysters, fresh fruit, other luxuries and delicacies which the Holts could rarely afford. We did buy ice daily, and occasionally Mama bought a loaf of bread, although she made most of our bread, the most delicious loaves, hot rolls and cinnamon rolls that were ever made. Both she and Mrs. Moore kept starters of yeast going and at least once a week made five or six loaves of bread. If either of them went away on a short trip and the starter was thrown away, they had only to borrow enough to begin a new starter to keep the eternal round going.

The Fort Smith & Western took back to the city the cattle raised on the ranches outlying the town, shipped them from Kinta to the stockyards in Fort Smith. It also took cotton and corn and it picked up coal cars from the mining towns of Lequire, McCurtain and Bokoshe and took them east as well as west.

There were four trains each day. Eastbound, toward Fort Smith, No. 4 came through Kinta at 8:16 A.M. The afternoon eastbound train went through at 3:44. This was No. 2. Westbound, toward Guthrie, the state capital, No. 1 went through at 9:26 A.M. and No. 3, westbound, stopped at our depot at 6:30 P.M. To go to Fort Smith, then, one usually caught No. 4, the morning train at 8:16. This got one to Fort Smith by mid-morning and gave a longer day for shopping. Unless there was too much shopping for one day, one could catch No. 3 back home and arrive at 6:30 P.M.

The train that had the most daily importance to us, however, the train which brought most of the world to us in Kinta, was No. 1, which arrived at 9:26 A.M. The biggest mail came on this train, the newspaper, the ice and the fresh bread. More passengers might arrive on the evening train, but the necessities of life, the freight, the printed word, the precious letters from family and friends usually came at 9:26 in the morning.

The trains marked the day into familiar segments and kept the time for us. Whatever one was doing, when the whistle blew for the first crossing — and there was a crossing for each direction — one knew immediately what time it was. It was No. 4, eastbound and it was 8:16 in the morning. School began at 9:00 A.M. in those days and one knew precisely how long one could dally before beginning to dress for school.

It was No. 1, westbound — 9:26 in the morning. During the school term one was usually well into the first class. In the summertime, one would shortly be sent for the mail.

It was No. 2, eastbound, 3:44 in the afternoon. Just sixteen minutes until school would be out for the day. Finally, ending the day for us, it was No. 3, at 6:30 P.M.

In the winter, this last train went through after dark. Dark outside, and cold. The lamps lit, the fire in the stove glowing through the isinglass door, supper over, the family gathered about, children studying, the mother perhaps rocking the smallest child to sleep, the father, in our home, beginning to grade papers, in other homes perhaps poring over the newspaper one last time. Suddenly there it was, the full-chested, deep-throated, long, long-drawn wail — No. 3 whistling for the grade crossing just outside the town. The fireman believed in using the whistle in those days. He blew three times, always, holding the cord down each time long enough for a shiver of pure delight to climb the spine. The sound rose, spread in the clear, cold air, filled it, entered the home, entered the mind, entered the heart. No other sound in the world ever like it. No sound so full of promise, expectancy, no sound calling so urgently to something new and different, something exciting and prophetic and adventurous. No sound, in time, so nostalgic as a train whistle, so full of longing, so full of wistfulness for time lost, for time gone forever — the old, husky wail of a train whistle the surest symbol of a part of the American heritage of which today's child has been cheated.

If one lived close enough, men left their homes and went to meet the train. Just to watch the last train of the day chug in, stop briefly, chug on. To see through the lighted windows people traveling, going from someplace to someplace else, their strangeness always mysterious — faces seen only briefly through a train window, then gone forever. To watch a few passengers get off — usually people of the town coming back from Fort Smith. To meet somebody special coming for a visit. There was a word or two of welcome, a word or two of news exchanged, then, the train having departed, each man went lingeringly back to his home.

There *were* men, of course, who met every train during the whole day. Men who either had business meeting the trains, or nothing better to do. A handful of them gathered at the station half an hour or so before a train was due. They sat about on the mail truck or on the wide ledges of the depot windows, or stood about in small groups. They were usually older men. It may have been they felt a surge of restlessness, a disenchantment with here and now, especially age, a longing to leave it behind, to go with the train, no matter where — just go, someplace new, see something different, do something new, be young again. More than the wind, a train made one restless.

There was always somebody to "let the train go through." That done, they drifted away until the next train was due.

The arrival, the departure, of the trains furnished the excitement of their lives, gave them point and meaning.

*

Our house, the Moore house, the Dick Rabon house and a fourth house rented to some people whose name I have forgotten filled the four corners of the two lanes which intersected at that point. In our corner there was only one house, ours. The vacant land which stretched down to the next lane was available to us and my father rented it and used it for an enormous garden each year and a small pasturage for the cow in the winter.

In the corner south of us lived Mr. Dick Rabon. There were no small children. The daughter, Hester, and two sons were grown. We were never allowed to call any adult by his first name alone. Married women were given their title, thus Mrs. Moore, Mrs. Puckett, Mrs. Johnson. Single women were Miss Lena, Miss Ada, Miss Cora, so Hester Rabon was Miss Hester.

Across the lane east of us, the Moore house and Dr. Johnson's house filled the block, both having ample grounds, only a fence dividing the properties. And at that time Dr. Johnson's house was the end of town. Beyond his house the road that ran in front of all our houses curved out onto the prairie, meandered across the prairie to Sans Bois (the ancient Choctaw town), to Stigler, the county seat of Haskell County.

Sans Bois — which was universally pronounced San Boy — took its name from the small river which rose clear and blue in the mountains of the same name, wandered across the prairie, accumulating silt and growing sluggish on its way and joined the Arkansas some forty miles north near the village of Cowlington.

Sans Bois was barely a village. There was a general store, at least for a while after we moved to Kinta. There was a church, a cemetery, a school and the ruins of a Choctaw girls' academy. Mrs. Moore had attended the Sans Bois Academy when she was a girl.

The school was called Edmond's Chapel. Most of the land thereabouts was owned by the McCurtain families, and Sans Bois was the seat of the Choctaw government in its last years before the Choctaw Nation was assimilated by the United States and the state of Oklahoma. My father taught summer school there frequently.

All travel going to Sans Bois or to Stigler or to Whitefield passed our house on its corner, passed in front of the Moore house, then bent beyond Dr. Johnson's house onto the prairie.

*

The most beautiful thing about Kinta was the prairie. Infinite, or so it seemed to a child, mysterious, beckoning, a little frightening. Not flat but gently swelling. Bleak in the winter and cold. The wind forever blowing over it. Prairie wolves coming almost into the town in the winter, filling the night with their desolate, desperate, lonelier-than-God howls. One at first, then the chorus, long, long deathly wails. Full-out and terrible. Then without warning, full-stop. Not one voice fading out alone. Just stop, all at once, as if on signal. Mystifying, terrible, fearful.

Snow covering the prairie, white shrouding, or white blanket. Dazzling white snow, unbroken as far as the eye could see, until some horseman was a black speck against the sky, looming gradually larger until a horse and rider could be made out. No travel with buggy and wagon when a deep snow was on.

Then the slow melt, the dry brown grass showing through again.

Bleak, but still beautiful, in some infinite, awe-ful way.

Spring on the prairie was a madness. A few days of sun and warm south wind in early April and suddenly the prairie was a carpet of flowers. The prairie flowers were the very first to bloom, all short-stemmed, blooming very close to the ground so that they gave the appearance of being matted, like a tufted rug. They were bluets, spring beauties, Johnny-jumpups and I don't know what all else, but they were all blue or so tinged with blue as to give a blue appearance from a distance.

They covered the entire prairie and for two or three weeks there was the holy sight of this vast spread of land turned entirely blue — the blue being bluer than the sky. Electric blue, sapphire blue, turquoise blue, violet blue, shimmering blue, sparkling blue, dancing blue. An entrancing sight, bewitching, intoxicating.

One walked on the prairie and crushed the small flowers under one's feet. It could not be helped. There was no place to put one's feet except on flowers. Crushed, they smelled, and the air was heavy with their smell. The heat of the sun also brought out their odor, and the air in the town, the air in one's home, the air one breathed was laden with it. Every breath was scented with this sweet, but light, smell. It was like breathing flowers.

One never wanted to be out of the sight of the prairie in the spring. One wanted to spend every waking moment on it. We and the Moore children pled, "May we play on the prairie? May we pick some flowers?"

Usually we were allowed. "But no further than the first gully. Don't go beyond the first gully."

By that first spring we knew why. We had been told why many times. The gullies crisscrossed the prairie in crazy pat-terns, leading into and out of each other. A child could wander up a gully, into another, wind and twist about in the senseless maze and soon be hopelessly lost, all sense of direction gone, all remembrance of a path lost. And adults might search for days, up, across, down, around the senseless patterns, then more by chance than anything else find a lost child, or tragically, also by chance, fail to find him until too late.

Another reason was that gypsies camped on the prairie. In all the months except the coldest months of the winter, a gypsy camp or two could always be seen far out on the prairie. Our mothers believed the stories that gypsies stole children. We were cautioned about gullies and we were cautioned about gypsies. It was shudderingly delicious to venture down into the first gully, then scamper back up to safety again. It was shudderingly delicious to watch a big, painted gypsy wagon come lumbering across the prairie toward town, to stay till the last safe moment to see them up as close as possible, then turn and race wildly for home.

Gypsy men were tinkers, going from house to house sharpening knives and scissors. Gypsy women were, by and large, beggars, colorful beggars in their gaudy clothing, but beggars nevertheless, going from house to house begging old clothes. They were also fortune tellers, reading palms and telling fortunes with decks of old greasy cards.

Screen doors were kept safely locked when gypsies were in town and children were kept in the houses.

But the first gully, where we were allowed to go, was a satisfying distance out on the prairie behind our house and the

Moore house. It was almost beyond hearing an adult call. Not quite. A mother's voice could be faintly heard or we would not have been allowed to go.

One lone tree, a persimmon tree, marked the rim of that gully. It made enough shade that when we grew tired we could flop down on top of more flowers and rest and cool off. We gathered the small flowers by the basketful, then gathered more and clenched them in our hot fists, to see them wilt before we could get them in water. We brought them home with us and our mothers found vases, glasses, teacups, fruit jars for our bouquets. Our homes were full of blue flowers during those few short weeks. We went on a blue binge, a rapturous, spring-fevered blue-flowered binge, never growing tired of gathering the flowers, never growing tired of having them in our homes.

*

The prairie had a mystique of its own for me which more than overlaid the town. A child playing on the prairie was suddenly still, moved away from the other children, to the edge of the gully, and stood frozen. Listening. For what, she never knew, for there was never anything but the usual sounds of birds, insects, a wagon coming down the road, a dog barking, a cow bawling. Nor did she ever learn for what she was listening. But there was something present, a life, a spirit, something which made it necessary to stand still and listen, as if it would speak to her. And occasionally the standing still and listening was accompanied by a strange exaltation, uncalled for by any foreknowing, simply a sudden radiant joy, a sudden boundless lift of the heart, a feeling of lightness and buoyancy, as if one had wings and could fly.

It came most often on days when the air was crystal clear,

so clear that the mountains were given a third dimension, of depth; when near objects were defined so sharply that they stood out distinct in every line, when one was nearly weight-less because of the clean, unweighted air.

One was lifted suddenly so joyously that simply to be alive was almost more than one could bear. Then one had to listen. Not hearing anything, then one had to run wildly, roll dizzily down the gully, climb the persimmon tree, or simply dance crazily about. Whatever it was, one *had* to do something, to move, to act.

A prosaic answer might be that on such days there was some atmospheric change which accounted for the clarity of the air — and in only one other place have I ever seen such crystal clarity of the air as we sometimes had in Kinta, and that was in Santa Fe, New Mexico. This atmospheric change may have thinned the air, as high mountain air is thin, so that we breathed less oxygen and were sent thus light-bodied and light-headed.

The trouble with that solution is that I never heard anybody else say they had experienced these things. My mother scoffed at me and I learned to keep these feelings to myself. I decided I was strange somehow and was a little embarrassed by the strangeness, a little ashamed of it, and eventually determined to keep these strange feelings to myself. No use having the whole town know I was weird. But the mystique of the prairie and the strange response in myself persisted all the years we lived in Kinta. I never had it again after we left. Not until fifty years later, returning and once more standing on the prairie, I found myself listening, feeling once again the strange exaltation and joy. I expect it was just as well that we did move from Kinta. An entire lifetime of some queer extrasensory perception might have been very debilitating.

To me the prairie was endless and the prairie was mysterious, but to everybody the prairie was central to the life of the town. Out on its swelling, gently rising and falling, slowly breathing bosom were the cattle ranches and the farms which were the reason for the town's existence.

From the prairie, if you looked east, a swell rose, over which the road to Lequire wound. A white house was on the crest of that swell. A white house with a white picket fence around it. Built in a rambling, one-story style, with gingerbread gables and gingerbread front across the porch. One knew that that white house was guarded, that men with guns kept watch night and day. Or so at least the town legend went.

Because in this white house lived Green McCurtain, the last Principal Chief of the Choctaw Nation, the last governor of his people. In his lifetime of brilliant, dedicated service to his people he had inevitably made many enemies. Although there was no longer any Choctaw Nation, although Green McCurtain himself had had to lead his people out of their national sovereignty into the state of Oklahoma, it was still said that his life was by no means secure. That it was constantly threatened and that devoted men guarded him well.

Governor Green McCurtain was Lena McCurtain Moore's father, the grandfather of Corinne, Inez and young Green McCurtain Moore and the later Moore children.

7

THE CHOCTAWS

✳

FOR HUNDREDS OF YEARS the home of the Choctaws had been Mississippi and southwestern Alabama. The Chickasaws were north of them, mostly in Tennessee, and the Creeks lived to the east in Alabama and Georgia. The Choctaws were the largest branch of the Muskogean linguistic stock. They were closely related to the Chickasaws, who spoke a dialect of the Muskogean language, and they were also, but more distantly, related to the Creeks and Seminoles.

As with all Indians there were tribal traditions about their origin. The Choctaw tradition said they came from the Far West in the distant past and, as with the children of Israel, Moses guiding them with his rod, their leader had a sacred pole which he carried during the daytime. When the tribe camped at night the pole was stuck in the ground. Every morning it was examined carefully. If it leaned in any direction, this was the direction they were to take. It seemed always to lean toward the east which meant they must continue traveling eastward.

When they reached a place in northern Mississippi they found the pole remaining upright one morning. This place they called Nanih Waya, the end of their journey, the place where their gods intended them to make their new home.

They built mounds and fortresses and the place became the ceremonial and ritual center of their nation. Nanih Waya is in present-day Winston County, Mississippi.

The legendary account for the Chickasaws says that twin brothers, Chahtaw and Chikasah, actually led them out of the west, but as they neared the end of their long journey the two brothers quarreled. Some of the people followed Chikasah, who branched off northward. The main group, however, continued to follow Chahtaw and settled in Mississippi.

For several centuries they lived peacefully and undisturbed. They were not a warlike people, usually going to war only in defense of their homes. They early became an agricultural people, raising corn, beans, squash, pumpkins and melons in little plots by their cabins. They were a very practical people. Although they owned less land than any of the surrounding tribes, they made better use of it, always raising more corn and beans than they needed and storing the surplus.

Corn was the most important element in their economic life, although they also appreciated the importance of fruits, nuts, seeds and roots from the woods and made use of them and stored them also. Every house had a corncrib, however, and corn in the form of hominy and meal was the staple of life.

They hunted, too, but hunting was always secondary to agriculture. The buffalo had long disappeared, but they hunted deer, sometimes as far afield as Arkansas and Louisiana. They valued the meat of the deer but primarily they needed the skins for clothing. The woods in Mississippi were full of small game which furnished them all the meat they needed. There were turkeys, pigeons, squirrels, beaver, otter, raccoon, possum and rabbits.

With great sense of organization they grouped their towns into three geographical divisions or districts: the Sixtown Indians, or *Okla Hannali*, in the south; the Long People, or *Okla Falaya*, in the west; the *Okla Tánnáp*, or the People of the Opposite Side, were in the east.

There was no tribal chief. Instead each district had a Head Chief. In war and other enterprises requiring a cooperative effort of the whole Nation, the three chiefs acted together. There was no capital in the modern sense, since any chief might be succeeded by one from another village in his district. Succession to chieftainship depended partly upon personal ability and position and partly upon inheritance. Very early, therefore, certain family dynasties of great power and influence emerged.

Each town in a district also had its chief who came somewhat under the authority of the Head Chief. Besides the town chief, each village had a *Tichou mingo*, who acted as the chief's speaker and arranged the feasts, ceremonies, dances and so forth. There was also a war chief who led the men of the village to war and two *Taskaminkochi*, assistants to the war chief.

Councils of a district were called by its Head Chief, and councils of the entire Nation by the three Head Chiefs acting together. Runners were sent to summon all the town chiefs to the assembly. The members of the council were greatly influenced by the judgment of the head chiefs, were usually guided by their suggestions and recommendations, but the decisions were always made in a democratic fashion and in accord with the wishes of the majority of those assembled.

The council usually dealt with such matters of public policy as peace, war or foreign relations, but it also exercised a certain judicial power.

Murder was the one great crime recognized among the Choctaws and was invariably avenged by the relatives of the victim. This was tribal law and a murderer expected to be killed, in turn, and either quietly awaited his execution, or fled the country. This tribal law, so old and so inevitable, was continued well up into the nineteenth century.

As practical as the Choctaws were, they were not a mystical people. They believed rather vaguely in some deity or Great Spirit, but they believed this spirit lived pretty far off, was not too bothered about them, and they had no religious ceremonials honoring the spirit, nor did they pray to it. They believed in immortality in a somewhat vague way also, in some distant land into which the deceased person eventually took up his abode.

They accepted the here and now and made the best possible use of it. They were greatly interested in all social activities and loved to gather together frequently for, games, dancing and feasting.

The first contact the Choctaws had with the white man was with De Soto and his men in 1540. The Spaniards were welcomed when they arrived by Chief Tuscaloosa in his town of Tuscaloosa. De Soto demanded carriers and women. The carriers were furnished and Chief Tuscaloosa promised them women at Mabila (Mobile). To reach Mabila, De Soto demanded canoes. The Choctaws had no canoes but made rafts for the Spaniards.

Then Chief Tuscaloosa was required to accompany the Spaniards. He managed to send runners ahead to assemble the warriors at Mabila. A pitched battle occurred when the Spaniards arrived. All the Choctaws were killed, but the Spaniards also suffered heavy losses. Twenty-two of De Soto's men were killed and 148 were wounded, suffering 688 arrow wounds. De Soto remained in the vicinity about a month, burning and ravaging the country, then he marched northwest across the entire Choctaw country and entered the Chickasaw domains. Failing to find the wealth he was looking for, he then left, making no settlements.

For a century and a half, then, the Choctaws saw no more of the white man. From 1700 on, however, the French were close neighbors along the Mississippi and around New Orleans, and the entire period of the eighteenth century was a time of French, Spanish, English and finally American intrigue and encroachment.

It was during this period the Choctaws became acquainted with European grains and garden vegetables and began to acquire horses, cattle, hogs and barnyard fowls. It was during this period, also, that white men started marrying into the tribe, taking up residence among the Choctaws, and began to influence the tribal councils. Among the most prominent of them were the Folsom brothers, who came from South Carolina; John Pitchlynn, the son of an Englishman; the French Canadians Louis and Michel Leflore; and a Scotch-Irishman named William McCurtain. William McCurtain, who is reputed to have come from County Ulster, Ireland, fathered ten sons. The brothers were Cornelius, Thomas, Daniel, John, Luke, Allen, William, Canada, Samuel and Camper.

All these men settled among the Choctaws during the last quarter of the eighteenth century and their descendants became leaders within the tribe.

Mississippi became a territory of the United States in 1798 and white men began to flock to the new territory. The Choctaws were pressured to cede parts of their domain to the American government. Through various treaties from 1801 to 1820, they were persuaded to cede most of their outlying lands, all of those in Alabama, all in the south and west of Mississippi. By 1820 they had remaining to them only their land in the north and the northeast. The payments for the land ceded were held in the Federal Treasury and issued to the Choctaws in annuities each year.

If they had lost most of their land, they had made great material progress. The practical-minded Choctaws adapted themselves quickly to the white man's way of life, following his customs in dress, in trade and in farming the land. Many of them had great herds of cattle and they learned to raise cotton, learned to card, weave and spin it and make it into clothing, and they learned to market their surplus crops. Some of them accumulated considerable wealth and, following the example of the white planters, owned Negro slaves.

Mississippi became a state in 1817, and the state could not abide a separate government of Choctaw Indians in its midst. It was also so crowded now that the Choctaw lands were coveted. In a series of treaties between 1820 and 1830, the Choctaws were persuaded to cede their remaining lands in Mississippi and to accept in exchange the lands set aside for them in the Indian Territory west of the Mississippi River.

The original land set aside for them was the entire southern half of the present state of Oklahoma, bounded on the north by the Arkansas and Canadian Rivers, on the east by the Arkansas state line, on the west by the Texas line, and on the south by the Red River. Before any of the Choctaws could remove to their new country, however, it was discovered by the United States government that white settlers were living in the eastern section and the Arkansas state line had to be redrawn farther west. The Choctaws were persuaded to cede this portion of their new country.

In time they were required to cede or lease the entire western half of their new lands, one portion to the Chickasaws, the farthest western portion to the Plains Indians.

The Federal government hoped the Choctaws would move voluntarily. An Indian agent, Major William McClellan, was appointed in 1826, and the next year he began to erect buildings for his agency about fifteen miles from Fort Smith, near old Fort Coffee, at what became known as Skullyville. By 1829, however, only 150 Choctaws had been induced to settle in the new land.

Mississippi state leaders were becoming increasingly impatient over the slow removal of the Choctaws. In 1829 they passed legislation abolishing the tribal government of the Choctaws and making them citizens of Mississippi.

This threat to their national life caused the Choctaws to enter into a final treaty at Dancing Rabbit Creek, in 1830, with the Federal government. At Dancing Rabbit Creek, Secretary of War John H. Eaton bullied the Choctaws, reminding them of their helplessness, and firmly declining to intervene in their behalf with the state of Mississippi. Hopeless and helpless, the Choctaw leaders signed the treaty on September 17, 1830.

The treaty provided that the United States would secure to them "the jurisdiction and government of all the persons and property that may be within their limits west, so that no Territory or State shall ever have a right to pass laws for the government of the Choctaw Nation of Red People and their descendants; and that no part of the land granted them shall ever be embraced in any Territory or State; but the U.S. shall forever secure said Chowtaw Nation from, and against all laws except such as from time to time may be enacted in their own National Councils, not inconsistent with the Constitution, Treaties, and Laws of the United States; and except such as may, and which have been enacted by Congress, to the extent that Congress under the Constitution are required to exercise a legislation over Indian Affairs."

For three quarters of a century this was the Magna Charta of the national existence of the Choctaw Nation.

The treaty promised numerous annuities for the support of their government and schools. It also gave every Choctaw head of a family the opportunity of remaining in Missssippi, selecting an allotment of land and becoming a citizen of the United States. Those who chose to move were to be paid for their cattle or other property left behind, and were to be provided with transportation to their new homes, and with food for twelve months after their arrival.

Most of the Choctaws elected to move and the main removals occurred during 1831, 1832 and 1833. Bids for the removals were opened to white contractors, who guaranteed food and transportation. But so ruthless were the contractors in their greed, so poor were the food and transportation that many of the Choctaws who could afford it bore the expense of removal themselves.

The sufferings of the emigrants were indescribable and beyond belief. The way was terribly difficult under the best circumstances — 350 miles through swamps, dense forests, impenetrable thickets and canebreaks and swollen rivers. The Choctaws were forced to walk most of the way. Crossing the Mississippi River they were crowded onto anything that would float. One ancient steamboat blew up, crowded to the rails with the Indians, and several hundred were killed.

A white child, a girl about thirteen years of age, lived with her parents on the road the Choctaws took through northern Mississippi. She witnessed the terrible sufferings of the Indians as, for weeks and weeks in 1831, the long, heartbreaking

lines filed past her home. The people were pushed and prod-
ded along like cattle. The old and the sick, all who weakened
and could not keep the pace, were abandoned. Of the old and
the sick, many were simply shoved into a hollow log and left
to die.

The white family helped those who could be helped, gave
them food and shelter until they could take up the march
again — and they buried those who died. They wondered at
the brutality of the white man in charge of this removal.

Elizabeth Woolverton, the white child, was to become my
great-grandmother. Her parents personally had nothing to do
with the removal of the Choctaws, but multiplied by hundreds
of thousands like them who had swarmed into the country,
they had everything to do with it and must share the collective
guilt.

Perhaps the figures tell the story best. Around 20,000 Choctaws attempted the removal. The population of the Choctaw
Nation in 1845 was 12,700. Their hardships did not end when
they reached the end of the trail in their new country. They
endured two or three years of starvation, sickness and death
after their arrival.

One cannot escape the thought that while in Washington it
may have been believed the most humane solution to the problem of Choctaws in Mississippi had been reached, in the hands
of local agents of the Federal government the best solution
seemed to be the death of as many Choctaws as possible.

Three centuries after their first contact with the white man,
the Choctaws were expelled from their ancient home. They
settled into their new home to work out their problems.

They took with them their own forms of national government. They divided the new land into the three familiar districts: the *Okla Falaya* along the Red River, in the southeast;

the *Moshalatubbee* in the north, bounded by the Arkansas River, and the *Pushmataha* to the west of the Kiamichi River.

As soon as they recovered from the trauma of the removals, the Choctaws began to prosper. Their new country was wild, but beautiful, and soon towns and settlements sprang up and trails and roads crisscrossed the country. The largest town was Doaksville, in the southeastern district. The Federal government established a post office there in 1832. Other post offices established were at Skullyville, near Fort Smith, in 1833; Eagletown in 1834; Perryville in 1841, and Boggy Depot in 1849.

These were small but thriving towns, with hotels, blacksmith shops, general stores and markets. They were located on important highways which flowed through the Nation toward Texas. A newspaper, the *Choctaw Telegraph*, was established at Doaksville in 1848, succeeded in 1850 by the *Choctaw Intelligencer*.

All lands were held in community. No Choctaw owned land, but he was free to settle upon the land where he pleased so long as he did not trespass upon land already fenced and worked by somebody else. He could fence as much as he pleased and let his cattle roam in the enclosure, he could plow and farm as much land as he had the funds, the equipment, the time and family members to farm.

Inevitably some families already grown wealthy by their efforts in Mississippi, already owning slaves, took over vast acreages and fenced and ran extensive herds of cattle on them, raised huge fields of cotton and became wealthier still.

Among these families were the Folsoms, Pitchlynns, Walkers, Leflores, Joneses and McCurtains. They were the leaders among the Choctaws, accepted, honored and respected by them. The people looked to them for leadership and the members of these families provided it in very much the same way the members of the aristocracy in England assumed political responsibility for their nation. They were better educated and better trained, by tradition and experience, for positions of leadership.

The Choctaws were fortunate in the appointment of a new agent shortly after the removal. William Armstrong was to prove a valiant and trusted friend. As soon as the Choctaws were settled in their new home, Armstrong urged them to build log buildings and organize the schools provided by the treaty annuities. Some of these schools were opened as early as 1833–34. By 1842 a comprehensive school system was established and every district had schools.

In 1834 the Choctaws, again following in the footsteps of their white brethren, changed their form of government. They wrote a constitution and they vested all authority in a General Council which should be composed of twenty-seven elected members, paid for their services from the tribal annuities.

The three District Chiefs were also to be elected and, *ex officio*, were to be members of the General Council. Any two of them could veto legislative enactments. The laws were in written form and a copy was deposited with the U.S. agent. In the central part of their settlements near the present site of Tuskahoma, they built a spacious log council house, which was given the sacred name of Nanih Waya.

This experiment in an elective form of government was amended in 1843 when a bicameral Council was decided upon. A Senate was established with four members from each district, holding office for two years, and a House of Representatives elected annually, based on the population of the districts.

But this form of government proved unsatisfactory. It was

too unwieldly and there was no central power. Finally, in 1857, a new constitution was drafted at Skullyville which abolished the office of District Chief and created a Principal Chief, or governor, for the entire Choctaw Nation.

This almost caused a civil war in the Nation because a considerable portion of the citizens objected to the abolition of the District Chiefs, and to the removal of the capital from Tuskahoma to Doaksville. A compromise was eventually reached and in January of 1860, at Doaksville, a constitution was written which satisfied all. The final constitution retained the district organization and the District Chiefs and courts, but provided for a national government with a Principal Chief.

The districts were now divided into counties which constituted an election district for members of the Council and served as a unit of local administration. Moshalatubbee District, into which John and Lucy Holt moved in 1902, consisted of five counties, Sugarloaf, Skullyville, Sans Bois, Gaines and Tobucksy.

The county officers were elected for a term of two years and consisted of a judge, a sheriff and a ranger. The ranger's duty was to attend to the advertising and sale of strayed livestock. The county judge appointed an official who served as clerk and treasurer, and the sheriff appointed his deputies.

The Principal Chief was elected by the people for a two-year term. He could succeed himself for another two-year term, but he then became ineligible for re-election until at least one term of office had intervened. He was the head of the National government and had great executive authority, partly through his constitutional powers and partly through legislative enactment.

Principal Chiefs actually never retired from politics. As

soon as they retired from their two terms in succession they entered the Council where their experience was much valued. It was also customary to seek election for a third term as soon as the constitutional ineligibility had expired.

The official title was Principal Chief, but unofficially the head of the Nation was usually called "Governor."

The other executive officers of the government were the National Secretary, National Treasurer, National Auditor and National Attorney. These officials were elected for two-year terms in the years between gubernatorial elections. Thus the Choctaws had national elections every year, on the first Wednesday in August.

With very few amendments, the constitution of 1860, which provided for a General Council of two houses and a Supreme Court and the executive officers, was the fundamental law of the Choctaw Nation throughout the rest of its existence.

The official seal of the Choctaw Nation, with its bow and crossed arrows and combined pipe and hatchet, now form a part of the Great Seal of the state of Oklahoma.

*

In the Moshalatubbee District in Mississippi the McCurtain family had been prominent since the last quarter of the eighteenth century. As has been said, the original William McCurtain who married into the tribe had ten sons. The most outstanding of these sons was Cornelius who was born in 1803.

As has also been said, in the new Choctaw country the Moshalatubbee District was located in the northern section of the Choctaw lands, near the Arkansas and Canadian rivers, near the Arkansas town of Fort Smith. Under the new constitution it became the First District, its largest settlement was

Skullyville. The post office was at Skullyville and annuities in the First District were paid at Skullyville. The name derives from the Choctaw word *iskoli*, which means money.

After my family moved from Kinta we lived for two years in the village of Cowlington, just twelve miles from Skullyville. Many times we drove to Spiro, the larger town which grew up near Skullyville, to shop. On the way we passed through Skullyville. I remember a school, a general store and the post office. It was in the post-office building that annuities had been paid to First District Choctaws for so many years. The old post-office building is still standing, the only building of old Skullyville left. It is now occupied by an antique shop. Skullyville died because the Fort Smith & Western Railroad bypassed it and everybody moved to the new town of Spiro, created by the railroad's route.

*

Cornelius McCurtain, one of the ten sons of William Mc-Curtain, came into prominence in the Choctaw Nation early. He brought his wife and small son, Jackson Frazier McCur-tain, to settle in Skullyville in 1833, the last year of the great removals. It is said that he paid his own expenses and moved his family in comfort. Immediately after settling in Skully-ville he began to take an active part in the affairs of the First District. As a member of the Board of Trustees he was a fac-tor in the establishment of the first neighborhood schools in the District.

He was elected to the General Council in 1844, in 1846 and again in 1848. In the fall of 1849 he was elected Chief of the First District, a position he held until 1854. When his term as District Chief expired he was appointed to the Board of Commissioners of the Nation to investigate what was termed the Orphans' Claims. He died shortly afterward. His wife, Mahayia, lived until 1869.

Cornelius and Mahayia McCurtain had seven children. They were Jackson Frazier, born in Mississippi in 1830, Isabelle, Elsie, David, Green, Edmond and Robert.

Of the five sons born to Cornelius and Mahayia McCurtain, three were destined to become Principal Chief of the Choctaw Nation: Jackson, Edmond, born in 1842, and Green, born in 1848.

Two of the sons, David and Robert, were assassinated. In April of 1874, David McCurtain was shot by a Negro named Charles Brown. He died a few days later.

In January of 1970, I sat in a restaurant in the small town of Spiro, Oklahoma, and listened to an old man, a descendant of Thomas J. Ainsworth, also prominent in Choctaw politics, tell about it. "The McCurtains were always in Choctaw politics," he said. "In the spring of 1874, a mulatto named Charles Brown shot David McCurtain. The word was brought to Green McCurtain by a friend who said, 'Green, your brother David has been shot.' Green said, 'Who did it?' The friend said, 'Charles Brown.'

"Green swore out a warrant for Brown and went and got him. He tied him on a horse and was taking him to Fort Smith, to Judge Parker's court, when he met a man who said to him, 'Green, your brother has died.'

"While the two men were talking the Negro kicked up his horse and tried to escape. Green shot him dead."

In August of 1874, Robert McCurtain was killed by Henderson Walker, a son of ex-Governor Tandy Walker. This killing occurred at the old Walker home near Skullyville over some slight provocation. Henderson Walker fled the country and remained away for three years. When he returned, Jackson

McCurtain (known as Jack) sought him out and avenged the death of his brother. The old tribal law of an eye for an eye and a tooth for a tooth had not completely died out.

The public career of Jack McCurtain was coincident with the adoption of the 1860 constitution. He was elected to the General Council in the fall of 1859.

But the Civil War broke out in 1861 and the Choctaws were the first of the Indian Nations in the west to join the Confederacy. Coming from Mississippi as they had, they were loyal to the South.

Jack McCurtain enlisted in June of 1861 in the First Regiment of Choctaw and Chickasaw Rifles, was commissioned captain of Company G in this regiment. In 1862 he was commissioned a lieutenant colonel of the First Choctaw Battalion and served in this capacity until the end of the war. His younger brother, Edmond, also served with this battalion.

Upon returning to his home, near Red Oak in Sugarloaf County, he was elected to the Senate and served continuously until February of 1880, when he succeeded to the office of Principal Chief on February 20, 1880. In August of that year he was elected Principal Chief and was re-elected in 1882.

He was an aggressive Principal Chief. His years in office were the closing years of rehabilitation following the Civil War and he was instrumental in closing the long controversy concerning the rights of the Negro freedmen. Under him they were granted full tribal citizenship.

The capitol of the Choctaw Nation had been moved twenty years earlier to the old Armstrong Academy at Chahtah-Tamaha, in the southern section of the Nation. Jack McCurtain moved it back to Nanih Waya, near Tuskahoma, where a permanent and beautiful building was built.

For some years more and more white intruders and renegades had been invading the Territory, to escape the law in the States. Judge Isaac Parker occupied the Federal bench in Fort Smith, with complete and final jurisdiction over the entire Western Judicial District, which included the Territory. Chief McCurtain made a vigorous effort, with the help of Federal troops, to drive the lawless element out of the Choctaw Nation. He made so many enemies during this period that for a time his life was in such danger that he moved his home down near Antlers. In 1883, however, he returned to live near Tuskahoma.

At the end of his second full term constitutional law prevented his running for Principal Chief again. However, the chieftainship stayed in the McCurtain family. In August 1884, Edmond McCurtain, his younger brother was elected. Edmond McCurtain's home was at Sans Bois. He had entered public life in 1866 as county judge of Sans Bois County. In 1872, he was trustee of schools for the Moshalatubbee District and in 1876 he was a representative to the General Council from Sans Bois County.

During the years Jack McCurtain was Principal Chief, Edmond McCurtain was Superintendent of Education for the Nation. There were no colleges or universities in the Choctaw Nation, but Edmond McCurtain worked diligently for appropriations with which to send qualified young people to eastern colleges and universities. He served two years as Principal Chief, then declined to run for office again. He was a good Chief but his term was overshadowed by the greater statesmanship of his elder brother.

Undoubtedly Jack McCurtain would have run for the office at the expiration of Edmond's term, but he died in 1885. Edmond McCurtain supported Thomas McKinney, who was elected. Then he continued to serve in the Senate as the senator from Sans Bois County. He lived until 1890 and is buried near his brothers David and Robert in Skullyville Cemetery.

*

Great changes were now rapidly occurring which created many problems in the political and economic life of the Choctaws. The influx of white settlers had assumed abnormal proportions — there were far more white people than there were Choctaws. But they could not buy land nor could they hold title to their businesses. They had to obtain a license from the Choctaw government to engage in any business. Inevitably this situation, as more and more white people came into the Nation, was one that chafed and irritated. The old order of things was beginning to slip and the sovereignty of the Choctaw Nation was being challenged. Although the Choctaws held tenaciously to their own governmental rights, by 1890 it became apparent that the United States had no alternative except to terminate the Choctaws' political and economic control.

The United States Indian agents, with one exception, condemned the Choctaw system of landholding, in commonality. The Commissioner of Indian Affairs declared in 1886 that the treaties should be disregarded if necessary, saying "the treaties never contemplated the un-American and absurd idea of a separate nationality in our midst . . . These Indians have no right to obstruct civilization and commerce and set up an exclusive claim to self-government, establishing a government within a government, and then expect and claim that the United States shall protect them from all harm, while insisting that it shall not be the ultimate judge as to what is best to be done for them in a political point of view."

He recommended the forcible allotment of the land in quarter-section tracts and the purchase of the remainder of the Choctaw lands for homestead entry.

With the opening of the Oklahoma Territory in the western area in 1889, a territorial government was provided for the new section. This provided an opportunity for introducing bills in Congress for the extinction of Indian titles and the dissolution of the tribal governments.

The Choctaws were extremely apprehensive and were divided among themselves now. There began to grow up a party of advocates of voluntary division of the tribal lands as a protection against unfriendly legislation. But a conservative element, unable or unwilling to appreciate the absolutely untenable position of the Nation, opposed any talk of voluntary allotment and a favorite ploy in Choctaw politics now was to charge opponents with favoring allotment.

*

Green McCurtain entered political life in the Nation just prior to all this disturbance. He was born near Skullyville in November 1848 and educated at the neighborhood schools in Skullyville County. He served as sheriff of Skullyville County and as representative of the county to the National Council.

From 1880 to 1884 he was trustee of schools for the Moshalatubbee District, thereafter becoming district attorney for that district. In August 1888, he was elected National Treasurer and was re-elected in 1890. At the expiration of his terms as National Treasurer he was elected to the Senate in 1893 for a two-year term.

While he was National Treasurer a vast sum of money was paid to the tribe — in payment of the western land leased to

the Federal government for the Plains Indians. Green McCurtain disbursed this money in a per capita payment of $103 to
the tribal membership with absolute integrity and efficiency.
This incident served to impress the entire Nation with high
respect for his staunch character and integrity and it enabled
him to marshal them behind him to follow a sane course in
the troublesome allotment days just ahead.

Green McCurtain was a member of the Choctaw Commission sent to Washington in 1893 when the bill to create the
Dawes Commission was passed.

If enacted, this Commission was to preside at the liquidation of all the tribal forms of government in the Indian Territory. While in Washington, Green McCurtain saw how
hopeless the Choctaw cause was and set himself to get the
most he could for his people out of the Federal government
and to persuade them to accept it.

The law was enacted on March 3, 1893, and the President of
the United States appointed three commissioners to negotiate
with the Five Civilized Tribes — Choctaws, Chickasaws, Cherokees, Creeks and Seminoles, to effect the extinction of their
titles to the land, either by session to the United States, by
allotment, or some other method. It was expected that
quarter-section allotments would be made and the remainder
of the land would be purchased by the United States.

The President appointed Henry L. Dawes of Massachusetts,
Meredith H. Kidd of Indiana and Archibald S. McKennon of
Arkansas, and the commission became known as the Dawes
Commission. They spent the year of 1894 traveling through
the country meeting with various groups of Indians. The
Choctaws were hospitable and courteous but absolutely un-
yielding.

During the winter of 1894–95, it was apparent that more

pressure was being brought to bear. By now a few Choctaw leaders began actively to work for negotiation with the Dawes Commission. They met at Hartshorne, near McAlester, in July of 1895. Green McCurtain was one of the leaders. He made a passionate and eloquent speech at the meeting, warning his countrymen that the Choctaws were already losing their independence and being crowded out by the white population, over which they had neither judicial nor economic control. He advised negotiating before it was too late. He warned that allotment was inevitably coming and that the only hope the Nation had was to treat with the Dawes Commission on the best terms possible.

But the opponents of treating with the Commission were more numerous and the Dawes Commission returned to Washington to report their failure to achieve an understanding with the Choctaws.

There was no mistaking the temper of Congress now. A number of hostile bills were introduced, that of Delegate Flynn of Oklahoma Territory being the most forthright. He advocated forcible allotment and throwing the rest of the land open for homestead entry.

Green McCurtain decided that the only way to defeat such legislation was to convince his people they must negotiate. He therefore called a convention of leading Choctaws at Tuskahoma.

In the convention a memorial was drawn up and signed by all but five of the members present, requesting Congress if changes were felt to be necessary to change only their tribal judiciary and postpone other changes for twelve months during which time they would make the utmost effort to convince their people to make an agreement with Congress.

This memorial influenced Congress to give the Choctaws another chance. No legislation was enacted to destroy the tribal government or titles.

Inexorably, however, the machinery of liquidation continued. The Dawes Commission was requested to investigate and make a full report on tribal and individual leases, and was authorized to make complete citizenship rolls of all the tribes.

The Choctaws in convention at Tuskahoma had organized themselves into a political party, taking the name of the Tuskahoma Party. Prominent Choctaws belonging were Green McCurtain, E. N. Wright, A. R. Durant, Wilson N. Jones, Peter J. Hudson, Wesley Anderson and S. E. Hotema.

The election that summer was a bitter one. There were four candidates for Principal Chief. Green McCurtain was the candidate of the Tuskahoma Party, and his election was widely hailed as a victory for allotment. The new administration secured control of both houses of the Council and for the first time the Choctaw government was now committed to a policy of dividing the land and negotiating with the Dawes Commission.

Green McCurtain was a man of great intelligence and of brilliant insight into the problems of his people. So great was his ability and so much did the people trust his integrity that it is doubtful if anybody else could have piloted the Nation through the turbulent days of relinquishing tribal institutions.

He patiently persevered in many conferences, with his people, with the Dawes Commission, until at last in April of 1897 a final agreement was signed at Atoka. It provided that the Principal Chief should deed to the United States the entire tribal domain, which should then be divided equally among the citizens except that each of the freedmen should receive only forty acres.

The allotments were to remain inalienable and nontaxable

for twenty-five years, except that provision was made for the sale of certain portions at stated intervals. The town sites, public buildings and mineral lands were to be reserved from allotments; the proceeds from the sale of town lots were to be distributed equally among all the citizens except the freedmen; and the mineral revenues, mostly from coal, were to be used by the United States government for the support of education.

The tribal government should continue until March 4, 1905, but acts of the Council would be subject to the approval of the President of the United States. The trust funds held by the United States would be capitalized and paid out on a per capita basis. Finally the agreement was to be valid when ratified by the Congress of the United States and by the Choctaw Nation.

This agreement was an issue in the election of 1898, but Chief McCurtain was easily re-elected. He was not eligible for election in 1900 and he supported Gilbert W. Dukes, of the Tuskahoma Party, who was elected. Chief Dukes' administration was distinguished by the ratification of the agreement.

In 1902, Green McCurtain ran for the office of Principal Chief again. Dukes bolted his party and supported another candidate. McCurtain was elected but by a very close margin and Chief Dukes tried to prevent him from taking over the reins of government. The United States Indian Agent and federal troops from Fort Reno were called in to protect the judges who counted the final election returns. Green McCurtain was declared the new Principal Chief.

The election of 1902 was the last election held in the Choctaw Nation and Chief Green McCurtain was its last elected Principal Chief, a title and office he held until his death.

One of the first changes made after the Choctaws signed the Atoka agreement was in the school system. Control of the schools was transferred from the Choctaw Nation to the Department of the Interior. The office of district trustee was abolished and under the new regime the Choctaw boarding schools became vocational schools for the training of full bloods.

Under the regulations of the Department of the Interior, by 1901 systematic provision was made for the first time for the education of white children. The incorporated towns began to establish public schools.

As has been said, in the summer of 1902 Professor John Holt was recruited from the neighboring state of Arkansas to teach in the new public school system, and he and his young wife, Lucy McGraw Holt, forthwith moved to the Indian Territory that summer.

The district and county governments in the Choctaw Nation were liquidated and ceased to function after 1906. But both the Dawes Commission and the Choctaws had underestimated the vast amount of work and time it would take to make the citizenship rolls, make the allotments and abolish the tribal government.

While the other branches of the government were fading out, the power of the Principal Chief became even greater for a time, partly because of the many details calling for executive direction, partly because of the extraordinary ability of Green McCurtain. He was continually busy with the details affecting citizenship rolls, allotment deeds and individual disbursements. He was constantly called to Washington by the authorities of the Interior Department where he was listened to with great respect. Well beyond the actual admission of Oklahoma as a state, in 1907, the tribal affairs continued to warrant his attention and direction.

In the history of the Choctaw people he stands out as perhaps the greatest leader the Nation ever had. He was a good executive, an incomparable administrator and a dedicated patriot.

He was married twice. His first wife was Martha Ainsworth, from whom he was later separated and divorced. They had one son, D. C. McCurtain. His second wife was Kate Spring. They had four daughters, Cora, Lena, Bertha and Alice. Lena married Herbert Moore of Skullyville.

Mr. Moore's people had been Alabama Choctaws and had been among the first to be removed from their homeland. They had settled at Skullyville, too.

Mr. Moore was one of the handsomest men I ever saw. Even as a small child I knew he was an unusually good-looking man. He was not very tall, but he was slim, with an erect figure. He had small feet and hands, and one of the things I remember most about him is his feet, slim and narrow, and always shod with the handsomest shoes he could buy.

He was working as a cowboy on the huge Frazier ranch near Skullyville when he met and began courting Lena McCurtain. I have been told that Governor McCurtain did not much approve the match, for he thought Herbert Moore was a rather reckless young man. Little did he realize that this son-in-law of his would become one of the leaders of the Choctaws after the Nation had ceased to exist and was part of the state of Oklahoma. Mr. Moore was one of the first state legislators. At this time the capital of Oklahoma was at Guthrie, and I recall that each time the legislature met he took his wife and children with him to the capital.

*

At some time during his public career Green McCurtain moved from Skullyville to Sans Bois. There he built a spacious eight-room, two-story home near his brother, Edmond. His office was on the second floor of his home, presumably for the sake of his personal safety, just off and above the front entrance porch.

Sometime before my family moved to Kinta, Governor McCurtain left his home in Sans Bois and moved to Kinta. Kinta, like Spiro, was a new town created by the route the Fort Smith & Western Railroad took down the Sans Bois valley. It bypassed both the thriving small community of Sans Bois and the little town of Whitefield and most of the people of those two communities moved to the new town.

*

Governor McCurtain was a big man, standing six feet two and weighing around 220 pounds. To my eyes, that saw all adults as very big anyway, he was an enormous man. We saw him riding into town from his white house on the hill out on the edge of town, a big, big man riding a big, big black horse.

Occasionally he stopped by to visit his daughter, Lena Moore. Once I was at the Moores' house when he stopped. He sat in a chair in the parlor, filling it to overflowing. He talked kindly to the children and pulled a paper bag of striped peppermint candy from his pocket and handed it around to all of us. We then ran outside to play.

Many years later, when I was doing research in Oklahoma history, I came across a photostatic copy of the Atoka agreement which Green McCurtain signed for the Choctaw Nation. He signed in a large, steady hand the agreement which ended the life of his people as a sovereign nation. To do so must have broken his heart, but he knew it had to be done and his hand had not trembled.

In my mind's eye, looking at the signature, I remembered the big hand that had reached into his coat pocket and pulled out a bag of peppermint candy for his grandchildren and their friends.

Green McCurtain was a very big man in every way that counted.

*

The Indian and Oklahoma territories petitioned for admission into the Union as one state in 1906. The state of Oklahoma was admitted on November 16, 1907.

THE EDGE OF THE WORLD

*

MEMORY began for me with the identification of myself, but a storehouse of unremembered memories was also strongly engraved so that I knew I had grandparents and aunts and uncles. As I had been with them much since babyhood, their identities were already established in my mind.

I knew I had a grandmother and a grandma. Grandmother was my mother's mother and I knew it, although I knew it only because I heard my mother call her "Grandmother." I knew Grandmother's last name was McGraw. I knew Grandma was my father's mother, for I had heard him call her that, and I knew that her last name was Holt. I knew I had two grandfathers, one I called Papa or Pappy, who was my mother's father, for she and all her sisters and brothers called him Papa, and I knew my Grandpa was my father's father and that his last name was Holt. At four, I thought these distinctions were common to all children and that my use of the names could be easily understood as identification.

I knew that my mother's name was Lucy, for my father sometimes called her that. I knew my father's name was John, for my mother occasionally called him John. But to me they were Mama and Daddy and for the most part they used those names in speaking of, or to, each other. In the old-fashioned way, as soon as there was a child, parents began speaking to each other, not only to the child, but in identification of each other, as Mama and Daddy, or Mama and Papa. My mother would say, "Daddy, can you reach that high shelf in the kitchen? I need a can of tomatoes."

Daddy would reply, from his five feet eleven, "You're such a shortie, Mama. Of course I can reach that high shelf," and he would. Mama was only five feet four.

Daddy was a fairly new term for a father in those days. Most children called their fathers Papa. I have no idea why we were taught to speak of our father as Daddy, except to distinguish him from Grandfather McGraw, who was already Papa to other grandchildren by the time my parents' children came along. To avoid eternal misunderstandings, probably, my mother chose to call him Daddy to us. Inevitably we shortened it to Dad before we were very old.

It was thus I believed I had made a very sensible and easily understood identification of both my Papa and my Daddy to Corinne Moore on that hot August day in 1909. If she was confused, she was too courteous to show it.

My memories of that year when I was four years old are confined mostly to highlights. There cannot be many such highlights, for life goes along fairly smoothly for a child so young and there are few peaks and valleys. There are just days and nights, and a little sister, barely two years old, whom I was often told to "mind."

Here in Appalachia, my present home, an older child is told to "tend" a younger sister or brother. We did not use that term in the southwest. Mama would say, "Janice, mind Mary C. now. She's coming outside to play."

Minding Mary C. was no great chore, for she was too young to have ideas of her own about play. She was usually docile and simply joined me in whatever I happened to be playing at the time. Later, when she became more of an individual herself, with her own storehouse of memories and her own will, it did become a chore which I often dreaded, and we frequently quarreled and even fought each other. But when I was four and she was two, there was some measure of amiability between us.

Our house did not sit squarely in the center of its plot of land. It was built along the left fence, with just barely room to pass between the fence and the house, and it was set into the left-hand corner of the yard. This gave the little house some space for a yard within the limits of the board fencing along the two streets which intersected. That there was no grass on the lawn made no difference to our enjoyment of it. In fact, it added to our pleasure because we could dig in the dirt anywhere we pleased.

The back porch seemed very high off the ground to us, although it was actually only three steps. But two small girls could stand under it and one of our favorite digging places was in the cool shade under that porch. Mama gave each of us an old spoon and I don't remember that we dug anything particularly. We just dug and dug — tunnels and holes which made mounds of dirt to sift through our hands, then we filled the tunnels and holes all up again and dug them over. It was endlessly fascinating because the dirt under the porch was soft and viable. Sometimes we found rusty nails or bits of old china. These were treasures, to be put in a pile all to themselves and kept. Sometimes we dug up a worm and put him in a tin can and tried to keep him alive for days. We had no idea it would have been much better to leave him in his natural environment. A worm was to fish with. Our parents loved to fish and many, if not most, summer weekends were spent on Beaver

Creek fishing. We always hoped to find enough worms to fill the can and have our own bait. I do not remember ever being taught to bait a hook with a worm. I just seem always to have known it. I would guess that the same is true of Mary C. and John.

That first year we were not freely allowed to go over and play with the Moore children.

"Why can't we go over and play with Corinne and Inez?" I would ask.

"You haven't been invited," Mama would say.

"But Corinne and Inez would be *glad* to have us come play, anytime," I would plead. "They said so!"

"Their mother didn't say so."

"But she wouldn't care."

"Inez might not be feeling well."

"She isn't sick today. I just saw her out in the yard playing."

Inez was a child who frequently ailed. She was paler in color than Corinne, although whether this was due to her various illnesses or to the fact that she took after her father's side of the family, I did not know. Mr. Moore's coloring from his Choctaw blood was considerably lighter than Mrs. Moore's. She had the same dark hair as Corinne and her eyes were just as black.

It never really did any good to plead with Mama. When she said no she meant it and she rarely changed her mind, but I would want to play with the girls so badly I could hardly ever resist the pleading. "Please, Mama!"

"Janice, Mrs. Moore has three little children of her own to take care of," Mama would reply, "and she doesn't need two more."

"Then let *me* go," I said, selfishly.

"Then Mary C. would be lonely."

"Oh, Mama, please!"

"Now, Janice, that's enough. You cannot go over to the Moores' to play, alone or with Mary C. You're too young and too little yet."

"Please! I won't bother Mrs. Moore, I promise."

"I said that's enough." Mama would suddenly become very stern. Her face would redden as her anger rose. "If you say another word about it I'll have to switch you."

When Mama said those fatal words, I said not another word, for I knew she meant what she said. If I opened my mouth about it again, I *would* get that switching.

Occasionally we would be asked to come over and play and Mama would say, "You may go for one hour."

Dutifully I would report to Mrs. Moore, "We can stay one hour, then we must go home."

Because she knew we would be punished if we stayed longer, even if we were being no trouble to her, Mrs. Moore always came to the door at the end of the hour and said, "Children, Janice and Mary C. must go home now. Their hour is up."

However reluctant we were to leave our fascinating games with Corinne and Inez, we always went straight home. Mama's hand on a switch or Dad's razor strap was heavy indeed and a licking from her was one to be remembered. When, occasionally, Mrs. Moore forgot to remind us when the hour was up she, herself, would take us home to tell Mama it was not our fault, that it was she who had forgotten to watch the time.

Mama was always the disciplinarian in the family. Our father was a soft touch. He rarely even scolded. He might say, "That wasn't very nice of you, Janice," or "You were told not to do that. You'll get in trouble if you do it again."

I do not remember whether it was we or the Moore chil-

dren who originated the term "Play like," when we made up
games. We never said, "Pretend," or "Let's pretend." We
always said "Play like," and inevitably it got shortened to
"P'like." We were always "p'liking" something.

Our home was clean and fairly uncluttered inside, mostly
because it was so sparsely furnished. Mama loathed housekeeping and she didn't mind a certain amount of clutter.

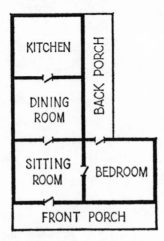

I have already told how there were two iron beds in the
bedroom. I think there was, besides, what Mama called a
bureau — a dresser with drawers for our underclothing. We
had no grand wardrobes so Mama simply hung a curtain across
one corner of the bedroom and our outer clothing was hung
behind these curtains on nails. Dad made newspaper and
baling-wire hangers for her and our best clothing hung on
these. I do not remember any rug on the bedroom floor except
one braided rug which lay between the two beds onto which
we could put our feet when getting out of bed in the mornings.
It was welcome on freezing cold mornings, too, for there was
no heat in the bedroom.

We had no parlor, as such. I badly wanted one and when all the furniture had been set in place I said, "Is this the parlor now?"

"No," Mama said, "this is simply the sitting room."

"But can't we call it the parlor?" I asked.

"That would be a false pretense."

"What's a false pretense?"

"A form of lying. This is a sitting room."

"Well, what is a parlor then?"

"A parlor is a very special room set aside for having guests and used only when there are guests."

"What are guests?"

"Company."

"When we have company won't they sit in here?"

"Yes, but that does not make it a parlor. We use it all the time ourselves. Look at it, Janice. You know the parlor at Grandmother's, and at the Moores'. Does this room look like a parlor?"

I had to admit it did not. There was no parlor set of furniture and no handsome library table in the middle of the room. There was matting, a kind of straw rug, on the floor, but I do not remember that it was wall-to-wall as were the matting rugs in Grandma Holt's sitting room. There were two or three rockers, the living room kind, a little rococo in style and none of them matching. At first there was no piano, although within two years that had been rectified, and cater-cornered in our sitting room was the much cherished, status-giving instrument.

The only distinguished piece of furniture my parents had was a beautiful old table which they placed against a wall, and they hung a lovely three-quarter-length beveled mirror framed in gilt over it. A few ornaments adorned the table, a pair of matching vases, with a tray of some kind between them. I have a dim memory of such an arrangement, and that the vases were blue.

My father and mother's wedding picture, in an enormous colored lithograph enlargement, hung on one wall of the sitting room, and the three famous horses' heads, the two black ones and the white one, in a steel engraving very popular at that time hung on another wall.

The cheapest kind of scrim curtains hung at all the windows. This room was only used in the summer. In the winter we did all our sitting about after supper, our studying when we reached school age, our eating and playing in the dining room where the big heating stove was. There was a couch in the dining room, the backless kind with two sides which normally were left dropped down but which when opened locked into place and made a full-sized bed. This couch had a brilliant red and green and black heavy cover on it. It was kept in the dining room instead of the sitting room because a sick child had to be in a heated room. We all had measles, mumps, chicken pox, whooping cough and endless colds on that couch. It was also the only guest bed in the house. A guest spending a night with us had very little privacy. But they were always members of the larger family and nobody thought anything about it.

The rest of the room was taken up by the dining table and chairs. Our dining table was round "fumed" oak. It was a sort of golden color. I never knew what the fumed meant except that it was newer and more stylish than the old-fashioned square black oak dining room tables such as my Grandmother McGraw had and such as I, myself, now have and would take no amount of money for.

In the summer the icebox was in the dining room. In the winter it was moved to the back porch because it was an im-

mense thing which my father had made in the form of a chest.
No child could get locked in it because there was no lock on it.
The lid simply let down and ice and food both were kept in
the one compartment which he had lined with zinc.

The telephone, on the wall, was also in the dining room, a
little difficult for an adult to use in the summertime because
the only place for the ice chest was directly under it. But the
ice chest made it very simple for a child to answer the telephone. All he had to do was scramble up on the ice chest.
My mother was always glad to get it out of the dining room,
but in the intense heat of Oklahoma summers she was just as
glad to get it back into the dining room about May of each
year.

*

The Moores' house was furnished quite simply except for
their parlor. One entered the house through a long front hall.
To the left a door opened into their parlor. As I remember it,
there was a piano against the hall wall, a parlor set of furniture,
which meant a settee and two chairs, upholstered in either
green velvet or black horsehair. And on the floor was a rug
very like the one in my Grandmother McGraw's parlor. I had
never seen what was called a velvet rug except in those two
houses.

By the time I was born my Grandfather McGraw had at-
tained a position of some affluence with the Western Coal and
Mining Company. The house in which I was born was their
first home. Shortly after my birth they bought a much larger,
more imposing house of some ten rooms, and it was this house
I remember and until quite recently believed I had been born
in. I have lately learned that the home in which I was born

was the first home and burned not many years after my grand-parents sold it.

At any rate, I believed my McGraw grandparents to be rich or quite well-off because they had a bathroom, electricity in the house and a beautiful parlor with a handsome velvet rug, which had a green background with lots of beautiful red cabbage roses all over it. It was a brilliantly colored rug and in my eyes the handsomest thing I had ever seen. They, too, had a piano, against the hall wall. All pianos were placed against an inside wall to keep them in tune and prevent damp and warping.

Now, in the Moores' home I saw the second of these velvet rugs. It had a green background, I think. It placed the Moores, whom I already knew were somehow important in the com-munity, in the same category as my McGraw grandparents. Only rich people could possibly afford that kind of rug, a real parlor set, a center table and a piano, such as my grandparents had and the Moores. I was a little smug about the fact that my grandparents, in addition, had water in the house and elec-tricity which the Moores did not have. I was probably impos-sibly boastful about it.

The rest of the Moore house was plainly and simply fur-nished. Their sitting room, for of course the parlor was used only on state occasions and was not heated, was actually the parents' bedroom. It opened off the front hall to the right and was used as a sitting room because it had a fireplace with a coal grate which threw out intense heat. Needless to say, with the coal fields all around Kinta, the fuel we heated with was coal. My mother and Mrs. Moore only cooked with wood.

Behind the bedroom was a small "lean-to" bedroom in which the children slept. It was called the side room. This room became very important in our lives eventually.

In the Moore house, one went down the hall, past the closed door into the parlor where the lace curtains were tidily never disturbed — except to be taken down and washed once a year — to another door that opened to the left. This door opened into the dining room. The Moores were still using a square, black oak dining table. The six chairs were always set up to the table as if ready to be used. There may have been a pie safe or cupboard of some kind in one corner, I do not now remember. On beyond, still to the left, was the kitchen, as sparsely furnished as ours — the big, black wood-burning cook-stove, the long deal table (at which we ate breakfast, but rarely any other meal), shelves built along one wall on which to put the everyday china and silver (our everyday was all we had!) and a chest or cupboard of some kind in which to keep staple groceries and canned goods — mostly home-canned.

I felt some envy of the Moores' parlor and devoutly wished we had one. But at least I could boast that my grandparents had one, which in truth was grander than the Moores' because it was much larger and it contained also a beautiful oak library table on which sat a Tiffany-shaded table lamp. And in one corner of the parlor at Grandmother's was a combination desk and bookcase. It was never used as a desk, but as a bookcase it housed many fascinating books which I was given permission to read when and as much as I pleased.

But if I felt envy for the Moores' parlor that was all the envy I felt. I was quite content with the rest of our house and would not have changed it for theirs. Most of my content came from being the child of my parents.

I liked Mr. and Mrs. Moore very much, but I truly thought that to be the child of Lucy and John Holt was the greatest privilege a child could have. I would never have traded places with any other child I ever knew and I sometimes wondered what other children felt, how they could bear not to be the children of Lucy and John Holt.

However long I liked to play with other children, and in time they included others besides the Moores, I was usually glad to come home, to see my father and mother again and be with them. That bubble of joy rose in my throat at the very sight of them. I envied nobody their wealth if it meant I must take their parents along with it.

I was a big girl before I realized that most children felt the same way about their parents and that nobody envied me mine. At four and five and six, however, I believed it to be a genuine hardship that all the children I knew did not belong to my parents!

*

In addition to discovering myself, and discovering from the barn roof where Kinta was, there are a few other memories of that summer I was four years old. One is that of Mama lying on the bed so much of the time, obviously suffering.

I was too young to be told my mother was going to have a baby, or to have understood it had I been told. I thought doctors brought babies in their little black bags. Not that my parents ever told me that, but other children had and I believed it. But I was accustomed to seeing Mama lying on the bed often, already.

She suffered from migraine headaches which began when she was a teen-age girl and continued most of her adult life. She was sometimes stricken for as long as three days, and during that period of intense, blinding pain, she could do nothing but lie in bed, and be terribly nauseated, and suffer the anguish that all migrainoids know so well.

At such times the bedroom was darkened by drawing down

the green window shades, and we were cautioned to make no noise. Noise was an agony to her. We tiptoed around, taking care not to slam doors, not to drop things, not to raise our voices in either anger, or tears, or laughter. "Sh-sh-sh," our father would say, finger on his lips.

At such times he did the cooking and washing up and took care of us. He was always so gentle and kind that in spite of the fact that I knew my mother was suffering and I felt so sorry for her, it was a joy to have Daddy in charge.

In my entire childhood, my father never once whipped me. He did one time pick up a dried dogfennel weed and lay it half a dozen times across my bare legs. But it only tickled and broke and that made both of us laugh.

Mama had sent me across the corner to get half a gallon of buttermilk from our corner neighbors. "Come straight back," she said, "I need the milk to make bread for supper." Our cow must have been dry at the time or we would not have been buying milk from a neighbor.

But these neighbors had a brand-new baby, only two or three weeks old, and I could not resist lingering a while after the milk was ready. I was even allowed to hold the baby and the minutes passed, about fifteen of them I would judge, for that would have been about the extent of Mama's patience.

Then here came Dad. I saw him coming across the road, quickly gave the baby back to its mother and scooted out the door with the milk jar in my hand. Dad met me with the piece of dried dogfennel in his hand. "You were told to come straight back!" A switch of the weed. "Why didn't you?" Another switch of the weed. In all, perhaps four or five tickling licks, then the weed broke into pieces and Dad stood looking at it, and I stood looking at it, then we both laughed and went to the house, he now carrying the fruit jar of milk in one hand, holding my hand with the other.

I think now he gave me my one and only switching from him to save me from a harder licking from Mama, who kept a supple green switch in the summer and Dad's razor strap handy in the winter with which to administer punishment. Either could hurt keenly on one's bare legs or bared bottom.

Mama was cross just the same. "Why didn't you mind me? I told you to come straight back."

"They have a new baby, Mama, and they let me hold it. I didn't think it was very long."

For once I think her understanding of the joy of being allowed to hold a tiny baby got the best of her determination that all her children should obey her instantly and without question. She just said, "Hmph. Next time do as you're told or there will be consequences."

Consequences was a word I had learned the meaning of quite early. It always meant punishment.

Accustomed, then, as I was to having Mama confined to the bed fairly often, I thought nothing of the fact that she spent every afternoon those hot months of August and September on the bed. Summers were always difficult for her. Heat bothered her more than it did most people and the brassy glare of the sun seemed to help bring on her migraines.

She must have suffered intensely that summer, from her pregnancy, her growing awkwardness and the unbelievable heat in that little house which had no trees for cooling shade and no grass to cool the hard-baked yard. I only knew that more and more often I was told to take Mary C. outside and play. We were warned not to play in the sun, to stay in the shade of the house or play under the back porch.

At two and four play consists mostly of dabbling in things. We did not yet play like anything or anybody very much. In addition to the two old tablespoons Mama gave us a battered pie tin and, I think, the lid of a lard can. This would have been a Cottolene lid (a shortening used in the south very much), and about the size of a pie pan. Now, in addition to digging holes and tunnels we spent hours making mud pies.

The watering trough was leaky and under it the ground was delightfully soft, oozy and malleable. It was not exactly clay but it was very nearly so. We dug up pounds of the stuff each day and carried it under the porch in our pie pans, then we made cakes and cookies and pies and set them out in the hot sun to bake. Playing in mud, thus, was an occupation we rarely tired of. It was always so gooey and cool and easy to shape.

In the corner of the barn lot was a refuse heap. We didn't play there, but we hunted for treasure there. It yielded nothing much but rusted tin cans and nails, bits and pieces of iron, leather straps, small steel rings and clots of hay and manure. To our great joy, however, it also yielded bits and pieces of china, part of a plate — one quarter, maybe — half a bowl, the bottom half of a cup, and so enamored was I already of the past, although it must have been subconsciously, that these bits and pieces of crazed, browned china meant more to me than all the tea sets in the world. I collected each little piece carefully, washed it at the watering trough, dried and shined it, and this old china became a very special tea set for me.

Once in a while, on a rare cloudy day, we played under the old watering trough itself. This usually ended in disaster for me. I could climb up on the well coping and from there onto the edge of the trough where I would perch with my bare feet in the water. This was heaven on a soggy, humid day — just to dangle one's feet in the water.

Rarely, however, could I resist the temptation to wade in the trough. That was when catastrophe overtook me usually. The trough was slimy with moss and therefore very treacherous for a four-year-old's bare feet. Almost inevitably they slipped from under me and I fell, getting my calico dress slimed all over, getting my underwear filthy dirty with the green moss, getting myself thoroughly sopped.

Mama's hand was quick to punish because climbing up and playing in the trough was forbidden. If I did climb up and successfully wade for, say, two or three minutes, Mary C.'s yells and screeches brought retribution shortly anyway. Mary C. was too small to climb, and I was too small yet to help her climb, and besides, being naturally a good and obedient child, Mary C. rarely wanted to disobey.

I never cared much and usually took my punishment with pretty good grace, knowing I had it coming to me. I found it a little difficult, however, to take it with good grace when it was Mary C.'s yells that brought the punishment. Had I slipped in the water in the trough, I was willing to trade the punishment for the blissful moments when I had successfully navigated from one end to the other before falling. But when I was just about to make it, to have Mama suddenly appear with her switch because Mary C.'s cries had roused her made me occasionally feel like drowning my little sister in the trough next time.

On rainy days Mama usually felt well. It was cool and gray and relaxing for her and although we children were confined to the house she never minded clutter and she could be extremely lenient with us in our play. She even let us play on the beds on rainy days, forbidden on other days. She would strip the white bedspreads from them, or at least one of them, and we bounced up and down, had pillow fights, climbed to the headboard of the bed (for me) and the footboard of the bed (for Mary C.) and jumped off.

"P'like we're diving in the creek," we would say.

We would dive and then swim by wiggling along the length of the bed. This could occupy us for hours. Mama had only to shut the door and if our shrieks of delight were muted enough they did not bother her.

When playing on the beds palled we were allowed to make a train of the dining chairs. We knew all about railroads from having ridden the Fort Smith & Western, so we chugged and tooted along happily. Mary C. was usually the engineer, which she invariably wanted to be anyway because she could make all the chugging and chuffing noises to her heart's content and make the brakes hiss when the train stopped.

I was far happier as the conductor. I knew all the way stations between Kinta and Fort Smith and would chant them the way the conductor did when he came through the cars — "Lee-quire! McCurtain! Bo-ko-she! Spiro! Braden! Fo-o-o-rt Smith! All out for Fort Smith. End of the line. Fort Smith!"

Seldom were Corinne and Inez allowed to visit us on rainy days. Four children cooped up in the house were two too many for either mother, and we were rarely allowed to visit them on rainy days.

But sometimes a rain would come up suddenly when the four of us were playing in our yard and Mama would come to the door, "Come into the house, quickly, before you get wet. *All* of you! Corinne, Inez, Janice, Mary C. Come right now!"

The Moore children obeyed my mother when at our house just as we obeyed their mother when at their house. So, without question Corinne and Inez would come trooping into the house with us.

Sometimes we played on the beds, both of them at such

times, but most often we played train in the dining room. Almost invariably then, Corinne and I butted heads over who would be the conductor. Inez and Mary C. would settle themselves in the engine of the train and somehow manage to be co-engineers or engineer and fireman, both chuffing and puffing happily, occasionally pulling on an imaginary whistle cord for a crossing and always for a station stop.

But there could only be *one* conductor. Corinne knew the names of the way stations as well as I did, perhaps even better. I sometimes forgot the last stop, Braden, before Fort Smith.

"*I'm* going to be the conductor," Corinne would say in that firm, I-mean-it way she could take on when her mind was made up.

"You were conductor last time," I protested.

"No — *you* were. I remember, because we had a penny and we called heads and tails and you won."

"No, *you* won. Corinne, I remember. You *were* the conductor last time. It's my turn now."

But there was not much use bucking Corinne over being conductor, for Mama was too near, usually in the kitchen, and could overhear the quarrel. She would step to the door and say, "Janice, Corinne is your guest. If she wants to be the conductor you must be courteous and let her be the conductor."

Oh, how I hated this being courteous to a guest. The fact that Mrs. Moore made Corinne be courteous to me didn't count at such a time. I always wanted to be the conductor.

Her way won, Corinne could now be gracious. "You don't have to be a passenger. You can be the brakeman."

Being a passenger was the dullest thing in the world. All you did was sit there. But the brakeman's job was to carry a lantern with which to signal the engineer, if it was a night train, and to put down the little stool onto which the "p'like" alighting passengers stepped off the train. Needless to say when either of us was brakeman passengers got off the train at every station. "We'll p'like it's the night train," Corinne would say.

Slightly mollified I would ask Mama if we could have Dad's lantern for a signal lantern. Sometimes, if it was empty or nearly empty she would let us have it. "All right. Don't swing it too hard, though. There's a tiny little bit of coal oil in it and you might spill it."

At other times, when the lantern was full, she would have to deny us. "No, I'm sorry. Dad just filled the lantern. It's full. You'll just have to play like you have a lantern today."

If she was in an especially good mood she would take a round oatmeal box, punch holes in the sides and run a string through. This made a good substitute lantern.

We could play train happily for hours, too, and usually Corinne, having got her way the first time round, would be nice enough to let me be the conductor the last part of the game.

Sometimes we were allowed to take blankets and make tents over the turned-upside-down chairs in the dining room. Then we camped out. We knew all about this, too, both from hearsay and at least one experience already. One of the ways our parents had always economized during the long summer months when there was no income was to go for a long camping trip in the Winding Stair or Kiamichi Mountains.

He and Mama would pay up the rent for the summer, then pack the grub box, which was an ingenious affair that fitted on the back of a wagon or buckboard, and take off for the mountains and their beautiful clear fishing streams and hunting hills.

Just that summer a fishing and hunting party consisting of our family and the Snodgrasses had spent six weeks back in the mountains before we moved to Kinta. From hearing about it I have a vague memory of the two big tents required, the half dozen big guns for hunting deer, wild turkey, bear and elk, and the fishing rods for trout, bass and crappie. I think this hunting and fishing trip was into the Kiamichi Mountains, southwest of Kinta.

The Snodgrasses son Robert was three years older than I. From hearing it told and from vague unformed memories, I know that on this month or six-weeks long camping trip I hung at his heels and became a great nuisance to him. Once he was wading in the shallow little creek that flowed alongside the camp. Water knee-deep on him was waist-deep on me, but stubbornly I followed where he led.

He was furious with me. He kept yelling at me, "Go back! Go back!" But I would not. It was great fun wading in the deep water. Finally, in sheer black rage he shoved me and I fell. Of course I strangled and came very near drowning. If the mothers hadn't heard Robert's screams, for by now he was frightened out of his wits and was doing his best to rescue me, that might easily have been the end of Janice Holt.

Robert got a good thrashing and I got a spanking, but the two young women friends had cross words, probably for the first time in their friendship. Aunt Annabelle was almost six feet tall and formidable at any time. Lucy Holt was five feet four, but nothing ever intimidated her.

Aunt Annabelle contended that Lucy should have watched her small daughter more closely, that she couldn't be responsible for *everything* Robert did. Mama argued that Robert was a bad-tempered, contentious little boy and had almost drowned her child.

The truth was that both mothers were too busy with camp chores to be paying much attention to their children and both felt guilty. Each had a good sense of humor, however, and it wasn't long before the harsh words ceased. No real harm had been done and they could laugh about it. But I was never allowed in the water again unless my father or my mother had hold of my hand, which was a great deprivation for me because until then I had been allowed to paddle about in six inches or so of water along the bank. This fun was now denied me, my punishment for disobeying and following Robert. I don't re-member that there was any story of further punishment for Robert, except the hard thrashing he got. And it *was* a hard one, to hear the mothers tell it.

My father said that he tried to make things up to me by fixing a fishing pole for me so I could at least sit on the bank of the little creek and fish in six inches of water. And he made me a small seine with which I could catch minnows. I would never let Robert have one of them, so the story goes, which made him furious. I suppose I actually got the best of the deal after all.

*

But that first hot August and September in Kinta there was a special fascination for me. Out where the horizon met the prairie was the very edge of the world, and it fascinated me intensely. I would haul the small wagon Dad had made for Mary C. and me past the Moore house, past Dr. Johnson's house to the end of the sidewalk. I was not allowed to go further.

Many times when I reached the end of the sidewalk I would stand and look with longing at the road which wound across the prairie. The edge of the world looked so near. If only Mama would let me go just once I was certain I could reach it in a very short time.

Inevitably there came the time when the temptation proved too much for me. Leaving the wagon behind I trudged out on the road. I hadn't gone a quarter of a mile before Mama caught up with me and gave me a good switching for "running away."

Mrs. Johnson had seen me and naturally she had gone to find Mama to tell her that I was out on the prairie alone.

"Why did you run away?" Mama said as she led me homeward.

"I wasn't running away," I said, still sobbing from the switching.

"What else do you call it? You were out on the road. You were going out on the prairie and you know you've been told never to do that alone."

"There aren't any gypsies out there now," I said.

"That doesn't matter. That isn't the point. That is only one reason you aren't allowed to go out on the prairie alone. Janice, you deliberately disobeyed me. Now, why?"

"I don't know," I said.

"You *must* know. Now, why did you do it?"

"I just wanted to see."

"See what, for heaven's sake?"

"I don't know. Just see . . . just see."

"Well, don't ever do it again. As far as I'm concerned you can see all that prairie anybody needs to see from our back porch and certainly you children can see all of it you need to see from the first gully *when* you are allowed to play there. Or from the buggy when we drive out on the prairie."

But we had never driven out on the prairie to the edge of the world. I did not say so, however. Mama was still too angry, perhaps too frightened, to give her credit, and she was still occasionally giving me a little extra cut on the legs with the switch to hurry me homeward.

"You are *so* stubborn, Janice," she said. "You *knew* you would be punished and yet you deliberately ran away."

"Mama," I could only repeat, "I wasn't running away. I just wanted to see."

"I don't want to hear any more of that," Mama said. "Now, hush crying. And if you ever go out on the prairie alone again I'll give you a switching you'll *never* forget!"

I wonder why children do not tell their parents more often what they are thinking and what motivates them. It never occurred to me to tell Mama about the edge of the world. I just took my punishment with as good grace as possible and said nothing. Had I had the good sense to tell Mama she probably would have explained to me about the edge of the world.

Perhaps I didn't really want to know the truth about it. Or perhaps I wanted to keep it my secret until I could learn the truth for myself. Perhaps there was a little doubt and I didn't want to know it. But I think children don't tell their parents many such things for fear of being laughed at. Mama might have laughed, it is true, but it would have been a loving laughter. But children can be terribly hurt even by loving laughter. They feel it is ridicule of themselves and their ideas and often they keep fears, anxieties, even anguishes to themselves rather than risk what seems to them to be ridicule.

Twice more that summer I could not resist this temptation to try to find the edge of the world and "ran away." Each time

I was caught before I had even begun to reach my destination (because of Mrs. Johnson's eagle eye once, and because Mama simply missed me once) and each time I was punished. And Mama was as good as her word. She waited until we got home then got out Dad's razor strap and strapped my legs good and hard. But I was never tempted, even to escape this punishment, to explain why I "ran away."

Mama finally forbade me the use of the little wagon outside the yard.

There finally came a Sunday when Dad hitched the horse to the buggy to take the family to Sans Bois for some reason.

As I have said, we really did not have a buggy. We had a buckboard. Everybody has seen Western movies and knows that a buckboard has one seat and a rather long traylike back end. Mama and Dad always rode in the seat and Mary C. and I rode in the back on a padding of hay covered with a quilt. The sides of the back end were very shallow and we were always cautioned to hold on. The dirt roads of those days could be rough and often were full of potholes.

Dad had a habit which irritated Mama intensely. He was a rather dreamy person anyhow, and driving along he would frequently get to pondering something, pondering evidently so deeply he would even forget he was driving. The reins going slack, naturally the horse would go slower and slower until he was merely ambling along at a very slow walk to match Dad's dreamy thoughts. Mama would put up with it as long as she could, then she would nudge Dad and speak to him sharply. "John, we'll never get there at this rate."

Dad would come to with a start, give the horse a sharp flick with the whip on his rear end, the horse would jump almost out of the shafts and start trotting briskly.

On this Sunday, for whatever reason, Mary C. had crawled to the very rear of the buckboard. She was holding on, as ordered, but when the horse gave that great forward leap, Mary C.'s hold was broken, she was bounced so high up in the air that the buckboard literally ran out from under her and she fell into the white dust of the road.

"Mama! Mama!" I screamed as loud as I could. "Mary C. has fallen out of the buggy!"

But the buckboard was old and rattly and by now the horse was galloping along and Dad was trying to rein him in. "Whoa, boy, whoa there, now."

I could not make Mama hear me, and I, myself, was bouncing around considerably, but holding tightly to the sides of the buckboard I made slow progress toward the seat until I could reach up and tug on the back of Mama's dress. "Mama!"

Mama turned, not releasing her own tight hold on the metal arm of the seat. "Janice, sit down, sit down this minute, you'll be thrown out."

"Mama!" I shouted over the banging and rattling. "Mary C. had fallen out! She's back in the road down there!" I risked turning loose one hand to point.

Mama grabbed it. "You're going to fall out! What did you say?" This time she bent toward me to hear better.

"Mary C. fell out of the buggy when Dad hit the horse with the buggy whip. She bounced clear out of the buggy!"

Mama clutched Dad's arm. "John, stop this horse right now! Mary C. may be killed. She's fallen out of the buggy. Stop! Now!"

The buckboard was stopped as quickly as possible. By that time it was evident that no harm but a bruise or two had come to Mary C. Highly offended, scared, mad as a hornet, screaming at the top of her lungs, she was chasing down the road toward the buckboard as fast as her two-year-old legs could carry her.

She was picked up, soothed, then scolded. "Sit right behind the seat! You've been told that a hundred times. Now see what happens when you don't mind!"

Her anger and hurt having been assuaged, Mary C. submitted to the scolding meekly. But she wouldn't speak to any of us for a long time because once the scare was over we all laughed. We should have realized this would hurt her feelings, but it was *so* funny — the great jump the horse had made, the buckboard literally rearing up onto its back wheels and running out from under Mary C. when she was thrown so high into the air, and her chubby legs churning the dust as, purple-faced, she tried to catch up with us. It could have been quite dangerous, she could have been badly hurt, but Mama had a way of saying, "All's well that ends well," and once a danger was averted she never dwelt, as some women do, on what might have happened.

We drove and drove and drove across the prairie, and as we reached the low swell of land which had marked the edge of the world to me and there was still just as much world ahead of us as there was behind, it dawned on me there was no end to the world at all. That it just went on and on and on and that what I had believed to be the edge of the world was simply the distant meeting of the land and the sky.

It was a tremendous relief to me, but at the same time it was a shattering experience, for if the world was all *that* big, then perhaps Kinta wasn't really right in the middle of it. I had my first doubts that I had personally made an earthshaking discovery on the barn roof.

I learned this without any doubt at all the first time we went to another town to shop — Quinton, I think. For Quinton seemed to be just as much the middle of the world as Kinta. For once I asked a question, but I asked it of my father, not my mother. "Are there many towns in the world?"

"Millions," he said.

"How much is millions?"

"More than anybody in the world can count."

I never knew my father to lie, therefore I knew there were more towns in the world than anybody could count. He also went ahead to tell me there were many countries in the world, not just the United States, not just Oklahoma and Arkansas, and that in many of those countries in the world the people didn't speak our language, they dressed differently and their religion was different. He told me many things about them, but from then on I couldn't wait to read about them.

TRAUMATIC YEAR

✳

ONE DAY IN THE JANUARY after our move to Kinta in August, the tenth day of January to be exact, Mama did not get up out of bed and cook our breakfast for us. This was not unusual. "Mama has a headache again," I told Mary C. in a whisper.

"Yes," Mary C. agreed, nodding her head. She could talk more plainly now. "Mama has a headache."

Dad was a fairly good cook himself and our breakfast was a hearty, good one of oatmeal, eggs and bacon. His biscuits, however, were fried instead of baked and tended to be a little flat.

When breakfast was over, and he rather hurried us, Dad said, "Girls, get your coats and put them on. You are going over to play with Corinne and Inez today."

We stared at him, not knowing what to make of this turn of affairs. Never before had we been allowed to go play with Corinne and Inez so early in the morning. But we did as we were told, for however unusual it was, it was certainly a delightful state of affairs. We thought it would be wonderful if we were allowed to stay an hour or two. But Dad himself took us over to the Moores'.

As Corinne and Inez greeted us, as surprised as we, Dad and Mrs. Moore went into the kitchen for a brief time. Then Mrs.

Moore got her own coat. Dad came back into the room where we were. "You girls stay here until I come for you. It may be some time, but whatever you do, stay right here. Mama is a little bit sick and Mrs. Moore is going to go with me and help her. Behave yourselves and don't make any trouble for Angeline."

Angeline was Angeline Folsom, the black cook of the Moores and she was perfectly capable of taking care of a dozen children. We loved her almost as much as Corinne and Inez did because she was always giving us cookies, or a piece of cake or pie, and she was a jolly, cheerful, happy woman.

She was the descendant of a slave who had belonged to the wealthy Folsom Choctaw family and bore, as did all slaves, the name of the owner. She was quite dark, rather short and very fat. Her lap could be most comforting when one had skinned a knee or knocked one's head against a post. She could not at all take the place of one's mother, but for something minor she was a very good substitute.

The day wore on and we grew a little tired of this long visit. I'm not sure the time didn't come when we were all so tired of each other we quarreled. "I want to go home," I said.

"You can't go home yet," Angeline said, "your daddy ain't come for you."

Something inside me told me an unusual event of some sort was occurring. What it could possibly be I did not know, could not imagine, but I began to worry, for Dr. Johnson was at our house by now. I suddenly felt a cold fear that something was terribly wrong, that perhaps my father or my mother was dreadfully sick, and I frantically wanted to go home and find out for myself. But Angeline was firm, and stay at the Moores' house I did.

I had never spent a night away from my parents in my life

and when dark came both Mary C. and I began to cry. Angeline sensed our fears and realized our homesickness. She took both of us on her ample lap and reassured us. "Your mama is just a little sick. She ain't coming to no harm, though. She just a little sick. Miss Lena is over there helping her and Dr. Johnson and it won't be long now till your daddy will come for you."

She fed us a good supper and shortly afterward, worn out with fear, homesickness and anxiety, we drifted off to sleep when she put us to bed. It was strange to go to bed in our underclothing. Nobody had thought to bring our sleepers over, naturally, so Angeline simply removed our dresses.

Sometime during the night — I know it was after midnight — we were wakened by Daddy. Never were we so happy to see anybody. He slipped our dresses on us and our coats and one on each arm he carried us home. His face was shining and he was beaming with joy. "I have a surprise for you when we get home," he said.

We begged to know what it was, but he wouldn't tell us. Instead he carried us into the bedroom where Mama lay on their bed with a swaddled bundle on her arm. Dad held us over the bed and Mama laid back the cover from the face of a new baby. "You have a little brother," Daddy said. "His name is John Albert Holt, Junior, and he was born at twelve-thirty this morning."

This was the first child my mother had had without the comforting presence of her own mother, or without going to her mother's home for the birth. As I have said, Grandmother came to Dow when the little stillborn baby was born, Mama had gone to Altus for my birth and to Paris, where Grandmother and Grandfather were spending the summer, for Mary C.'s birth.

But I suppose my father and mother decided the time had come when they could risk a normal birth. Also Kinta was larger and Dr. Johnson may have been a primitive old doctor by today's standards, but by the standards of those days he was a good general practitioner.

I remember protesting, "It isn't morning! It's still night."

"January eleventh began at midnight," Daddy said. This was a strange new fact, but I was so happy to be at home again, so excited over a new brother that I didn't ponder it long.

Mama said, "We wanted him to be born yesterday so badly because that was Daddy's birthday, but he just wanted his own birthday, I guess."

I thought it was wonderful that so tiny a baby could decide he would have his own birthday. He was as small as a doll, although I think he weighed ten pounds and gave our mother a very hard time. To Mary C. and me he was the most beautiful little live doll we had ever seen. We wanted to touch him, we wanted to hold him, but while we were allowed to pat his hands and touch his face, Mama wouldn't let us hold him. "Go on to bed, now," she said, "and let this little fellow and his mother get some rest."

Dad put us to bed in our own bed, thank heaven, and we slept soundly. The sound which woke us early the next morning was one that was strange to us. Not the old dominecker rooster crowing, or the cow bawling, but a baby crying. It took several minutes for us to take this in, then Mary C. whispered to me and said, "That's John crying, isn't it?"

We were up in seconds. "Is something hurting him, Mama?"

She laughed. "No. He's hungry and all babies cry when they're hungry."

We were to learn eventually that John cried many times when he was not hungry, for no good reason that we could tell. We didn't know that babies did that either and we would rush to his crib anxiously and search for a pin that might be sticking him. Most often he had simply lost his pacifier! We would hunt around and find it among his blankets, stick it in his mouth and the crying magically ceased.

Mama said babies needed to cry occasionally to exercise their lungs and that if they were picked up and petted every time they cried it would spoil them to the point they would never lie in their cribs and somebody would have to hold them all the time.

Mama refused to allow John to be called Junior, nor did we call him Johnnie. After he was grown and married his wife called him Johnnie, but we never did. Daddy was Daddy to us, and he became Big John to the older members of the family. John became Little John. This is what we called him, as if he had two names, and we continued to call him Little John long after he was a grown man. I think perhaps he did not cease to be Little John to us until our father died in 1940.

He must have been about three months old the first time I was allowed to hold him. I had a small red rocking chair. I sat down in it and carefully Mama put him in my arms. I felt like a young mother myself as I sat and rocked him. I wasn't at all afraid of dropping him. I had watched Mama hold and rock him too often. I simply cradled him carefully in my arms, making sure his head lay against my chest and rocked him in utmost delight.

He *was* a beautiful baby. To his chagrin when he was a young man, Mama used to tell about the time she entered him in a baby beauty contest at a county fair or festival of some kind when he was nine months old and he won, hands down.

He did not long remain a perfect delight to me. All too soon, and all too often it seemed to me, we would be engrossed in some entrancing game, such as a war, or our version of a ball game, when there would come that dreaded call, "Janice! Come mind the baby!"

All the other children would go ahead with the game, but Janice had to trudge to the house to mind that now most unwelcome little brother.

To do Mama justice, it occurred only when she had to leave the house for some reason — go downtown on some brief errand I couldn't do for her, or to help some sick person for a short while. Minding John did not mean I had to hold him, and I was never allowed to change his diaper. This was partly Mama's innate modesty and partly her fear I might stick him with a pin, I imagine. A bottle was always left to stick in his mouth if he got hungry. Otherwise his pacifier sufficed to keep him quiet. Minding him meant only the boresome job of staying in the room with him, just watching over him. Once I was terribly angry at being called to mind him.

Mr. Moore was planning to build a new barn. The lumber had been delivered and piled back of the old barn and it was the most fascinating place to play. It was often a battleship for us, or a fortress, or simply a mountain to climb. We never tired of clambering over it, that nice, big pile of lumber. We were playing some enchanting game on the lumber when Mama called. At the house she said, "I won't be gone more than half an hour, but you'll have to mind the baby for me."

There he lay, perfectly happy, making crowing noises. He was about five months old now and could have soft toys tied to his crib that he would bat around. He was having a beautiful time. I could hear the other children shouting and laughing at their game and here I was stuck with this tiresome little brother.

I was so sick of him all at once and so angry that to my eternal shame I walked over to his crib, got a good hold of his upper arm and pinched him just as hard as I could.

He screamed, naturally, and he cried so hard that it frightened me almost out of my wits. And I had sense enough to know the pinch might make a bruise on his tender white flesh. Also I was afraid Mama might come home early and find him crying, and I would have to tell her what I had done. We never lied to our parents. In fact the word "lie" was never used to us. One of the nicest things about our parents was that they detested that word and it was anathema in the family. If one told a small lie or exaggerated a little bit, it was a fib. If one told a big one, it was a "story." "You storied to me, Janice!" And to be caught once or twice storying, which brought a very stern punishment, was enough for each of the three of us as we grew up.

For once I broke the rule that I was not to pick the baby up and I did pick him up out of his crib and held him and rocked him trying to comfort him. I thought he would never quit crying! It couldn't have been more than five minutes, if that long, that he cried, but it seemed like hours to me.

Finally he hushed and I put him back in his crib, but his face was red and splotched from crying and his eyes were also red and splotched. I knew Mama would notice. But if he wasn't crying when she came home she would think nothing of that, for she often let him cry out a temper spell and she would think probably he had missed her, wanted her and had cried for her. She would simply feel of his diaper and if it was wet, send me on out to play and change him.

I was safe at last, for the pinched spot also faded quickly. It was the first, the last and the only time I ever deliberately hurt him. It taught me an unforgettable lesson.

*

I was not yet five years old when John was born, but my fifth year was memorable for other things. First, and most traumatic, I learned about death. Not just the fact of death. I had known animals that had died but I learned that people must die, too.

My mother had a lovely alto voice and I think my father had the sweetest tenor voice I ever heard. Inevitably they were members of a quartet which sang in church, at weddings and at funerals, anywhere the music of a quartet was wanted or needed. They were both accomplished musicians and while other members of the quartet may have sung their parts by ear, both my parents read music.

An old man of the community died. I don't remember who stayed with John, but Mary C. and I were taken along to the funeral. It made no impression on me until the procession moved to the cemetery. The quartet, with Mary C. and myself hanging onto Mama and Dad, stood there beside the grave. I saw this deep hole in the ground. I saw the casket in which the old man lay. Then to my utter horror I saw the men put the casket in the hole in the ground and begin shoveling dirt on top of it. I asked no questions, I just froze with terror. I asked no questions when we got home. The man was old and I thought only old people died — sometimes. I had no idea everybody had to die sometime.

But that summer a little girl about two years older than I was spending the day with me. I imagine her mother was having a baby. Mama was no midwife, but she did seem to be the one everybody sent for when a baby was being born and more children came to spend the day with us than anybody else in the community.

We were digging, as usual, under the porch when the subject of the old man's death came up. This little girl then told me that not only old people died, but everybody, everybody in the world, even I, had to die at some time. I would not believe it. I argued fiercely, cold with fear that she was right. She tried to prove it to me by mentioning small children who had died. I had not known them, but she said, "It's true. I've got to die sometime and you've got to die sometime. Everybody that lives has got to die."

"Even my Mama and Daddy?" I said.

"Even them," she said, "and probably before you because they are older."

The rest of the day was a nightmare to me. I couldn't wait for Mama to come home. Fortunately she came fairly early and the child went home. For once I asked. I *had* to know the truth. I was too horrified. Mama did her best to explain kindly to me that it was true. "It's nothing to be frightened of," she said, "it's just like going to sleep," and because she believed in immortality she added, "and you wake up in heaven."

"But will I have to be put in a box and put in the ground and all that dirt piled on top of me?" I asked. "I couldn't stand it, Mama. You know how I hate to be shut up in things."

"You won't know," she said. But I *knew* I would know. Nothing would keep me from knowing I was down in the ground covered with dirt and locked in a box.

It was so traumatic for me that for years I would wake in the night and feel that I was already dead and buried. I would break out in a cold sweat, assure myself I was still alive, but I would lie there and shake and wish I could wake somebody to talk to me, or that I could go and crawl in bed with Mama and Daddy. I would snuggle near Mary C., sound asleep, and she was warm and alive. But we both had to die sometime!

Many years later I learned that Mary C. had suffered the same trauma and that it lasted with her for many more years than it did for me. This was one of the few times our parents did a very unwise thing. We were not old enough to be taken to a funeral yet, and had we not been taken, the child spending the day with us might never have thought to tell us this haunting fact, for it came about as a result of our discussion of the old man's death.

Later that year there was another tragedy to reinforce the trauma. Mama came home from the Moores' one afternoon and at supper that night told Daddy, "Little Green isn't well. He's feverish and fretful."

Green was Corinne and Inez' baby brother. He was about two years old now.

"What's the matter with him?" Dad asked. "Cold?"

"No," Mama said, "he doesn't seem to have much of a cold. But he's feverish and awfully restless and fretful."

"Maybe it's the grippe," Dad said. This was the term used for what we now call influenza.

"I just don't know," Mama said, frowning. "The symptoms are rather vague. But perhaps that's what it is."

We heard, we felt sorry for him, but we really didn't worry about little Green. With six children, one of us always had something wrong. Besides Green was such a truly beautiful, fat and healthy baby I don't think it even occurred to our parents there could be anything seriously wrong with him.

Mama continued to go over each day to see how he was, to

help if she could. Each day she returned, more and more worried.

After several days of this Mama came home one afternoon quite pale and she seemed herself to be almost in a fever — of worry, of fear, of just what we did not know. She reported to our father, "Dr. Johnson isn't sure, but he thinks Green has spinal meningitis. Oh, John! John!"

She collapsed in Dad's arms, bursting into tears.

Dad patted her tenderly. "Now, Lucy, now, Lucy. There, there."

To see Mama cry at all was devastating. Mary C. and I both burst into tears. We had no idea what spinal meningitis was, but if it made Mama cry it must be awful, terrible, horrible!

"Lucy," Dad said, "you must get hold of yourself. The children are frightened."

Mama, with great effort, stopped crying, straightened her shoulders and even managed a weak, watery smile at both of us. Then the tears flowed again and she could not keep herself from gathering us into her arms. All three of us sobbed and I'm not sure Dad didn't wipe away some tears, too.

Finally, Mama got complete control of herself. She put us away from her, wiped our tears with her apron and said, "I must work up my dough for the bread for supper."

Dad smoked an old corncob pipe. He stuffed it full and tamped the tobacco down. When he had it lit and was puffing on it, he said, "What are they going to do?"

"They are taking him to Fort Smith. To see a specialist. They're taking the afternoon train up."

Dad gave Mama's shoulder one more pat. "That's the most sensible thing they can possibly do. And remember, Lucy, it may not be spinal meningitis at all."

But it *was* spinal meningitis and little Green McCurtain Moore died in the dreadful agony of that disease the day after he was taken to Fort Smith. I thought he died in the hospital there, but one of his sisters has told me since that he died in the old Main Hotel. I am glad I did not know it as a child. It would have given me a horror of that old hotel which we had to use so much that I should have felt all my childhood — perhaps all my life.

When he was brought back and buried, we were not taken to the funeral. Mama knew and felt terrible regret at the damage that had already been done to us over the old man's funeral. But I could imagine it all too well. The baby was buried in the Skullyville Indian Burrying Ground. I don't believe my parents went all that way to the cemetery, for Skullyville was near Spiro, but of course they went to the funeral service held either in the home or the Methodist Church, I do not know which, before the little body was taken to the cemetery.

This was the utmost in horror to me. Not only could I not bear the thought of little Green being buried, it meant that children, too, could die. That not only old people died, but babies and young children, too, not only could but did die sometimes. That it might happen anytime to our own baby, Little John, or to Mary C., or to me. It was then I took to waking in the night with a suffocating feeling I could not control. I would do my best to get death out of my mind, but I felt buried already myself, and when finally I could no longer bear it I would call out, "Mama! Mama!"

Mama would be instantly awake, as she always was when any child of hers called in the night, and instantly she would be beside me. She would smooth my hair, which would be wet with the sweat of fear, talk to me, kiss me, rearrange the covers and stay beside me, sitting on the edge of the bed until my trembling and crying ceased. The suffocating feeling would leave and I would drift back off to sleep.

But it was many years before I lost my fear of death — and I am not sure I have ever lost it. Nobody wants to die. But now my feeling is more that I just don't want to leave this beautiful world and have things go on that I know nothing about. I want to keep my own identity and keep living in this exciting world and know what is happening.

*

In December of that year, 1910, Governor Green McCurtain died. But he was, to me, an old man, and there was not as much horror as there had been over the baby.

In those days nearly all outside doors of homes had a transom over them and the transom was worked with a fixed rod which opened and closed it. Governor McCurtain ran into one of these rods one dark night and bruised his eye and forehead. Erysipelas set in and within a week or ten days he had died. Today it would not have killed him, but medical knowledge in those days was very limited.

He died on December 27, 1910 — the last of the McCurtain dynasty, the last of the Shak-chi-homa chiefs, and the last elected Principal Chief of the Choctaws. He is buried in the McCurtain lot in the Sans Bois Burying Ground. A grateful people erected a lasting monument of granite at the site of his grave. He was enrolled as number 8535 on the Choctaw rolls.

Thus Mrs. Moore lost her baby and her father in the same year. She must have been pregnant with the little boy born in

1911, named for his father but always called H.M. to distinguish him from his father. I am sure he was some comfort to her, but he probably brought almost as much grief, reminding her of the baby she had lost.

*

It was a tragic, dreadful year for me, that year I was five years old. I feared for every member of our family constantly. The only bright spot was our own baby and to make certain he hadn't died in his sleep I used to tiptoe to his crib and listen to make certain he was still breathing.

Old Angeline was right when she told my mother, "That child's nerves are too close to the skin. She gonna have trouble all her life with 'em."

I certainly did that year and to some extent, more than I like, all my life.

10

HALCYON SUMMER AND CABOOSES

*

OUR SUMMERS were different from those of most families because, as a teacher, my father was beset every summer with the
problem of how to support his family during the three months
when he received no salary.

In those days, at least in Oklahoma and Arkansas, teachers
were only paid nine months out of the year — the nine-month
school term. We never knew how we were going to spend a
summer. As I have said, sometimes he solved this problem by
packing us all up and taking us on a long camping trip. Other
summers he taught a summer school, usually nearby, which
for the most part lasted only two months. One month of the
summer was usually divided between visits to the two sets of
grandparents.

Usually Dad announced early in the summer what plans
were being made, but the summer of 1911 most of June went
by before a word was said about what we were going to do. I
did not wonder about this, for at the age of five I did not really
understand why our summers were different from those of
other families. But at supper one night Dad announced,
"Well, we are going to have a little trip and a little different
summer from those we usually have."

"Are we going camping?" I asked quickly.

"No, not this summer . . . not in the usual way. We *are* going camping but we'll be living in a house."

This puzzled me. Camping meant living in a tent. Even on our weekend fishing trips Dad always took the big tent . . . "Just in case," he would say, "it rains." How could one camp in a house?

"But you said we were going on a trip!"

"We are. Not a very long one, though."

"Where? Where?"

"Near Stigler. Just five miles from Stigler, in fact. I am going to teach the summer school in a little town called Kanima. And we are going to camp out because we will back here in Kinta when the summer school is over and there is no need taking all our furniture." He leaned back in his chair and smiled his lovely, gentle smile. "Now, do you think that might be fun?"

"Oh, yes!" But there were qualifications and I thought the fun sort of depended on them. Kanima. I had never heard of it. The name was Choctaw, of course. "How big is Kanima?" I asked.

"Oh, Janice," Mama interrupted, "you always ask so many questions. What difference does it make how big Kanima is. We will be there only for two months."

"Let her ask questions," Dad said. "It's her way of learning. Kanima," he continued, "is not really a town at all. It's really a little mining village. Do you know the difference between a village and a town?"

I nodded. "San Bois is a village. Kinta is a town. A village is smaller."

"You're right," Dad said. "Kanima has just one general store, a fairly big store, but there's just one. I think there may be a blacksmith shop, and perhaps a dozen or so homes."

"No bank? No restaurant? No drugstore?"

"No. None of those things. I said it was a village, remember."

"Is there a railroad?"

"Yes," Dad said, "there *is* a railroad. All mining camps have railroads. How would they get the coal out without a railroad?"

"Is it our Fort Smith and Western?"

"Well," Dad said, weighing his words, "I think it may be a branch of it. But you must not expect our nice passenger cars. It's only a coal and freight train which passes through going to Stigler each day."

"Every day?"

"I'm not sure it runs on Sunday." Dad laughed.

"A freight train!" I said, entranced. Freight trains had cabooses. We saw them go through Kinta. It was the dream of my life to ride in the caboose of a freight train. I would gladly have forfeited all the comfort of the red plush seats of the Fort Smith & Western passenger train to ride in the caboose of a freight train — at least once, although I had no idea what the interior of a caboose looked like.

"Will we get to ride on it?" I asked, bouncing with excitement.

"I doubt it," Mama said. "Stigler is only five miles from Kanima. We'll probably go to Stigler only once or twice all summer and I think the horse and buggy would be much nicer than a dirty, cindery old coal train."

Dad winked at me and said carelessly, "Well, we'll see."

This satisfied me completely. When Mama said, "We'll see," it meant no, usually. When Dad said, "We'll see," nine times out of ten it meant yes. I knew that if it was at all possible, in spite of Mama, Dad would see to it that we made at least one trip to Stigler on the freight train.

"When are we going?" I wanted to know.

"In a day or two," he said, "as soon as Mama can pack what we are going to take. School starts the first Monday in July, so we must leave as soon as we can."

Mama and Dad moved the barest necessities for keeping house to Kanima in one wagon. The house we moved into was not even finished. It was three bare little rooms, with the studding uncovered on the inside. But it did have floors, outside walls, windows and a roof. Mary C. and I looked around in dismay. "It will do for the summer," Dad said, "remember I told you we would be camping out."

Well, reminded of that it was fine with us, especially when Dad ingeniously made most of the furniture we needed, aside from the beds, from crates. Mama cooked on a kerosene stove.

The house sat right in the middle of an immense wood. There were no woods near Kinta and perhaps it is only in my memory that this wood seemed so thick and dense and the trees so huge, but there was one felled oak tree behind the house which Dad made into a play place for us. It was so thick in diameter that he had to make a small set of steps for us to clamber on it, so thick and wide there was no danger of our falling off. He cleared cockleburr, jimsonweed and pokeweed from that end of the log, but about a third of the way down the log these weeds grew so rank and tall they made a jungle around the log. The log was at least forty feet long.

"Always climb up here by the steps," Dad cautioned us. "Don't ever go down into those weeds." Then he chuckled and quoted an old slave saying, "Come in outta them jimsonweeds, boy, don't you know you'll git snakebite!"

Mama was more worried about the pokeweeds which were already beginning to have berries on them. Eaten, pokeberries are poisonous. When they are ripe they look delicious, a little like clusters of ripe grapes.

"Don't eat those pokeberries," she said to us, much too often we thought. "Remember they are poison."

"We won't," we promised, and indeed nothing would have made either Mary C. or me eat one. It would have had to be forced down us.

Fully ripe they did make awfully good ink, however, and Indian war paint. But when we asked about using them that way Mama said, "No. You might forget and put your fingers in your mouth before washing your hands."

So the joys of painting ourselves purplish red and writing pokeberry ink letters were denied us, also.

Mary C. and I spent hours playing on this immense log. "P'like it's a ship," I would say, "and we're on the ocean."

"How big is the ocean?" Mary C. asked.

"About a million times bigger than Grandpa Holt's pond," I said.

Mary C.'s eyes rounded for Grandpa Holt's pond was a big one.

I cinched it by saying, "You can't even see the other side of it. It takes a week, maybe, or even maybe longer to cross even in a big ship."

We played like the log was almost anything we could imagine that summer. We even picked big pieces of the dried bark off, climbed down the steps and made mud pies on the bark dishes, then climbed back up and let them bake in the sun and had tea parties. Then the log became the mansion of some very rich people. We played train on it. But mostly, I'm sure, we just took great delight in it and ran up and down it, yelling, having a wonderful time. I don't recall that either of us ever fell off.

Another reason I feel certain the woods were tall and dense is because there must have been thousands of squirrels in them. We had squirrel meat for meals so often it's a wonder I wasn't forever turned against it.

For some reason I had always loved the gizzard of fried chicken, although I can't imagine why, for it is tough and practically inedible. But my teeth were young and good and I could chew it and it must have had a flavor I liked. For whatever reason I liked it. I was most disappointed when I learned that squirrels didn't have gizzards and learned it in a most embarrassing way.

We had guests for supper one night — in fact, the first night we had a huge platter of fried squirrel. Confidently I passed my plate and said, "The gizzard, please."

Everybody whooped with laughter and I turned beet red and wanted to crawl under the table. What had I done wrong?

Dad, seeing my embarrassment, was kind. He said, "Honey, squirrels don't have gizzards, but you didn't know that, did you?"

I admitted I had not, but I certainly learned it once and for all that night. I never developed a favorite piece of squirrel and, to tell the truth, don't much care for any of it to this day although Henry, my husband, is as avid a squirrel hunter as my father was.

All my father had to do that summer was go out in the yard and about a hundred feet into the woods and shoot half a dozen squirrels. Henry doesn't have it that easy. He has to walk miles through our woods to find them and some summers they are so scarce he is lucky to find a dozen. When I tell him about Kanima he groans at such abundance.

One huge oak tree grew immediately in front of the house. Its lowest limb must have been twenty or thirty feet from the ground. Nevertheless, Dad climbed a ladder up into the tree and hung a swing for us from that long, straight lateral limb.

Mama thought the swing ropes were too long and that we swung too high in it. A fall from its top swing would certainly have broken some bones. At its very highest, we swung up into the leaves of the tree, which we thought heavenly.

Dad had no such fears for us and when Mama was busy and wasn't looking, he would push us as high as he could. Then we would plead, "Run under, Dad! Run under!"

This meant he got a good hold of the seat of the swing, took off running and pushed as high as he could, running out under the other side of the swing. These were the times when we went clear up into the leaves.

About half an hour of swinging was all we ever wanted, however. Children like to do things together, "play like" together. Even the most thrilling times, when some adult was willing to push us, grew wearisome after a while. Then we would play on the big log behind the house or play hide and seek in the woods, or pretend we were hunting squirrels. I think Dad even whittled out play guns for us for this game.

We missed the Moore children and although other children came to play with us, nobody could take the place of Corinne and Inez. Nobody knew our special games with them, and although we tried to teach the Kanima children, they were never as satisfactory playmates. Otherwise, the summer in Kanima was a halcyon time for us. There was such a variety of interesting things to do, things which were such fun to do.

John was eighteen months old that summer, Mary C. was four and I was six — a heavenly six because I would start to school that fall and I had been looking forward to it for at least two years.

I don't remember learning to read. My mother has said that I picked it up for myself when I was about four, by asking what this letter was and that letter from the headlines in the Fort Smith paper and from the titles of stories and articles in magazines. Before she realized it I was putting the letters together properly and beginning to read, with some peculiar pronunciations, but nevertheless truly reading.

The first book ever given to me was a child's book called *The Sunbonnet Twins*. It was mostly pictures with short sentences under them. Dad took me on his knee that Christmas morning and started to read it to me. With great dignity I crawled down and announced that I could read it for myself, and I did. As impossible as it seems I had read *David Copperfield*, in my Grandmother McGraw's library, by the time I was eight years old. I was simply born to be a reader.

But all the adults in the larger family of aunts and uncles read constantly and my parents would have been lost without magazines, books and newspapers. There was never anything lacking for a child filled with curiosity as to what words meant and how they were put together to learn, and we were all encouraged to read for ourselves as early as possible.

I started to school sooner than I thought I would be allowed to. I had been looking forward to the fall term in Kinta, but at supper, the Sunday night before the Kanima school was to begin, Dad suddenly said, "Janice, how would you like to go to school with me this summer?"

I could hardly believe my ears. "Really? Really go to school?"

"Well," he said, in the slow manner he had when weighing matters, "it won't count when you start to school in Kinta, but you might learn something, and you can recite with the primer class if you want to."

I almost exploded with joy. "Oh, I'd love it, Daddy. I'd just love it. Every day, you mean? Go to school every day!"

Mama said, a little dryly, "If you start you most certainly *will* go every day. There won't be any backing out when it gets tiresome for you."

"It won't get tiresome," I promised. I couldn't imagine school ever getting tiresome.

"You'll see," she said, and then uttered one of her innumerable clichés, "but what you begin you have to finish. You'd better be sure you want to go."

"Oh, I do! I do! And I won't even want to back out!"

I could hardly eat another bite I was so excited. The very idea of finally going to school was overwhelming. I had been yearning to go to school for so long, and the days at home in Kanima did grow tiresome and tedious. I thought school would be sheer heaven.

I know now that my parents thought the summer experience, a little like kindergarten, would prepare me for real school, but also Mama welcomed the idea of having me, mostly the mischief maker when there *was* mischief, out from under her feet for two months. Two small children at home were as many as she really needed.

It was a walk of one mile from our house to the schoolhouse, which was a one-room affair built of logs. Mama packed a good lunch for us, put it in an attractive basket, and

I was allowed to carry it. Dad held my hand. As we walked along the dusty road on those dewy mornings (I was always barefoot and if there is anything more satisfying than walking barefooted on a bedewed dusty road early in the morning I am not aware of it), Dad taught me many things about the natural beauties along the road.

"That weed," he would say, "is really a beautiful flower. It is bouncing Bet."

"And that one?" I would ask.

"Wild aster."

"And that one?"

"Ironweed. It has a pretty purple flower in the fall."

He tried to teach me to distinguish between the various trees, hickory, oak, elm, pecan, walnut and others by breaking a small limb off and showing me the differences between the leaves. It is still the only way I can distinguish between trees. In the winter I couldn't tell you the difference between a walnut and a hickory to save my life. The bark of all trees looks so much alike to me.

Just before we got to the schoolhouse we had to cross a little creek on a footlog. I loved this because the creek was so shallow that if my foot slipped the water was only about six inches deep and it was fun to splash in. Once, however, I came to grief and splashed too hard and sat down in the water. Dad laughed. "It's a good thing your mother can't see you. You're going to have wet panties and a wet dress most of the morning."

"Well," I said, "it's summer and I won't take a cold, anyhow."

"No, you'll just be a little uncomfortable and some of the big girls may tease you."

They did, but in a nice way, and I didn't mind.

As well as some things that were good for me and useful to me, I am afraid I learned some things not too good for me. A little snobbishness, for one. The "professor's" daughter was the favorite and pet of all the older girls and they vied with each other to push me in the swing, to have me sit beside them at the big old-fashioned double desks, to loan me their crayons with which to draw pictures. There were some quarrels among them over me.

"Sit with me this period, Janice."

"No, it's my turn. She sat with you this period yesterday."

"But I have a whole box of new crayons. I'll let you use them if you sit with me."

New crayons were always pointed, had not yet been blunted, and more often than not the girl with the box of new crayons won out with me.

Or they would vie with each other as to who was to push me in the swing. I always got more than my share of the swing. "I'm the tallest," one would say. "I can run under and push you the highest in the swing, Janice!"

"But I'm the strongest and I can push you the hardest and fastest!"

If I fell and skinned a knee there were half a dozen big girls to sympathize, to wash my wound and improvise a bandage for it. They brought me good things to add to the lunch Mama fixed for Dad and me — peaches, wild grapes, cookies, cake, candy from the store.

In other words, they bought me, and it all went to my egotistical little head and I thought school was wonderful. I became a little arrogant and picked and chose sometimes unfairly. Whoever offered the biggest bribe received my favors

all too many times. I should have known better, and they
should have known better.

Had Mama and Dad known about it they would have put
a stop to it, but my father was a gentle man who rather dream-
ily often didn't see what was plain under his eyes. He was
simply grateful to the older girls for putting up with me and
taking such good care of me. I don't suppose he ever noticed that I had the use of the swing oftener than anybody
else, with somebody to push me, or that there was always
a crowd of older girls gathered around me at recess and noon.

I completed what was known as the primer class in that
two months and actually could have done the work of the first
grade, but Dad did not allow that. He wanted me to begin
with other first-graders in Kinta that fall.

School got a little boresome before the summer was over,
but I was not permitted to stop. What I had begun so joyously I had to finish even if I was learning very little now, and
was weary of it as the end of July and its intense heat came
on.

There were two bad frights that summer. While I went to
school in the morning with Dad, he often allowed me to walk
home with the older children, knowing that once we reached
the path that led into the woods to our house I was only a
few hundred feet from home and could not get lost. We were
all romping along the dusty road one afternoon when we spied
a snake lying in the ditch which bordered the road. One of
the girls screamed, "It's a blue racer!"

"What's a blue racer?" I asked, my heart up in my throat.
I had heard Mama and Dad tell of rattlesnakes in the mountains, but a blue racer was a new snake to me.

"If he sees us," the girl said, "he'll chase us and they can
outrun even a train. They're the fastest things on earth."

About that time the snake stirred. "Run!" everybody shouted. "Run as fast you can!"

The big girls deserted me and I was left alone to run as fast as my short, chubby legs could carry me. I kept looking over my shoulder to see if the snake was catching up with me, but he never stirred from the ditch, and finally some common sense came to my rescue and while I continued to trot along, still fearful, I was no longer frantic with fear.

When I got home and told Mama about it she laughed. "That's pure nonsense," she said. "There is no snake that chases people and there's no such snake as a blue racer. It was probably just a plain common variety of black snake and you know they are not poison and do no harm to people. It was probably lying in the shade in the ditch to escape the heat. Snakes like cool places."

This was very reassuring to learn, but my faith in the older girls was badly shaken by the incident, especially by the way they had run off and left me to my fate and I was pretty cool to them for a few days. But it was not in my nature to hold grudges long and within a day or two we were all friends again.

The other frightening event happened to John. As I have said, he was eighteen months old and enchanting and we all adored him. But he was just old enough to get into a lot of mischief.

One Saturday Mama made some candy, the kind called taffy. It is made by boiling water and sugar, flavored with vanilla, until it spins into a hard ball in cold water. Then it is poured into a long platter or onto a marble slab and allowed to cool until it has reached a stage where it can be taken in the hands and pulled, over and over again, to a shiny whiteness. Then it is stretched into a thin rope and allowed to harden, when it is cut into small pieces. It is a hard, chewy candy and we all loved it. It was also simple to make, especially if one did not have chocolate with which to make fudge. We had taffy candy oftener than any other kind.

The candy had just been poured, boiling hot, into a long platter. Naturally we did not have a marble slab. John came toddling into the kitchen. He was too short to see what was on the table. The top of his head didn't even reach the table top. He stumbled suddenly and threw his hand up onto the table to catch himself and that little hand plunged into the boiling hot candy.

He screamed with the sudden pain. Mama and Dad were both in the kitchen, fortunately, but it was Mama who whirled about first and saw what had happened. "John! John! The baby!"

Dad, who was a tall, lean man, could move very quickly when he needed to, although usually he took his time doing anything. He was at Little John's side almost instantly, stripping the hot, sticky candy off the baby fingers. He burned his own hands, heedless of the pain as he got off all the candy he could. Mary C. and I stood, appalled, not yet quite taking in what had happened but knowing by the baby's screams it was something terrible.

The pain must have been agonizing. It was agonizing to us to hear him screaming. Mama and Dad did what they could to ease it for him, which couldn't have been much, then they bandaged the hand. Not thinking to bandage each finger separately, they bandaged the entire hand.

One day when Mama was changing the bandage, she called to Dad, "John, come here."

He went and looked at the baby's hand. "The fingers are growing together, aren't they?"

"Yes," she said. "This is our fault, John. We should have bandaged each finger separately."

They both knew it now, but the damage was done. Dad patted Mama's shoulder. "We shall have to take him to the doctor in Stigler and have them cut apart and stitched separately."

Tears came to Mama's eyes and she hugged the baby to her. "I hate to think of more pain for him, especially when it's our fault. Oh, the whole thing is *my* fault. If I had set that platter of candy farther back on the table . . ."

"It does no good to say if I had done so and so, now, Lucy. We'll hitch up and take him to Stigler today and get this immediate damage remedied."

When they came home with him (we had been left with friends during their absence), Mama told us, "The doctor put him to sleep and he didn't feel any pain at all. His fingers will be a little sore for a while and that's all."

She was glowing with happiness that they had caught the damage in time, that it had been a simple thing to correct and that her baby had had to suffer no pain from its correction. And we glowed with her. He was *our* baby, too, and we could not bear for him to be hurt.

*

Our parents had their tenth wedding anniversary that summer in Kanima. Remember they had been married on August 31, and it was the hottest part of that hot summer in that little mining-camp town.

Nothing was said about any wedding anniversary, however. Mama just suddenly said one day, "We are going to Stigler Saturday."

Mama and Dad had been to Stigler several times that summer on the coal train, leaving us with a neighbor, so we had never been.

"You and Dad are going?" I said, automatically.

"No. We are *all* going," she said.

"Even the baby!" I couldn't believe it.

"Even the baby." Mama smiled at me. "You're going to get your wish. At least one time in your life you are going to ride in a caboose!"

Both Mary C. and I were almost beside ourselves with excitement and joy. Riding in a caboose was the thing we had most wanted to do all summer and it had begun to look as if it were not going to be allowed us. We were especially good the rest of that week, suspiciously good, for we were afraid that if we got into trouble, to punish us Mama would change her mind and leave us behind.

The day finally came. The coal train pulled in and stopped, the engine watered at the water tower, then the train crept on up to where we could board the caboose. "Now remember," Mama warned us, "I expect you children to make no trouble. Be quiet and obey."

"Yes, ma'am," we promised quickly. But I couldn't resist adding, "Do you think the conductor will let us ride up in that little cab on top the caboose?"

"I don't know," Mama said, "but you must not ask him if you may. If he invites you to ride up there with him, you can do so, but *not* unless he invites you. Do you understand?"

"Yes, ma'am." But I crossed my fingers and made a wish — a devout wish that we would be invited. The caboose itself was wonderful, but to ride in that little cabin on top of the caboose would be simply heavenly.

The train couldn't have gone faster than eight or ten miles

an hour with its long heavy load of coal cars, but *we* were in the caboose. It had long benches down both sides, a chair or two, a potbellied coal-burning stove and a tiny little stairway which led up into the little cab on top.

We dutifully and quietly sat ourselves down on one of the long benches, well-behaved children as we had been taught to be. But my heart was thudding and I couldn't keep my eyes off that little stairway in the corner. Would we be invited to go up into the cabin? Riding in the caboose was great fun and in itself was something to boast about for the rest of my life (especially to Corinne when we returned to Kinta), but it was nothing compared to being allowed to go up that little corner stairway and ride in the cabin.

When the train was under way and his duties performed (this included collecting cash for our fares from Dad — no tickets were sold at Kanima), the conductor (I suppose freight trains have conductors — at any rate he was the official in charge of the train) looked at Mary C. and me, and at John sitting in Mama's lap and as courteously as if we had been adults he said, "Would you like to ride up in the cab with me?"

Quicker than an eel I slithered down off the bench. "Oh, yes, sir!"

Mama said, "Not the baby, I think. He would be too much trouble for you, but the girls may go up with you."

John, I think, was a little frightened of the entire experience, for he made no fuss over staying on Mama's lap. But picking Mary C. up in his arms and leading me by the hand, the official negotiated those narrow stairs easily.

Inside the cubicle were two chairs, one at each window, on either side of the car. The official installed me, alone, in one, and he took Mary C. on his lap in the other chair.

I was awed at being so high and was silent for a time. Then, as usual, I began to want to know things and to ask questions about them. "Whose chair is this?"

"The brakeman's," the official said, "but he is busy right now. Besides he won't mind letting you ride to Stigler in his chair."

There was a short silence, then I remembered to say, "It's very nice of him."

"Oh, he's a very nice man," the conductor said, laughing.

Another silence and then another question. "Why is this little cabin built up here so high?"

"Because I must be able to look out and see the entire train — the tops of all the cars, the engine, the whole train."

"Oh."

From the caboose windows one could only see straight out, as in a passenger train. It was easily understood with such an important load as coal or other freight the conductor should be able to see the entire train.

I had noticed there were no screens on these windows and it wasn't long until I leaned out, just a little, pretending secretly I was the conductor looking over his entire train. But by leaning out just a little I couldn't see very far up the train, so I tried leaning a little farther.

My skirttail was caught immediately and the friendly official became very stern. "Young lady, if you do that again you'll have to go downstairs. I am a grown man and I can lean out these windows safely, but you can't. If you tried to lean out far enough to see the entire train you would fall. Now, don't do that again!"

I certainly did not try it again, for the last thing I wanted was to be banished down into the caboose. Not only would I miss the most heavenly ride of my life, but I would most certainly incur Mama's wrath at such shame and be punished when we got home.

We finally reached Stigler. As we neared the town the conductor conducted Mary C. and me down the stairs. He would be very busy from now on. "Did they give you any trouble?" Mama asked, as we sat down beside her on the bench.

I think my heart stopped beating altogether. I had given some trouble, no doubt about it, but that beautiful man said, "Not a bit. They were as good as little angels. They can ride in my cab anytime they want to." I could have kissed him. He hadn't told on me. As young as I was I knew he hadn't lied. For after one warning I *had* been perfectly obedient. So maybe he didn't truly consider that I had given him any trouble.

It was a long hot day in Stigler and Mama seemed to have an interminable amount of shopping to do. Dad went in one direction, to see the county school superintendent on some business probably, to take care of other duties, to do his own shopping, which usually consisted of nails or screws or screen wiring, or something else dull.

Mama kept us with her and we trudged along with her, getting hotter, stickier, dirtier by the hour. We were bought candy, ice cream and some kind of lunch, but before the day was over we were thoroughly sick of Stigler and wanted to go home. But we had to wait for the evening freight back.

Mama seemed to have an endless amount of groceries to buy, and she spent what seemed like hours to us in one of the department stores. We thought perhaps something would be bought for us, but nothing was. It was just a long, hot, dull day which finally ended and we could go to the station to take the train back to Kanima.

The same official was in charge of the freight train going back and he let us ride up in the cabin with him again. It was so cool and lovely up there. It never occurred to us that we were adding cinders and coal dust to our already dirty faces, hands and clothing.

When we finally came to Kanima we remembered our manners. "Thank you," I said, nudging Mary C., "for letting us ride in the cab with you."

"Thank you," Mary C. added.

That conductor was a gentleman. He bowed to us a little, as if we had been ladies and said, "It was a pleasure to have you. I hope you'll be going to Stigler again with me sometime."

But we never did. That was our one and only ride in the caboose of a freight train.

The first thing Mama did when we got home, after she had put her purchases away, was to fill the washtub with water and give each one of us a thorough scrubdown. She even washed our hair. We were covered with coal dust, mixed with peppermint candy stickings, ice cream stickings and the like.

The next day she let Mary C. and me in on the secret of her heavy shopping.

"Next Thursday," she said, "is Daddy's and my tenth wedding anniversary. On that day we will have been married exactly ten years and I'm going to make it a very special occasion and celebration."

"What?" we clamored. "What are you going to do?"

"Well, I'm going to cook a special supper, with a cake with ten candles on it, and I'm going to make myself a very special new dress to wear."

"Just like a birthday," Mary C. said.

"Just like a birthday," Mama said, laughing, "only more

important to Daddy and me. Part of my shopping in Stigler
was for the material to make the new dress. I want it to be
as beautiful as my wedding dress."

We were too awed to say one word. A special supper, with
a cake and candles. A beautiful new dress for Mama, who got
so few new dresses. A tenth wedding anniversary. "Why,
you've been married longer than I've been born, haven't you?"
I said, suddenly figuring it out.

"Well, I should *hope* so!" Mama said, laughing. "I should
most certainly hope so. We had been married four years before you were born."

I nodded. I had figured that out, too. "Why did you wait
so long to get me?"

"Babies come when God sends them," Mama said.

"When God can spare an angel?" I asked.

"I wouldn't exactly call you an angel, Janice," Mama said.

"But I was before I was born, wasn't I?"

Mama ducked the issue. "Perhaps."

I didn't really know what a wedding was. I had never been
to one. A man and a woman got married, I knew, and then
the man was the husband and the woman was the wife, and
pretty soon there were children, but what happened at a wedding was a total blank to me. I wanted to know, naturally.
"How do people get married? What is a wedding like?"

Mama explained as best she could. "A man and a woman
love each other. They want to live together the rest of their
lives. So the man buys a marriage license, the woman makes
herself a beautiful dress, and when the wedding day comes they
stand in front of a preacher and they promise to love each
other all their lives and then the preacher tells them they are
'man and wife.'"

"How do they learn to know they love each other?"

"They just do."

"Will I ever have a wedding? I don't think I'll ever know when I love sombeody. I'd have to leave you and Dad and I don't think I'll ever want to do that."

"Oh, yes, you will. When the time comes."

"When will that be?"

"Not for a long time. Many years yet. Not until you are a grown woman."

"Were you a grown woman?" I asked.

"Not as grown as I should have been. But, yes, I was considered a grown woman. I was eighteen years old."

"Where did you get married?"

"At home. In the parlor."

"Was everybody there to see? Grandmother and Grandfather and all the aunts and uncles?"

"Yes . . . now, that's enough questions. But I want this to be a surprise for Daddy. Both of you promise you won't tell him a word about the special celebration or the dress."

We promised, but we were so full of the secret we almost let it out a dozen times and nearly burst trying to keep it from our father.

I was in school and did not see the dress being made and Mary C. was still too inarticulate to describe it to me. By the time Dad and I got home from school each day, of course the material had been put safely away.

Finally the beautiful day came. Going home from school that day I felt as if my heart would burst with happiness, for I knew Mama meant to have the dress on when we arrived.

We came up the path from the road and Mama stepped out the door and came down the steps of the porch into the yard and waited. Just for a moment Dad paused. No, he came to a full stop and I looked up at him. I think it was one of the first times I ever saw tears in his eyes.

The dress was lilac-colored. I don't know what the material was, probably the same silk mull as her wedding dress. The little tufts were a deeper lilac in color, but the crowning touch of glory was the sash. It was actually not a sash, but a deep purple braided silk rope wound three or four times around her slender waist, ending in long silk tassels.

In front of all three of us children my father went straight to her and took her in his arms and kissed her. This was something we rarely saw, either. They often gave each other an affectionate pat or peck on the cheek, but we had never seen them act like lovers before. It was a long and loving kiss and we three children stood, turned to stone, awed and full of wonder. It may be we felt a little left out of things.

It is to his everlasting credit that my father had not forgotten this tenth anniversary either. A part of his business in Stigler had been to go to a jeweler's and buy what was then called a lavaliere. It was a tiny jeweled pendant locked on a gold chain. By some stroke of good fortune he had chosen a purple or amethyst stone which went perfectly with the lilac-colored dress. He went in the house and brought out the little box, which he had carefully hidden away, opened it and put the lavaliere around her neck, and then again we saw these two young people, old to us, embrace and kiss each other tenderly.

Then they broke apart, laughing and crying at the same time, and hugged and kissed all three of us, said we were the best part of the ten years.

"What would ten years of marriage be without three lovely children?" Dad said.

"Three such good and fine and splendid children," Mama added, giving each of us another hug and kiss.

"We're so lucky to have such a fine family," Dad said.

And *we* felt like members of the family again, quite swollen with pride to be so praised, so wanted, so loved.

I don't remember what kind of feast there was for supper, but I do know one thing. There was *no* squirrel and there *was* a beautiful white cake with fancy white icing and ten lovely candles on it.

MISS LENA THURMAN!

✳

HAD I KNOWN what lay ahead of me in Kinta I would have dreaded our return perhaps. We had only a week of freedom before the regular school term began. I had been spoiled by the summer school in Kanima and thought real school would be the same. It wasn't. Not by a long shot.

Corinne, a year older than I, had started to school in the little white frame building that had been the old schoolhouse, but by the time I was ready for school the new building was finished and I proudly entered the first grade the first time it had ever been held in the beautiful new building.

Real school was not like Kanima at all. It was work, hard work, with numbers, and spelling, not just reading and writing. And it meant study, study, study all the time in order to make the good grades my parents thought I was capable of making and should make.

"Why must I make such good grades?" I asked.

"Because we think you can," Mama said tartly. "Second best is never good enough, Janice. You come from a line of smart people (she meant her own family, naturally) and you are capable of making good grades."

"But what if I *can't!*" I wailed. The very idea of Mama looking over a report card of mine appalled me.

"If you really can't," she said, "that's different. But you did excellently in Kanima this summer, and we think you can do just as well in Kinta, *and*," she added emphatically, "we expect you to."

"Because I'm the professor's daughter," I said. I did not know what the word bitter meant, but I certainly felt bitter about *having* to make good grades because I was the professor's daughter. Why should *I* have to be an example?

Mama's face flushed, as it always did when she grew angry, but she only said, "That's *one* reason, certainly. I won't deny it. The principal reason, however, is that we think you have a good mind and we believe that mind should do its very best. If you do that, your very best, we shall be satisfied."

I felt more satisfied myself, then. The very best one could do was reasonable enough.

Another difference between Kanima and Kinta was that there was no favoritism showed me. I was merely one more pupil. Nobody paid me any special attention, certainly not Miss Lena Thurman, the teacher. I had got in the way of being petted, and I missed it, but I think even I knew it had not been good for me and in time I completely forgot it.

Kinta was an eight-grade school, and there were four teachers, my father teaching the seventh and eighth grades. Most of the students were part-blood Choctaws, of course, although by now Oklahoma was a state and white people could buy and own property and there were a few children in school with no Indian blood at all. One or two of our merchants were not Indian, the town doctors were all-white, the ministers of the churches were, also, and while we were part-blood it was such a small part that we were considered non-Indian.

The first few days at school were confusing. Miss Lena taught the first and second grades, so Corinne and I were in the same room. But the second grade was on one side of the room and the first grade on the other side so that I was not even seated near my best friend.

Nor did Kinta have the comforting double desks where two sat together and studied together. It was more modern and each child had his own lonely desk. Mine felt very lonely as I put my reader, arithmetic, speller and writing tablet and pencils in the desk. There was nobody at all to help me, apparently.

I have told in other books how fortunate Henry, my husband, was to have for so many years a truly inspired teacher in Miss Lorena Grant. I had that same kind of inspired teacher in the first and second grades in Miss Lena Thurman.

I don't know her age at that time, but she was not a young girl. She was perhaps in her late twenties, or early thirties, experienced, patient and a born teacher. She was a strict disciplinarian, as I am convinced all good teachers should be, and she put up with no foolishness. When you got into trouble with her, she switched you. In those days parents did not object to the punishment of their children at school. In fact, they stood so solidly behind the teacher that a youngster who got a "whipping" at school usually got another one when he got home for being troublesome at school.

But Miss Lena never humiliated a child in front of the rest of the children. The child to be punished was kept in at recess and the punishment was administered quickly and privately. She switched hard enough to hurt, but not hard enough to raise welts or streaks on one's bare legs. In the winter this would have been impossible anyway, because we all wore long underwear and long black stockings. I think she used a ruler on our behinds then.

Miss Lena was eminently fair. She announced the rules of

her classroom to us the very first day. "There will be no whispering," she said, "there will be no passing of notes, no throwing of spitballs, no moving about the room without permission. Permission to come to my desk to ask a question, or to ask for help with some problem, may be had by raising your hand. Permission to leave the room [we all understood this euphemism for the need to go down to the basement to the newly installed chemical toilets] may also be had by raising the hand, coming to my desk and explaining your need. Now. Do all of you understand the rules?"

With one voice we chorused, "Yes, ma'am."

The rules were very simple. You just raised your hand for everything!

But because she was so fair Miss Lena went slowly over the rules again. "Now, there will be no excuses for disobedience. You understand the rules perfectly. See that you obey them and everything will be fine. But if you disobey, you will be punished, either by a switching, or by being kept in at recess, or by being kept in after school."

I never got but one switching. It humiliated me so much and it hurt me so much to disappoint Miss Lena that I never again needed one.

I turned out to be a good student and after I became accustomed to the habits of study, truly liked to study. I think I must have been born with a question on my lips and studying answered many questions for me. Mama kept some of my old report cards, especially for that first year, which I still have. In those days numbers were used for grading. Rarely did I make less than 100 in spelling, 99 or 98 in reading, writing and what we called numbers, instead of arithmetic. The one bad mark that some of my report cards carried was in Deportment. All too often there was the remark, "Whispers too much."

Evidently, even at the risk of Miss Lena's disapproval I was already a chatterbox.

The whispering was what I had been switched for. Miss Lena had told me sternly each time, "Janice, stop whispering."

Finally she said, "Janice, if I catch you whispering across the aisle one more time I'll have to punish you."

Well, she did catch me whispering across the aisle one more time and Miss Lena never broke her word, so I was kept in at recess and punished — with the switching.

I could hardly face the class when recess was over and the other children came trooping in. "Did you get a whipping? Did you?"

I nodded. "Yes."

There was no use lying about it. I *had* gotten one and to try to brazen it out by lying would only make it worse. Undoubtedly Miss Lena would hear about the lie, too, and then I should only forfeit more of her respect. Maybe even get another switching for lying.

I was teased about the switching for several days, as all children so punished were teased, but it was finally forgotten by everybody but me.

After that I confined my whispering to the very minimum I could manage and Miss Lena never again had to threaten me, although my report cards continued to show that she was well aware that all too often the minimum of whispering I could manage was all too much to suit her. To give me credit, after my switching, most of my whispering was brought on by other students wanting some help with a problem, or how to spell a word, or pronounce one.

"I don't like this constant 'too much whispering' on your report cards, Janice," Mama said each month when I handed her my card. "What on earth is there to whisper about?"

I tried to explain to her. "The other kids want help of some kind."

"Can't you just shake your head that you can't whisper back. You can't help them? They can go to Miss Lena."

Which just proved that Mama didn't understand the code of children. You helped if you could. You even risked the disapproval of the teacher. You did not, under any circumstances, refuse help, nor did you say, behind your hand, "Ask Miss Lena." You just answered the plea for help, and risked the anger of what seemed, sometimes, to be the entire adult world.

School began at nine o'clock in the morning. In Kinta there was a saying that "books" took up at nine. At 10:30 we had a fifteen-minute recess and only rain or snow kept Miss Lena from making us bundle into our coats and get outside for some fresh air and exercise. But nobody wanted to stay inside anyway. Recess was too much fun. Of course if one had a cold or looked or felt feverish, Miss Lena kept him in. She was all things to us during the school hours — doctor, nurse, teacher, friend, parent.

The boys and girls were segregated on the playground, the boys on one side of the building, the girls on the other. We played strenuously and hard. Even the girls played such games as Pop the Whip, Red Rover and a strange group game I never knew to be played in any other school. It was called Shiloh, and to this day I have no idea why.

Two leaders were chosen and they chose sides until all the girls were chosen. Then the leaders found a rock, spit on one side and flipped it to see which group could go and hide first. As a group we had to hide in a group, and a bare schoolground with just a few nooks and corners of the building in which to hide offered us plenty of room for ingenuity. We could not, naturally, go inside the building.

When we were hidden, our leader advanced to the waiting side and said, "Ready." The waiting group then began to search, and they had to search as a group. Our leader would carefully watch and she would call "Cold," if the searching group was on a very cold lead. She would call "Warm," if they began to approach us. She would call "Hot," if they were practically upon us. If they found us there was a mad race to the base, usually the lowest step of the front steps of the building, and the first person reaching the base yelled, "Shiloh!" and the game was won.

Occasionally, although she was not allowed to lead the other group in any way away from us, if they got "cold" enough that our leader thought we could beat the other side to the base, she would yell, "Go! Go!" And we went, like crazy. Sometimes we beat the opposing team to the base, yelled, "Shiloh!" triumphantly and it was still our turn to hide. It was merely a group form of Hide and Seek, naturally, but why it was called Shiloh I don't know to this day and can't possibly imagine why it bore the name of that famous battle.

We played, as all children do, blindmans buff, drop the handkerchief, Farmer in the Dell, and one of our favorites was London Bridge.

In the spring we played marbles, just as the boys did, we flew kites, we played mumblety-peg and we played jacks. I was never any good at marbles, fairly good at mumblety-peg, but in jacks I was excellent. Nobody really liked to play jacks with me because I usually won. Why I was nimble-fingered enough to pick up jacks however crazily they fell when thrown and so stupid at marbles I don't know, unless it was because marbles involved sighting and shooting. Perhaps even that young my eyes were not as strong as they should have been and I needed glasses. But very few children wore glasses in those days and while occasionally I had a headache from studying, especially at night, it probably never occurred to my parents to have my eyes tested.

We played baseball in the spring, also, just as the boys did. And here again I was good. I was an especially good and hard and fast pitcher, pitching with a side-arm motion just like a boy. There was nothing girlish about my baseball.

But I grew up on baseball. My Grandfather Holt was an ardent baseball fan and Dad was so good a shortstop and hitter that he occasionally earned a little extra money in the summer by playing semipro baseball. My mother says the first word I learned to say after "Mama" and "Daddy," was "baseball." She was an ardent fan, also, and even when I was so small she had to push me in my baby buggy (which I called a go-buggy because when she put me in it I knew we were going somewhere), she never missed one of those sandlot or semi-pro baseball games.

Even at Kinta, remember, our recess and noon baseball games were real baseball games, played with official baseballs and bats. It had nothing to do with the softball the young people play in school today. I never played a game of softball in my life until we moved to Fort Smith and I was in high school and it was required as part of gymnasium. I was no good at it. I couldn't pitch fast and hard. The ball had to be thrown underhand and to me it was too big, too soft and too awkward.

I was never a good fielder, although I could catch behind the bat well, and was never afraid of the ball. My hitting was a little better than average and I was so strong and sturdy that when I connected with a good hard pitch I usually hit a home run. This was one game in which the captains' first choice was always Janice Holt. And not because she was the professor's daughter, but because she was a doggoned good baseball player.

I have not said that while boys and girls were taught in the same room with the same teacher, they were segregated in the schoolrooms, as on the school ground. When the bell rang for "books," we formed in two lines, one of boys and one of girls, and marched in. When recess ended and the bell rang again, the lines were formed again precisely as before.

We had an hour for lunch and needed it because the school was right in the town and only the children from out in the country brought their lunches. The rest of us went home for lunch, and begrudged every second of the time away from the school ground. If we lingered overlong at home, if lunch was not quite ready, we fretted. The other children would be back on the school ground already and the games begun and we were missing them. Fortunately we lived only one block from the school, I could eat in about ten minutes (if Mama allowed it) and be one of the first ones back.

Even though the boys and girls were segregated in the schoolroom and on the school grounds, at the very early age of six or seven they were very much aware of each other. They frequently passed notes to each other and eyed each other much too often and too long.

A family in Kinta had moved there the year I started to school. Their name was Willard and they operated the only restaurant in the little town, *The Busy Bee*. They had a seven-year-old son named Mitchell, and a very handsome seven-year-old boy he was. For some reason he had a crush on me.

There was a rule against passing notes and while he passed notes to me, I never answered them. Just looked at him and nodded to acknowledge his note had reached me. What important message they could possibly have contained I can't imagine. They were certainly not "love notes" in any sense. But he caused me the most embarrassing moment of my life up to that time one day at noon.

As we all came trooping out for the lunch hour, he suddenly dashed up to me, with another small boy to help him. One boy held me tightly by one arm and Mitchell held me just as tightly by the other and right in front of the whole school he gave me a quick kiss on the cheek. Then both boys turned me loose and ran. I wished for the ground to open up in front of me and just let me sink out of sight. Everybody laughed and mocked me, naturally.

I fled home as fast as my legs would carry me. And I was crying by the time I got there. But when Mama asked what was the matter I told a small lie. Not for anything would I have told her the shameful truth. I said I had stubbed my toe. She examined it to see if the skin was broken and it needed a bandage. She looked at me suspiciously when she could find no damage, but she asked no questions. I imagine she thought somebody had said something unkind to me and hurt my feelings, and my feelings were certainly my own private affair.

I don't know whether Otway Rabon, now the husband of my dear Corinne Moore, remembers that he was the friend Mitchell Willard inveigled into holding one arm while Mitchell could implant his meager little kiss or not. But it was Otway. He must have been amost as embarrassed as I was, and he must have liked Mitchell as a friend very much to consent to help him with this plan.

I have Otway's permission to tell of an embarrassing moment of his own. He was, as he says, "sweet" on a girl named Ouita Eden. Otway's home was farther from town than that of most of us. It seemed very far to me, but couldn't have been more than half a mile from our house, straight on out the road to the big white house of Otway's father, Mr. Wesley Rabon. The Rabons were considered very well off, and indeed Mr. Rabon must have been a good rancher and farmer. Otway has told me that their name Rabon is probably a corruption of the French name Rabonne. It is very likely because so many of the first people to marry into the Choctaws were French.

One of Mr. Rabon's mules needed shoeing and he told one of his hired men to take it to the blacksmith shop and have it shod. He told Otway, "You may as well go along and help." Mules have a way of balking when being led and a lad with a good stick could help "unbalk" him rather quickly if he laid the stick on hard enough.

On the way into town the road passed Ouita's home and Otway says he was gawking to see if he could see her. Of course he was walking behind the led mule. His mind full of Ouita and his anxiety to see her, he did not notice that the mule had suddenly balked and, blindly, still peering intently for a glimpse of Ouita, he ran smack into the tail end of the mule. His entire face was buried in the mule's rear flank.

Then he hoped and prayed Ouita hadn't seen him, but for weeks it haunted him that she might have been at a window in the house, or in some other place hidden from his view and witnessed the worst humiliation of his life.

*

I have said there was no form of favoritism shown me in the Kinta school, and there wasn't. On the other hand, being the professor's daughter brought some hardships. I would walk up to a group of children busily talking about something and suddenly there would be a dead silence. I realized they had been talking about my father — probably criticizing him. I was thus excluded from the give-and-take of ordinary school talk and criticism.

Maybe the children meant it kindly, but I am more inclined to think they were afraid I would tell tales at home. Their criticism of him might have made me angry. In fact the few times I did hear any criticism of him it did make me angry, but I would never have told tales on the girls. They had no way of knowing that. They were never actively unkind to me. They just quit talking until somebody thought of another subject which could include me.

I do think, also, that some of them thought the good grades I made were at least partly the result of the teacher's partiality to me as the professor's daughter. This was never true of any teacher I had. In fact, I am quite sure I had to work harder for my grades than the other children because the teachers did not want to be thought guilty of any partiality. I was simply a naturally good student, worked hard, studied hard and there was no way I could have kept from making good grades.

Some of the children believed our parents helped us at home, too, and so of *course* we made good grades. With a sniff a schoolmate would say to me, "I could make one hundreds, too, if my father was the professor and helped me at home."

"He *doesn't* help me," I would reply.

"Hah! That's what *you* say. Naturally you *would* say that!"

"Well, I do say it and it's true. He does not help me!"

"Then your mother does."

"No, she doesn't. My daddy has so many papers to grade at night he wouldn't have time to help me, even if he would. And Mama is always busy with the baby."

"You mean they don't help you at all?" This was always said in that critically unbelieving tone which infuriated me. It would make me almost angry enough to fight.

"No, *they don't!*" They don't believe in helping me study, even if they had time. They say I must learn for myself."

I don't think I ever convinced anybody, however, and I went through all eight grades of the elementary schools, as did Mary C. and John in their turn, with most of the schoolmates believing the good grades we made were mostly because our parents taught and helped us with our homework at night.

It was never true. When Mary C. was old enough to go to school Mama and Dad began the habit of gathering us around the dining table after supper. There was usually a bowl of popcorn and apples to munch on as we studied. But we got no help from either of our parents. We had it all to do ourselves and nine o'clock was bedtime. If we hadn't finished our homework by then (and there was such a lot of it in every subject!) we had to suffer the consequences of incomplete preparation.

When I was old enough for history to become part of my course of study I loved it, except for memorizing dates of battles and the like. My father loved history, too, and his memory for it was infallible. I would forget occasionally and ask, "When was the Magna Charta signed, Dad?"

He would look up from his everlasting paper grading and across the table at me. "Look it up for yourself."

"But, Dad, you know. Why can't you tell me?"

"Because you must do your own homework. You must get into the habit of using reference materials. Besides, what you look up for yourself you are more likely to remember. The effort you put forth in doing things for yourself will pay off someday."

I would have preferred it to pay off a little at that very moment, but my father *was* right. An early training in the use of reference materials is a good thing for any schoolchild.

We *were* allowed to help each other to some extent. We could not work each other's problems, or do the actual studying for one another, but Mary C. and I could give out our spelling words to each other, and, when we were old enough, we could say the multiplication tables to each other. But Mama and Dad never offered one least bit of help. If we got a wrong answer, they did not correct us. They let us make the error again in school the next day. All they did was see to it that we *studied* until nine o'clock.

I am sure, however, that the atmosphere of study was helpful to us. There were no distractions from our study. Dad always had so many papers to grade and when Mama began teaching she did, too, so the entire family was gathered around the dining table with the big Rayo lamp, which gave such a nice bright light, in the center. Other children rarely had this advantage. They had to study in the middle of many family distractions. To the extent, then, that a study atmosphere was provided us, we did get help from our parents. Much, and invaluable help. It was nice to sit with the stove glowing in its corner, the big lamp giving its bright light, Mary C. and me on one side of the big, round table, Mama and Dad on the other. Sometimes the entire study period passed without one word being spoken by anybody. By standing and reaching, which we were allowed to do rather than distract anybody else's attention by asking for them to be passed, Mary C. and I could reach the popcorn bowl, the platter of taffy candy, the parched peanuts or the big bowl of apples. In this way we munched and did our problems, studied our spelling, did our reading assignments. So, it was not quite true that our parents did not help us with our homework. By providing an example and the proper atmosphere, they helped us far more than by answering our questions or helping us with a hard problem or telling us how to pronounce a difficult word.

Reading was always my favorite subject and nothing could keep me from reading straight through the McGuffey readers. I don't remember who edited them, but they were full of excerpts from the classics. One got a smattering of Thackeray, Dickens, Longfellow, James Russell Lowell, John Greenleaf Whittier. I remember having to memorize *all* of that long Whittier poem that begins, "The sun that brief December day/ rose cheerless over hills of gray." *Snowbound*. We were not very often snowbound, although we had snow in eastern Oklahoma; almost every winter there were a few good snowstorms, with enough snow on the ground so that Dad would make sleds for us.

We have much more snow in Kentucky, and I never see the snow falling that the first line of that Whittier poem doesn't come to mind. I have long since forgotten most of the rest of the poem.

I was not called on to read aloud at school any oftener than any other child. I merely took my turn, as was the habit in teaching reading in those days.

One day, when Miss Lena was the monitor on the girls'

side of the school ground, I happened to pass near her as she stood talking to my father. I could not help hearing her say, "Janice reads aloud as well as an adult, Mr. Holt. I wish I could call on her oftener."

"See that you don't, Miss Lena," my father said. "Don't do any favors for her."

Miss Lena smiled. "I shan't. I imagine the child has a hard enough time as it is. But it's a joy to hear her read."

This did not make me feel smug, but it did make me feel proud. It was sheer agony to me to hear some of the children read aloud, so slow, so stumbling, with such dreadful mispronunciations. I couldn't imagine reading being difficult for anybody. But then I had been reading for a long time and, to tell the truth, except for the games at school and the play with the Moore children, I usually preferred a book to people.

When families with children came to visit us, I was often rude enough to take my book and hide some place so I could continue reading. Mama would have to hunt me out to make me be courteous enough to go through what to me was the boredom of playing with strange children.

Too often they had no imagination and I would have to invent games for them, then put up with their awkward attempts to play them. All too often, I'm afraid, I simply gathered them on the back steps and told them stories I invented. I had a vivid imagination and I occasionally took my revenge on these strange children by making up the most ghastly and horrible ghost stories my imagination could conjure up. I am sure some of those children had nightmares after an hour or two of my invented stories. Mama scolded often and even punished me. "You must be courteous to guests," she insisted.

But they weren't my guests, I hadn't invited them, and the call of the books was just too strong for me.

*

When I was six we finally obtained the long-coveted piano, and music which I myself could make became a part of my life, for of course I was given piano lessons. All little girls whose families had pianos took piano lessons as a matter of course.

The way we obtained the piano is a testimonial to Lucy Holt's indomitable will. We were going to have a piano! No home was complete without music. Dad played the violin, but that was not the same thing at all. Lucy McGraw Holt's daughters were going to have a musical education.

About that time the Fort Smith paper offered a prize of $100 on a good upright piano to the person who sold the most subscriptions to the paper. A piano in those days, especially an upright, only cost about $150, and Lucy felt certain they could borrow the extra fifty dollars or arrange terms to pay it out.

"I'm going to try for it," she announced.

"Lucy," Dad said, "do you have any idea how many subscriptions you'll have to sell to win that hundred dollars?"

"Well, I know it will take a lot," she said.

"Some person in Fort Smith, a city with a large population, will win that advance payment and you'll just work yourself to the bone for nothing."

Mama had a way of tossing her head when her mind was made up. She tossed it now and tossed off another of her clichés. "Nothing ventured, nothing gained," she reminded Dad. "I *am* going to try for it. I am determined the girls shall have a piano and learn to play. You know what music has meant in *our* lives. We want the children to learn to make their own music, don't we? And have the same pleasure?"

Dad agreed he did. "Yes, but I think you have set yourself an impossible task this time. You just don't know what you're letting yourself in for."

"I'll soon find out," she said.

Dad should have known better. Like her mother before her, whom I remember as having the same endless repertoire of clichés, *nothing* was absolutely impossible to Lucy McGraw Holt.

She got out and sold the *Southwest American* to practically the entire population of Haskell County. I can see her yet, saddling up the horse and starting out, a copy of the paper tucked under her arm. Mrs. Moore helped by allowing us to play at her house when Mama was gone, if it was a Saturday. Dad and I would be at school on weekdays, so Mary C. and Little John went to the Moores'. Occasionally, if she didn't mean to be gone very long, she took John with her, seating him firmly in the saddle in front of her.

She won the $100!

"You see," she squealed, happily waving the letter notifying her she had won in Dad's face. "I told you it wasn't impossible! I *did* it! I *did* it!"

Dad gave her a big hug. "You most certainly did and I am eating crow right now and very happy to be doing it. Really, Lucy, I didn't think it could be done — in this little town? In this county!"

"Hard work, my friend," she laughed happily. "Just sheer, dogged hard work. I never let a day but Sunday go by without going out and selling those subscriptions."

"Yes, I know."

We children were not surprised. We would have been surprised if she *hadn't* won. We were accustomed to seeing Mama do what she said she was going to do, and if she said she was going to sell enough subscriptions to that Fort Smith newspaper to win us a piano, we believed with absolute faith she would do so. And she had done it.

The Bollinger firm was agreeable about terms for the other fifty dollars — I believe the payments were five dollars each month until the piano was paid for. I do remember it took less than one year to own completely, entirely, with no more payments due, our own piano.

The piano came within a few weeks after Mama won the subscription race. What a great day that was! It was shipped down from Fort Smith in a big wooden box shaped like the piano itself. Dad looked it over when it had been slid carefully off the wagon which had brought it from the depot into our yard. "If we take the front off that crate," he said, "the piano can be slid out and we needn't disturb the rest of the crate."

"What will you use it for?" we asked. "Kindling wood?"

He grinned. "No. That's good lumber. I think . . ." and he paused long enough for his grin to stretch further, "I just think it can be a playhouse for you girls!"

"A playhouse! You mean it, Daddy! Our very own playhouse! Can we put our doll furniture in it? Can we have it for our very own?"

"Your very own. But you mustn't be selfish with it. Corinne and Inez must be allowed to use it, too."

We couldn't imagine having anything that Corinne and Inez couldn't use, too, so we raced into the house to tell

Mama. "May we go over and get Corinne and Inez so they can see the piano moved into the house? And can we tell them about the playhouse?"

"I think you should do exactly that," Mama said. "Tell them to hurry, though, or you'll all miss seeing the piano moved into the house. The men are about ready."

Corinne and Inez were almost as excited as we were and we all came flying back across the road together. Dad had already carefully taken the front of the crate off with a crowbar and chisel and a crew of men were ready to lift the piano and carry it into the house. It must have weighed a ton, for it was a solid oak Milton piano. It took eight men to lift it and carry it across the yard to the front porch. It took four men just to shove it across the porch and into the sitting room.

We children tagged along behind until the men had pushed the piano across the corner Mama designated. Then we just stood there in awe. Mama said, "You can touch it if you want to! You can't hurt it. It's hard oak and it would take a hammer or saw or ax to make a dent in it."

It was a very dark oak, and so shiny we could see ourselves in it. We ran our hands across its shining surface and marveled that anything could be so smooth to touch. "Are we going to take piano lessons, Mama?" I asked.

"You certainly are. *You* will begin next week. Mary C. will begin when she is six."

Doubt assailed me. I touched a key tentatively. "Mama, what if I can't? Suppose I can't learn to play it?"

"Nonsense. Anybody who wants to can learn to play the piano. I could teach you myself, but I don't think children should be taught piano or any other kind of music by a parent. I'm afraid I wouldn't have the patience, anyway."

"I'll try very hard," I promised.

Corinne, who was already taking piano lessons and could even play simple pieces, said, "It's not very hard, Janice. It's mostly just practice."

"Yes," Mama said. "Once you learn the notes that's mostly what counts. Practice and more practice and more practice."

I fully expected her to continue with another of her adages, "Practice makes perfect." But she didn't. And it was just as well. Practice never made a perfect, nor even a really good musician of me, but it did suffice to give me many hours of pleasure during my lifetime.

Dad stood the box, minus its front, in a corner of the side yard where for years it was the children's playhouse. Nobody else in Kinta had a real playhouse, so we had extra status for a while and other little girls we did not know so well angled for invitations to come play in our playhouse.

Corinne and Inez loved it as much as we did, and although we sometimes quarreled over whose turn it was to sweep the floor or wash up the tea dishes, or get our doll children out of bed, the quarrels rarely lasted very long. They would march angrily home, but perhaps later in that very same day they would be back over to play in the playhouse. Even on rainy days, if the front of the crate was stood up at a slant to keep the rain out, we could make use of the playhouse.

I have told in A Little Better than Plumb how our bedtime hour was spent, now that we had a piano. When we had finished our study, been undressed and tucked into bed, winter or summer, Mama went to the piano and Dad took his violin and they played for us. Literally they played us to sleep. As long as one child could drowsily call out, "I'm not asleep yet," they played, anything and everything they could think of, sometimes repeating several times our favorites or something especially soft, sleepy-sounding, waltzy and soothing. From the time I was six until I was twelve, when we moved to the city of Fort Smith, this was the way Lucy and John Holt's children went to sleep every night of their lives except when we were away from home.

And now, about the middle of the year I started to school, we had a piano and I could begin to learn to play for myself.

It may be that she only came to Kinta that year. It may be that she had been in Kinta several years, but I did not know Miss Isabel Duncan until she began giving me music lessons.

In my memory she was one of the most beautiful young women I ever saw — dark hair, merry eyes, a matte skin that was lovely and creamy, vivacious, charming, young and, at least for Kinta, an accomplished musician. She had a large number of pupils but she somehow wedged me in.

She went to the homes of her pupils to give the lessons and gave a thirty-minute lesson for a very small fee. I think it was fifty cents.

Pianos, in those days, had no benches, or very few of them did — only grands and baby grands as I remember. All up-rights had piano stools. I sat on the piano stool, wound up almost as high as it would go, and Miss Duncan sat beside me on a dining-room chair.

Within a few weeks it was evident that I had a small gift for music, a very small one but nevertheless one that was to be important to me all my life. We had no metronome to tick out the rhythm or beat of my music and scales for me. For a few weeks Miss Duncan's hand, lovely and small, would beat time for me. But she soon learned that I did not need anyone to lead me or beat time for me. I had a natural ear for rhythm. Most of the beginning pieces of music, naturally, were plain

¾ or 4/4 time. I could not go wrong on these and I quickly picked up quarter notes, half notes, eighths and even sixteenths, learning how much time to give them.

One day Miss Duncan said to me, "You may not have a *great* gift for music, Janice, but you have a natural ear for it, a natural sense of it, that will make it worthwhile for you to take music as much as you can all your girlhood. If nothing else, it will always make *you* happy and be a great source of joy and happiness to you."

I was so excited, so thrilled to hear Miss Duncan say this that I almost fell off the piano stool. "Will I ever be able to play as well as my mother?"

Miss Duncan laughed. She knew something I did not know. A lot of Mama's music was played by ear, was really faked. She could read notes but not rapidly enough to play really well. But Miss Duncan was kind. "If you work hard at it, you can not only learn to play as well as your mother, but I think you can learn to play better."

I had no real desire to be in competition with my mother, but I did want to be able to sit down at the piano as casually as she did, and ripple off the kind of music she played with such ease.

I progressed so rapidly that it was not long before I was playing short pieces of real music. It may not have been wise of Miss Duncan, but I think it was. Too many studies and too much of scales for too long a time, when a small child is wanting badly to play pieces with a tune, discourage the child and he loses his interest in learning to play at all. Miss Duncan, on the other hand, gave her pupils short, easy pieces as a challenge, almost as soon as they had learned their notes and the major scales.

Along toward the end of the year Miss Duncan asked

Mama to come into the sitting room when we had finished my lesson. "Mrs. Holt," she said, "I think Janice is far enough along that she can play in the recital I am planning for the end of the school year."

What happens inside a child when sudden fear and great pride are simultaneously touched? Whatever it is, a sinking feeling, a feeling such as one has in a fast elevator falling, mixed with surprise and emotion, happened inside me. In my stomach! It bounced, first up, then down, then up again and I thought I was going to be sick.

"You don't think it's a little too soon?" Mama asked.

"No, I don't," Miss Duncan said. "She's musically inclined by nature. She comes of a musical family. She's worked hard and she's made excellent progress. With your permission I would like to have her play a simple piece, one that she can easily master, in the recital."

"There's plenty of time?" Mama wanted to know.

"Oh, yes. I like to take my summers off and lessons will come to an end at the end of the school year. That's about six weeks yet. I suppose Professor Holt will have no objection to having it in the school auditorium?"

"I'm sure he won't," Mama said. "It will be a lovely event to crown the school year."

By the end of the school year I was seven. There may have have been one or two six-year-olds among Miss Duncan's pupils, but if there were I do not remember them. Corinne was one of the pupils and the only one I knew really well. They ranged from my age up to girls old enough to be wearing their hair up and their dresses down to their ankles.

It was thus that I found myself, so scared I truly was sick at my stomach, one Friday night early in June sitting on the stage of the school auditorium in the semicircle arranged for

Catherine Babb McGraw,
aged forty-eight

Daniel Murdoch McGraw,
aged fifty-three

John Albert Holt,
aged seventeen

Wedding picture of
John A. Holt and Lucy
McGraw, August 31, 19c

Part of the Holt family, late fall of 1905. *Back row:* Aunt Belle, her husband, Ed Northum, Cousin Verna Darr, Aunt Billie, Aunt Emma and her first husband Coy Northum, who died about six months after the picture was taken. *Middle row:* John A. Holt, holding Janice (aged about seven months), Lucy McGraw Holt, Aunt Grace. *In front:* Grandpa and Grandma Holt

Janice in her "go-buggy," taken the same day
as the family picture

Mary Catherine Holt,
at about nine months, and
Janice, three years old

Mary C., about two and a
half years old, Janice, about
four, and Robert Snodgrass,
about seven years old

The Moore home shortly before the Holts moved to Kinta. Mr.
and Mrs. Herbert M. Moore and Corinne and Inez on the porch.
Courtesy of Inez Moore Von Derau

Governor Green McCurtain,
last Principal Chief of the
Choctaw Nation. *Courtesy of
Corinne Moore Rabon*

Corinne Moore, aged five years, Green McCurtain
Moore, aged about one year, and Inez Moore, aged three
years. *Courtesy of Inez Moore Von Derau*

Janice, aged five, Mary C., two and a half, and John Albert Holt, Jr., about six months. On the back porch at Kinta

Kinta School. Courtesy of Corinne Moore Rabon

First and second grades, Kinta School, Miss Lena Thurman,
teacher. Janice, second from left in third row from bottom.
Corinne Moore was absent from school the day the picture
was taken

The blacksmith shop. From left: Will England, who was later
to marry my cousin Verna Darr; Herbert M. Moore; the blacksmith, George Lantz. *Courtesy of Inez Moore Von Derau*

The home of Grandfather and Grandmother McGraw, Altus, Arkansas, in 1970. The two rooms with chimney were built by Catherine McGraw with money she earned herself. The two big ash trees Grandfather planted are shading the fireplace ell.
Photograph by Mike Hancock

Mary Catherine Holt, aged eight, Janice, aged ten, John, Jr., five.
Taken in our Easter finery

Holt house at Kinta, 1970. Ell to left was built on after the Holts left Kinta. John Holt, Jr., was born in bedroom at extreme right. *Photograph by Mike Hancock*

Main Street, Kinta, Oklahoma, 1970. Old bank building on right. Two tallest buildings on left were in Kinta when the Holts lived there. All other buildings unrecognizable; many of the old ones are missing, probably torn down. *Photograph by Mike Hancock*

Ruins of the McCurtain home at Sans Bois, Oklahoma, in 1970. Foothills of San Bois Mountains in background. In front of house, below: Corinne Moore Rabon, left, Janice Holt Giles, right. The Oklahoma Historical Society is restoring this old home as a State Shrine. *Photographs by Mike Hancock*

The Skullyville Post Office and Pay Station, in 1970. The only
building remaining of the once thriving village of Skullyville.
Photograph by Mike Hancock

the music class. I *think* I sat next to Corinne, which was a sort of comfort to me. But the most comforting thing was that Miss Duncan had said to us, "We will begin with the youngest pupils, those who have been taking music the shortest time, and work up through those who are more advanced.

With that arrangement, my turn would come very early and be over with and I could enjoy the rest of the recital.

I had a new dress for the occasion, a white one with a blue sash. I wore white socks and black patent leather pumps. We were all asked to wear white, although no specifications were made as to our shoes, or the color of the sashes, or whether there should be sashes. There were children taking piano lessons for whose parents it was such a sacrifice they might not have been able to afford anything but the white dress. But Miss Duncan did think that if everybody wore white it would look nicer and the recital might be more effective.

Not a single child forgot his piece. I got through mine with my heart pounding, but without a stumble. The applause was most rewarding. But I'll tell you who did forget her piece! Miss Lena Thurman, of all people!

She had never had the opportunity to take music as a child and she had determined this year to do it. The community thought so highly of her that nobody even thought it odd of her to be the only adult taking piano and learning to play child's simple pieces. The piece she was to play that night was no harder than mine or any other child's. It was a simple first-year pupil's piece.

She came out, in her pretty white dress, took her place at the piano (there was a stool, not a bench and her feet were the only ones that could reach the pedals. The rest of us dangled). She started out confidently, got about halfway through, then stumbled. She made a valiant effort to recover by repeating the measure. She stumbled again. Once more she tried to recover by repeating the measure. Then, realizing our agony for her, and not the slightest bit embarrassed, she got up from the stool, made a little bow and said to the audience, "I'm sorry, but I have forgotten my piece." She made a dignified exit and I am certain the applause for her courage was greater than for the success of any of the rest of us.

I never did get over my fear of recitals, although I took piano twelve years. I was always scared, nervous, fearful I would forget. I never did forget but that didn't mean there might not come that time when I would. And I was sure I could never manage the aplomb with which Miss Lena had met her defeat!

*

We put that revolving piano stool to a use which was strictly forbidden and we had to sneak to do it. Usually we had to wait until Mama was over at Mrs. Moore's or downtown on some errand or busy in the garden.

Once the stool had been well broken in, it whirled as easily as a merry-go-round and this was precisely what we made of it. It was strictly understood that if one got so dizzy he fell off, got hurt even, he would make no sound. Crying would bring Mama and punishment would follow.

Even Little John loved to be whirled on the stool. "My turn," he would say, usually first, and he usually got his way. Being the eldest, the strongest, I did most of the whirling, carefully with John, with Mary C. usually holding him on by the arm. He was satisfied with a slow walk-around. He would break into a big grin and laugh gleefully. We would have to tell him, "Sh-sh-sh, Mama will hear you!"

The trouble was getting him off so Mary C. could have her

turn. Sometimes he would be just dizzy enough to be glad to get off, but more often than not he got whirled longer than any of us.

With Mary C. I could run and make the stool whirl very fast. I am afraid that I sometimes took some revenge for a small grudge against her by whirling her as fast as I could run and throwing her off. I remember one time when I ran so fast I stumbled and fell and Mary C. went flying off the stoll clear across the room and banged her head against the wall. It must have hurt badly. She did cry, but not very loudly. "You did that on purpose," she accused me. "You wanted to throw me off."

"I did not," I said. "You are always telling me to run as fast as I can. And I fell down myself I was running so fast. You saw me fall down!"

"Not as hard as me," she sobbed quietly, doing her best not to make much noise. "My head hurts now."

I was afraid she would have a bump on her head and went over to examine it. But Mary C. had a very heavy head of hair and while she had banged into the wall very hard a bump had not been raised. All that hair had absorbed a lot of the fall. "I'll go slower next time," I promised. "Do you want to ride again now? You can have an extra turn if you want it."

Mary C. pondered it a moment. Then she said, "Yes. But only if you promise not to run so fast."

I had another mean trick I occasionally played on Mary C.

Because the fence around our yard was a slat board fence instead of a paling fence we had a seesaw by the simple expedient of running a broad plank between two of the lower slats. Dad actually found the right width board and showed us how to seesaw with it.

I was so much heavier than Mary C. that I had to be very careful not to let my weight ride her up too high. And I had to be careful, also, coming down with her to keep her from bumping. Corinne could hold her own with me, although she was not as heavy as I was. She was very strong, however. We enjoyed seesawing with each other, even when we played tricks on each other. But seesawing with Mary C. was tiresome and tedious, and Mama insisted that I do it.

Things would go along fairly well until I became too bored with it. Then I would suddenly come down with all my weight, which threw Mary C. up so high that she would bounce, and sometimes bounce clear off the seesaw. "You did that on purpose!"

"Oh, Mary C., it's just no fun seesawing with you. I have to be too careful."

"Don't do it again, or I'll tell Mama!" Then she would doggedly crawl back on the seesaw.

The opposite of this was to slide off the seesaw when she was high up in the air and let her bump the ground very hard. Children are really little savages, and childhood is all too often a jungle through which they tread, wary of adults and cruel to each other. Brothers and sisters do truly love each other. I fought for John and Mary C. both many times. But I also fought *them*, when they wouldn't play what I wanted them to play, or when they dogged my footsteps and I wanted to be free of them. There was, on the other side of the coin, though, a lot of fun to be had with them — and I suppose we did no more scuffling and fighting and quarreling than all other children do. And little savages do learn, in time, to be tamed.

*

Several years after I had moved out of Miss Lena Thurman's room, into the fourth or fifth grade, she married Mr. Will Jones, the insurance man in the county. Everybody called him Mr. Will.

I think they went to Fort Smith to be married and came home on the late train. The whole town turned out to meet them, including my family, and there were firecrackers and Roman candles, much banging of tin pans, much shouting and yelling as they got off the train.

But then occurred something which appalled and frightened me. The women surrounded Miss Lena and put her in a buggy and drove off in one direction. The men picked up Mr. Will, carrying him on their shoulders, and put him in a different buggy and drove off in a different direction. The crowd laughed hilariously at this, even my father and mother laughed. I was appalled because I knew married people stayed together and here the crowd was separating Miss Lena and Mr. Will the very first thing. I was frightened because I did not know what they were going to do with them.

Finally, because I had begun to cry, Mama said, "Don't worry, Janice. This is just a prank. They are just being driven separately and by a longer and more roundabout way to their house. Both buggies will get there about the same time and Miss Lena and Mr. Will won't be harmed."

"It's just a joke?" I said, wiping my eyes.

"Just a joke."

"I don't think it's a very nice one," I said. "What will happen when they get them to their house?"

They had rented and furnished a small house before they married and I knew this must be their destination.

"When they get them there," Mama said, "Mr. Will and Miss Lena will invite everybody in and there will be a party."

Well — that was different. "Are we going?" I asked.

"No," Mama said, "I don't really approve of these stunts. I don't think they're kind, and it's way past you children's bedtime anyway."

I was a little disappointed not to be going to the party — parties usually meant ice cream and cake — but I was much relieved to learn that nothing dreadful was going to happen to Miss Lena and Mr. Will.

I don't know when Mr. Will died, but Miss Lena lived to be ninety-six years old. She only died in 1970, and while I never saw her again after we left Kinta I was told by Corinne that right up to the last she lived in her own home in Quinton, five or six miles from Kinta, and that she remained mentally alert. Miss Lena *would!*

*

There were no amusements in Kinta at all. Occasionally one of the churches had an ice cream supper or an oyster supper. Usually the women of the church sponsored the affair to raise money for new hymnbooks, a new communion service or some other church-related need.

Ice cream was ordered from Fort Smith. The affair was usually held on the church lawn with Japanese lanterns lighting it. It looked so beautiful. An ice cream cone could be bought for five cents, a big heaped-up delectable cone of vanilla or strawberry ice cream, or both if you wanted a double cone for a dime. Small tables were set about for older people who paid ten cents for a generous bowl of ice cream. In addition to parents, courting couples were always prominent at the tables. Sometimes the town was made aware of a quarrel between a couple who had been going together for months, were fully expected to become engaged and marry, when the young woman showed up with a different man, who ceremoniously escorted her to a table and bought her ice cream. Similarly the young man might show up with a new girl.

An oyster supper was usually held in the winter, but the same group of churchwomen, and for the same good cause, usually sponsored it. They ordered their oysters from Fort Smith, never sold fried oysters, but the oyster stew, for ten cents a bowl, was the best I ever ate.

No entertainment at all was ever furnished at these affairs. People went, ate, lingered an hour or so to talk, then went home.

About once a year, in the summer, a tent show came to town. Some of the townspeople thought these were sinful and would not attend, but our parents always took us. They saw nothing wrong in a ham version of *East Lynne, St. Elmo,* or *Uncle Tom's Cabin,* all of which I remember seeing at tent shows in Kinta. Eliza crossing the ice always had me sitting on the edge of my chair, although having read the book I knew she would make it. I always wept when Little Eva ascended to heaven. I think I was about nine before it occurred to me to wonder how she ascended into the upper reaches of the curtain. The next time I saw the show I didn't weep. I looked for the wires which I knew must haul her up. So much for illusions.

During intermission there was a clown act, or a dog act, or a solo singer performed. I have never forgotten the first dress suit I ever saw a man wear, and it was full dress, white tie, tails and all. He came on stage during intermission wearing an opera hat and cape. These he laid aside as the pianist played the overture to his song. He was an extraordinarily handsome man to begin with (although fully made up and his curly brown hair probably was a wig). When he began singing he had a full, beautiful baritone voice. In my opinion, then, the song he sang had to be the most beautiful song in the world. It was also one of the corniest — "Till the Sands of the Desert Grow Cold." But it was so well received he had to return and sing the chorus again twice!

I was not satisfied until Mama, much against her will, ordered the sheet music for me and I learned to play it for myself. Just the music gave me cold chills of delight, for each time I played it that gorgeous baritone voice was singing it.

About once a year a tired, fourth-rate circus came to Kinta. There was usually an elephant or two, a mangy lion, perhaps a camel. There was always a parade of these foreign animals, and there was always the calliope and the tired, middle-aged women, much made up and spangled.

All the acts — and there was never but one ring — were poor imitations of the big circuses, but we didn't know the difference. I hid my eyes during the high wire act, though it wasn't a very high wire, but I was certain somebody would fall. Most of the acts were dog and horse acts, with the decrepit elephants going through the usual balancing routine. The clowns were always fun. We sat and ate popcorn and peanuts and had the most wonderful time in the world. Never having seen a big circus, we were certain this was the biggest and best to be seen.

Local boys were hired to help put up the tents and were given passes to the show. These little circuses traveled by road. The morning after a performance they were gone. All that was left to show they had visited Kinta was the sawdust and litter where the big tent had been. How they got the tent down and left so rapidly by morning I couldn't imagine. But of course they were trained to do just that and they never lingered once they played a town. There was never a carnival or side show with these little circuses. Once the main performance was over, usually by ten o'clock, the crowd left and had I not been lost in the dream of its splendor I might have noticed that even as the crowd was leaving, men were knocking the tent down and the animals were being loaded into their vans.

My parents, the Moores, the Tidwells, Rabons and several other families were instrumental in getting one season of Redpath's Lyceum Company into Kinta. The concerts, the monologues, the lectures were held in the high school auditorium. Unfortunately the town did not like the Redpath Lyceum Company and one season was all that money for it could be raised. The events weren't enough fun, not nearly as much fun as the tent shows or circus. A concert of classical music left a Kinta audience cold, sitting on their hands. A lecture found the school auditorium half empty, even though people had bought season tickets. Only when a comedy skit was scheduled, and there were one or two, could one be sure of a full and responsive house. Then, as now on television, people wanted to be amused rather than edified.

Most small towns had at least a band, but Kinta did not. There weren't enough people who could read music, much less play an instrument. We were accustomed to the weekly band concerts in both Carleston and Altus, held in the Confederate Park in Charleston and on the high school lawn in Altus. Everybody went, sat on the grass and thoroughly enjoyed the mostly brass, oompah, oompah of the town band. But remember both places had a considerable German element in the population, which may have contributed to the type of bands so popular and the type of music they played.

In Charleston, admittedly about three times as large as
Kinta, there was even a fancy, gingerbready, white-painted
bandstand. To play in the Charleston band was an honor
all the men coveted, and many young men took up the cor-
net, the trombone, the tuba just for the prestige of playing
with the band. I don't really know how good a band it was,
but in my memory it was very good and even now I don't
remember any great discords. We usually heard the same
music over and over, but about once a month the band
came up with a new number. One of my favorites of every
summer was "Auf Wiedersehen," in which the audience
joined by singing. The band never failed to end their concert
with that song, and as the people reluctantly brushed the
grass from their clothing and started home, they would still
be singing "Auf Wiedersehen" softly, now to each other in
place of saying good night.

My parents did their best to get at least a small orchestra
started in Kinta, but when three men, a drummer, a cornetist
and a fiddler, showed up for the first practice, held in our
home, they knew it was a lost cause. They kept trying for
about a month, then they had to give it up.

Families were thrown very much on their own for providing
entertainment of any kind. We had books, magazines and
music in our home and were thus not totally isolated. I recall Scribner's, McClure's (about the time Willa Cather was
on the editorial staff), and for its fashions Mama always took
the Ladies' Home Journal.

She was clever at sewing and in those days enjoyed it. She
could look at one of the fashion illustrations and duplicate
it perfectly. She made her own clothing and all of ours, including John's pretty little suits. The only clothing we ever
had to buy were coats, shoes and caps, her own suits and

coats, and of course most of Dad's clothing, although I believe she made his underwear, nightshirts and some of his shirts.

For several years our parents belonged to some sort of card club. I think there were four couples and they took turns meeting weekly at each other's homes. They mostly played a game called "Pitch." There were no babysitters in Kinta so we were inevitably taken along to the card games. Usually we grew sleepy early, were laid crosswise on a bed and slept through the games, but I can still remember being awakened by somebody's triumphant shout, "High, Low, Jack and the Game!" This would probably be Lucy. She wasn't a poor loser, but she certainly did love to win.

I remember when the word game Scrabble came in, nobody could ever beat Henry Giles. Mama spent several weeks with us one summer and I have never forgotten how hard she concentrated on beating him just one game. If she could just have beaten him one game she would have been happy. She was good, but she never did.

I don't think it ever dawned on her that he won mostly because he played Scrabble the way he would have played checkers or chess. He just constantly blocked you off. He does have an excellent vocabulary, but that would not have been enough to make him win so consistently. But you could never make a move toward finishing a word that he wasn't there ahead of you, blocking you off.

The nearest I ever came to seeing her lose her temper with him was in a game which she was very near winning. He blocked her in a corner which would have given her the game with the little word "too." She slammed her hand down on the table and said, "You don't play fair, Henry! You always block me instead of trying to win yourself!"

"But that's the way I win," he said, laughing, "and it's perfectly fair. It's part of the game. Seeing far enough ahead to block."

"But that was my corner," she protested, "and I had the tiles for it!"

"It was my corner, too," he insisted, "if I could keep you from getting it."

There weren't many more Scrabble games after that. Mama gave up and admitted he was the champion. As I said, she was a good loser, but she certainly did not like to lose consistently.

*

Usually at Christmas one of the numerous uncles or aunts gave us children a card game of some sort. I remember when we came into possession of our first deck of "Authors." The cards were dealt out and the winner was the first to collect all the works of one author. It was supposed to be instructive. Perhaps it was. Certainly I knew who wrote *Kenilworth, The Autocrat of the Breafast-Table, Martin Chuzzlewit* long before I ever read them. The author's picture was on the cards and even a child who could not read could recognize the picture and try to collect all six cards of that author. Thus John, who did not start to school until we moved to the city, Fort Smith, could even play, awkwardly it's true, and often in tears when he lost, but at least he wasn't left out.

I much preferred books as Christmas gifts, and from our parents, at least, they were always forthcoming. The Christmas after I was nine, an ill-advised aunt-in-law gave me a novel written by Mary J. Holmes. I have forgotten the title, but it concerned two girls orphaned by a wreck at sea and taken as township wards in some little town in Massachusetts.

The elder girl was strong and she was indentured to a cruel farmer and his wife. The younger girl was beautiful and a wealthy family took her in and reared her as their daughter. The younger girl danced her way through life and in the end died of tuberculosis. The elder girl survived her hardships, grew up to be a strong woman who educated herself and became a teacher. Of course the book ended with her marrying a wealthy man.

Mama let me read it (no reading was prohibited us except her "doctor's book" and that only because the whole process of childbirth was illustrated in it — I learned this much later, in my teens), but she told me it was not a very good book and not to take it seriously. That life was not like that at all. The good did not always become rich, nor was becoming rich the sole purpose in life.

She did not really like for me to read the Horatio Alger books either, but she did not prohibit them. She wouldn't buy them for me, but there was always some boy in town who would loan them to me as fast as they came out, which was awfully fast. In time, I think I read them all.

*

Once a year, at the close of school, there was a school entertainment. It was held in the auditorium on the last Friday night of the school year. This was the same semicircular auditorium, on the third floor of the school building, with a good stage and curtains, in which the entire school assembled every Friday morning of the school term to pledge allegiance to the flag, to repeat the Lord's Prayer, to sing "America" which we thought was the national anthem. Then we sang the state song:

> *Oklahoma, Oklahoma, fairest daughter of the West:*
> *Oklahoma, Oklahoma, 'tis the state I love the best.*

I have forgotten the rest of the words but I can hum the tune through in its entirety to this good day.

The end-of-school entertainment usually consisted of a short one-act play — never very good, of course, but much loved especially by the parents of the young performers — a chorus of young singers selected usually from the lower grades, a piano solo or two and very occasionally a solo sung by a badly frightened child.

There was always, also, something we called a tableau. It usually came last on the program before the presentation of diplomas. It consisted of a posed group with some special theme — patriotic, Hope, Faith and Charity, Spring or some other season. It was a perfectly silent performance. The young people, mostly from the upper grades, got into their costumes, took their poses while the curtains were closed.

There were no stage footlights in this auditorium, but for the tableau, men of the community who knew how to set them, put magnesium and sulphur flares around the circular edge of the stage. As the curtains parted, showing the posed young people, these flares lit up, very brightly, burned brightly a short time then slowly died down and out.

Curtain! It was a great grief to me that I never got to be in a tableau!

The entertainments rarely lasted more than an hour, but they were by far the best attended entertainments held in Kinta. Since a great many of the people in the town were related to each other in some way or other, nearly everybody who came had a special interest in some special child and was convinced that that child had been the star performer of the evening. I don't recall that the auditorium ever had an empty seat on those occasions and often there were men standing in the back.

The climax of the evening came when the diplomas were presented to those who had graduated from the eighth grade. To me they were always young men and women, the girls in their long, angle-length dresses with their hair done up, the boys in their long-pants dark suits, with high, stiff-collared shirts.

Dad would present the Chairman of the Board: "Mr. Luke Allen, ladies and gentlemen, who will present the diplomas."

The diplomas, already made out, rolled and tied with blue ribbons (why always blue, I wonder?) were waiting on a table. The graduates always sat in the front row — there were never more than ten or twelve — and one by one, shy, but so proud and happy, each young man, each young woman came forward to receive the little roll of paper which told the whole world he had graduated from the eighth grade of the Kinta School.

Education is taken so much for granted now, indeed has become almost a travesty to the young, that it has been forgotten what a privilege it used to be to be educated, and no one who has never known a young man or woman with a considerable amount of Indian blood can imagine the tremendous pride these young people took in their educational privileges.

Not all young Choctaws, or part-blood Choctaws, could afford to continue through the eighth grade. Some of them had to stop at the end of the sixth. But to each who finished and received that precious diploma it was one of the most important documents in his life. In almost every case the diploma was framed and hung in some prominent place in the home.

*

Athletics were not much stressed in the school and parents took little interest in them. Baseball was the biggest sport in those days and there were intramural baseball games, held after school, but they were rarely attended by any adults and the schoolchildren had to have permission to stay and watch the game.

We had never heard of football, and basketball played a long second place in interest to baseball. Volleyball was simply a recess game. There were too few teams for matches to be held in any sport.

Once a year a county field meet of sorts was held, usually in the county-seat town of Stigler. One year, however, it was held at Whitefield, which was only ten miles from Kinta. My father persuaded several fathers to take their wagons to convey the teams and he worked very hard for at least two months that spring training the boys and girls, mostly for track events, high jumps, pole vaults.

Kinta won two events that year — the relay race and the baseball championship. We came home elated over having won anything at all in our first participation.

"Will we get to go again next year?" I recall asking my father as we slowly drove home.

"I hope so," he said. "It's a good thing for Kinta to participate in. We *ought* to do it each year, but it will depend pretty much on the school board and the interest of the parents."

I don't recall that we ever participated again, so presumably the interest of the school board and the parents was not enough. But one could understand why. Education to them was classroom work. Sports, of any kind, was play. School was a serious business and there ought not to be any time for play except of the kind one played during recess periods.

*

No doubt about it, Kinta was a difficult town in which to interest people in anything but cows and cotton. But as I knew no difference it was still the hub of the universe to me. It was home and I loved it.

12

CHARLESTON, MY CHARLESTON

*

PRECISELY WHEN a Confederate Reunion began to be held in Charleston, with Grandpa Holt very prominent in it, I don't know. But it was when I was still very young — not more than six or seven years old. It may even have begun before I was born and I only begin to remember them at that age.

At any rate, at that time in my life there were some sixty-odd veterans of the Confederate army who gathered for the Reunion annually. A group of them near Charleston must have gotten together and decided that they should meet thus and rehash those proud days, now some fifty years behind them, when they wore that old gray uniform so proudly and fought so valiantly for their "lost cause."

They determined it would be more than a get-together of veterans. They decided it would be a two-day picnic. There was a sort of park or fairgrounds about two miles outside the little town, where the town band played once a week in the summer and where people went for family picnics. It was beautifully wooded and the grounds were level. In fact the baseball field was located there and during the summer the road to the park was well traveled by the people going to see the games on Saturday afternoons. Naturally, Charleston had a baseball team. Every southern town had one. I think the entire south must have been mad about baseball!

I have heard my Grandpa Holt say that a gentleman was a Southerner, a Democrat and a National League baseball fan! The St. Louis Cardinals were the National League baseball club a gentleman preferred, because St. Louis was considered more of a southern city than a northern one. There were some dissenters but they weren't very vocal about it. And the south was so strongly Democrat that you had to shake the bushes to find a Republican and even then he wasn't very likely to admit he was one. The Solid South was truly solid in those days. I can vouch for that personally.

The two-day picnic was held in the park, families bringing their own picnic lunches. A meager little carnival, mostly with nothing but a merry-go-round, a shooting gallery, a few shell games, was always invited to come for the two days and for some reason one always showed up.

The various women's auxiliaries in the little town — the UDC (United Daughters of the Confederacy), to which most of the women in our family proudly belonged, the women of the Eastern Star — to which most of the women of our family also proudly belonged, for most of their men were Masons — and a few church missionary societies set up cold drink and food stands. To a child, the best home-cooked food, and it *was* the best home-cooked food, was nothing to compare to a hamburger and a strawberry pop bought at a food stand.

Coca-Cola had not yet appeared on the market apparently. I don't recall ever seeing it at any rate. And the only two flavors of soda pop available were strawberry and sarsaparilla. The bottles were glass and they had that funny little glass cap held tightly in place with a metal spring bar. The soda pop was kept cold in tubs of water in which ice was placed — huge hundred-pound blocks of ice renewed several times a day.

Once the Confederate Reunions began it was required of every living child of Grandpa's that he attend. No excuse but illness or some other disaster was ever accepted. The reunion was always held the first week in August. I don't believe it was ever once rained out and usually the weather was about 110 in the shade and the wagons and buggies constantly traveling over the road to the park and around inside it kept a dusty veil hanging over the entire picnic ground.

No one can possibly imagine how much fun Reunion Week was with all the children of the Holt grandparents, and their children, jammed together in the big farmhouse. It was built for coolness, with wide cross halls intersecting in the middle.

The halls were at least fifteen feet wide. They had big double doors at all four ends which could be shut against the weather in the winter and thrown wide open in the summer. They must have been icy in the winter, but we rarely visited in the winter so I have no memory of how cold those halls must have been. I do remember how beautifully cool they were in the summer with the breezes from any direction blowing through.

There were four main rooms in the house each at least twenty feet square with high ceilings. Three of them were bedrooms, and there was one enormous dormitory bedroom upstairs. The fourth main room was the parlor, naturally. It was rarely used except when people came calling.

Each of the main rooms had a huge fireplace, which was the only heat in the house. But they were strangely built on inside walls, so that the enormous chimneys seemed somehow to pin the huge square house to the ground. Once the house had been painted white, but the paint had weathered and it was a dingy gray by the time of my memory, almost as if it had never been painted. I don't suppose anybody ever thought about repainting it. We all liked it just the way it was and to have seen a pristine white house with those enormous mulberry and locust and walnut trees thickly all around it would have been so startling as to make it seem unreal to us.

One could not call the front yard a lawn. I think it must have been planted in orchard grass or something similar and it was hardly ever mowed. It was heavenly cool to roll and play and hide in. Just before the Reunion Grandpa cut it with the hay mower, swearing as he did so because it was Grandma and Aunt Grace who made him do it. It was an immense yard, fenced with an unpainted paling fence, and the front walk led from the gate by way of a slate-stone walk to the front stoop. Grandpa never mowed the yard close or very well!

The tree I loved most in the yard, as did all the other children, was a huge mulberry with great knobs or knots growing every foot or so up the trunk. This made it an easy tree to climb. The huge leaves made it easy to hide in. Swings hung from two of the trees. Not the long rope swings such as Dad had hung for us at Kanima, but what would today be called porch swings. One could swing fairly high in them, although we were discouraged from doing so for fear they would overturn with us. They were usually occupied by the adults anyhow, who found their slow gentle swing comfortable. A toe could keep the swing swaying gently and it was cool sitting there under the shade of those giant trees.

The yard, the trees, the swings, the deep grass, the long

cross halls and the big apple orchard made the place a Garden of Eden for children. I regret there is no picture of that lovely old place.

There was a small front porch, little more than a stoop, with lattice work at either end on which the most beautiful red roses climbed thickly. The real working porch and the porch where most of the men in the family sat during the summer was in the ell formed by the house and the dining room and kitchen.

The kitchen had once been entirely separate from the house and it had been built of logs originally. But it had been weatherboarded over the logs outside and ceiled over them on the inside. It had the biggest fireplace of all, for at one time all the cooking had been done on it. But now it was used only on special occasions, as when Grandpa wanted to roast a whole mutton (of which he was very fond) or pig or calf in it. Otherwise the cooking was done on a wood-burning range.

The floors in all the rooms but the parlor were bare except for the braided rugs which Grandma and the aunts had made. On the parlor floor was a plain straw-colored matting from wall to wall. It was padded with straw or hay and once a year it was taken up and carried outside, hung over the clothesline and beaten. The straw padding was then also renewed. The furniture was very plain, but comfortable. I only remember deep comfortable chairs and, I believe, a cane-backed settee.

The kitchen floor was bare and was scrubbed so often, with lye soap, that it was almost white and it was worn very slick.

This was not true of the cross halls. Their floors were rather rough and splintery. Once, running down the main hall, I slipped and slid several feet, without falling, however. But I did run a big splinter in my heel. I thought I had pulled it all out, so I said nothing about it to anybody. We didn't make a fuss about such things.

About a week later Mama noticed that I was tiptoeing on that foot. Some small piece of the splinter had been too deeply embedded and it had escaped me. By that time the heel was so sore that I knew it would hurt badly to have the piece of splinter taken out. Only the barest tip of it could be seen and in my ignorance I thought it would have to be cut out. I couldn't face that. So I eased the pain by tiptoeing. The heel was also feverish and throbbed at night sometimes until I couldn't get to sleep easily.

When Mama examined the heel she said the splinter must come out. I thought she would do it herself (and Mama didn't have much patience with fear of pain) or she would take me to the doctor who would hurt me much worse.

To my great relief Grandpa stepped in. "I can get it out," he said, "you won't need to go to the doctor."

"But it will hurt!" I protested. "It will hurt even if you take it out."

"No, it won't," he said. "I promise you it won't hurt. Well, maybe just a little prick, about like pulling a thorn out. That's all. Now, you've pulled out many a thorn from your feet or hands, haven't you? That's all it will amount to. I never broke my word to you in your life, did I, Janice?"

"No-o-o-," but I was sobbing already.

"Hush, Janice," Mama said, "no use crying before it hurts."

It was Dad who said nothing but picked me up and held me on his lap.

Grandpa went into the kitchen. "I'll be right back."

I did not know it but he was sterilizing his big pocket knife. It took him some little time and as the minutes passed my fear grew and I hid my face on Dad's shoulder and cried. He patted me and tried to comfort me. "It will be all right, now. Don't cry sweetheart. Grandpa will get it out and you'll hardly feel it at all."

But I couldn't imagine how anybody could even *touch* that dreadfully sore place without nearly killing me. I couldn't even bear to touch it with my finger!

When Grandpa came back onto the porch from the kitchen he was careful to hide the big pocket knife, with its long, sharp, pointed blade, behind his back. He sat down near Dad and said, "Now, put her on my lap, John."

I was still crying, but I made no protest at the transfer except to cling tightly to Dad's big hand. Grandpa said, "Now, turn your head the other way. Don't look and you won't even know when it comes out."

And except for one sharp little pain, I didn't know when it came out. He had slid the sharp point of that knife blade so quickly, and yet so carefully, under the tiny protruding edge of the splinter and pulled it out so surely and quickly that it was precisely as he had said. Many a sticker-bur had hurt worse being pulled out!

"Now, there you are," he said. "Turn around now and look at it! It's all out and you didn't feel it hardly at all, did you?"

I looked at the stub of the splinter which had caused me so much agony — of fear and of real pain. I could hardly believe it was all over. "Is that all there is to it?"

"That's all there is to it. It's over."

Oh, what a hero Grandpa was to me! How could he have done it so quickly and without hurting me unbearably? But he had and the relief was immediate, for a lot of pus came out with the splinter.

Mama took charge then. "John, carry her into the kitchen now."

"What are you going to do?" I asked, immediately apprehensive again.

"I am only going to bandage it," she said. "We can't let it get infected. You don't want any more trouble with it, do you?"

"No, *ma'am*."

Mama put some kind of medicine on it, which stung a little, then without touching it at all except carefully to wrap a bandage around the entire heel, she was as good as her word. She did say, however, when she had finished the bandaging, "Next time you'll know to come immediately when you've hurt yourself and let Dad or me take care of you. You see what happens when you let fear take over. Things only get worse."

I wondered how one managed not to let fear take over — especially fear of pain, but I did not say so. I only said, meekly, "Yes, ma'am."

Within two days I could walk on the heel again, but the bandage did not come off for nearly a week.

*

The real living room of the old house was Grandma and Grandpa's bedroom. It was so big that the huge wooden bed in which they slept only took up one corner. This left plenty of room for chairs to be grouped about the fireplace. In the inside chimney corner was Grandma's chair, a square table — homemade and rather large — on which she kept her Bible, the few magazines she read, the newspapers the family read and her sewing box. A kerosene lamp was also on the table, for this house had no electricity.

I can still see Grandma sitting in that corner, usually piecing a quilt (blankets were unheard of in those days) or mending a dress or some other garment. She was short, rather plump, dark-skinned and dark-haired, and very quiet-spoken. I cannot remember her ever saying a sharp word to anybody and she certainly never reproved any of her grandchildren. If we stubbed a toe or hurt ourselves a little in any way we usually ran to her. She shoved her glasses up on top of her head, laid down her sewing and took us into her ample lap to comfort us. She wore very plain cotton dresses except for special occasions when she had a beautiful plain black silk. In the summer her dresses were white sprigged with tiny lilac, purple or black flowers scattered over the material. In the winter the dresses were black with tiny white or yellow flowers. She always wore an apron over her dresses to keep them fresh. Both dresses and aprons were starched and perfectly ironed. I have seen my aunts iron all day long, with a hot fire in the wood-burning range to heat the irons, on their cotton dresses, their shirtwaists and skirts and the many petticoats they wore. How they stood it I cannot imagine, but they were a proud-looking and perfectly dressed group of women when they went out!

Since the house had no electricity, of course it had no indoor plumbing. Water for use in the house was drawn from an open, dug well. It was always very cold when freshly drawn.

The outhouse, or closet as we called it, was well away from the house. To reach it, one went down a path which ran beside the garden fence, turned a corner with the fence, then ran along a very thick plum thicket which was overhung with wild grapevines. In the daytime this was a lovely cool place to play, because we had literally to crawl under the vines to the middle of the plum thicket where it was open enough to make a playhouse. We spent many happy hours playing in that plum thicket, where the sun never struck, where it was always a little dim and dark. It was a marvelous place for spooky games, too, because of its dimness.

There was only one drawback to the plum thicket. There was a small grave to one side, marked with a slab of natural rock on which nothing had been engraved. It had to be a baby's grave, it was so small, and it was slightly sunken. We often wondered whose grave it was — how old the baby had been — what had happened to it. Nobody at all knew anything about it, not even Grandpa or Grandma. When we asked, as we certainly did ask more times than once, "Whose grave it is?" all Grandpa, or Grandma, would say was, "We don't know. It was here, just like it is now, when we came here." They seemed to have no theories about it nor would they conjecture on it.

The idea which we developed among ourselves and liked best was one I voiced one day. "I'll bet it's an Indian grave." I think the other cousins agreed mostly because it was, to us, a very romantic idea to believe some tiny Indian had been buried in our plum thicket.

The plum thicket was fine in the daytime, but if one of us had to go clear to the closet at night, a parent must be wakened, he had to light the lantern and accompany us. There was not a single grandchild who would go past that dark plum thicket, with that tiny grave in it, after dark alone. Until bedtime, three or four of us might manage it, with many shiverings and by running fast until we were past it, but in the middle of the night? No, sir! Some adult, usually one's own parent, had to go along and hang tightly to one's hand.

During the week of the Confederate Reunion the adults occupied all the bedrooms including the upstairs dormitory.

The children were bedded down in the halls, the little boys in one section, the girls in another, on pallets thick with half a dozen quilts. Those pallets never felt hard or uncomfortable to me. And the cross halls at night were the coolest sleeping place in the house. We certainly thought we had the best of the deal. The bedroom doors and windows were always wide open all day and night, to get the cross ventilation, but compared to the cool breezes that blew through the halls they were ovens and many a time we woke up with an aunt who had crept out and joined us on our pallets rather than lie sleepless in the heat.

I don't remember having any favorite cousins, although I think all of us who lived rather near each other, that is, within twenty or twenty-five miles, and saw each other more frequently, were a little partial to Aunt Emma Hartzell's daughters, Frances and Virginia. Frances was near my age and Virginia was near Mary C.'s. They lived in Mississippi and we only saw them once a year, at Reunion time. Frances and I usually managed to sleep next to each other, and I feel reasonably sure Mary C. and Virginia did the same. I do not recall any quarreling, ever, over who was to sleep where, among the Holt cousins. I do not recall much quarreling among the Holt cousins of any kind, and this was directly opposite to our relationships with the McGraw cousins. There was constant bickering among us and them. Perhaps with the Holts, the even-tempered, rather easy-going Holt genes predominated. With the McGraw cousins, the volatile, high-tempered, easily angered McGraw genes predominated. Whatever the reason, that's the way it was.

*

The Reunion opened the same way every year. There were three business blocks in the little town and all the people of the town lined themselves up along the sidewalks by nine or nine-thirty along the main street. Promptly at ten a bugle blew, out of sight, where two blocks farther west the veterans had gathered on the schoolhouse grounds.

Next we could hear the ruffle of the drums and we knew the parade had formed and begun. The children were always put in the front row to watch. No child was ever pushed back where he couldn't see. Then we could see the thin gray line in formation coming down the street, the drum rolling out the cadence. About half a block before the parade reached the crowd the band broke into the stirring strains of "Dixie" and it played that Confederate rallying song over and over the entire three blocks on which the crowd was gathered. There was rarely a dry eye as the veterans passed. I was always so proud because out in front of the rest of the veterans came the color bearers stepping smartly. The United States flag was flown, the old Confederate flag and several colors of various units borne usually by men who had carried those colors for that unit during the war.

Grandpa carried the Confederate flag. To me he was the most beautiful sight in the world in that battered old gray uniform which he had worn for four years, carrying the flag he had believed so honestly was the flag of *his* country. His head was always high, his feet moved with beautiful high-stepping precision. You would never have known he was sixty-five years old.

When the colors passed every man in the crowd took his hat off and every woman wiped tears away. It was still too soon for them not to weep over that long, wasting, lost war.

They may have lost that war, and it broke their hearts to know they had lost it, but they were never truly defeated. To the day he died my grandfather believed the southern states had a right, under the very Constitution of the United States, to secede and form their own government if they wanted to. To him, it was as much their right as it had been the right of the colonists to break away from England. I am sure most Southerners truly felt that and those who lived through that war and fought it continued to believe it always. I grew up saturated in that belief and not until I was a mature woman did I quit quoting the Preamble to the Declaration of Independence as the basis for that belief.

The parade consisted only of those sixty or seventy Confederate veterans. No high school bands, no important people riding along interspersed in the column. It was the Confederate parade and nobody else had any part in it. The men stepped quickly to the tune of "Dixie," heads up, forage caps and cavalry hats tilted jauntily until they came to the end of the lines of the people. There, just about where the little Catholic Church was located, they stopped, broke ranks, furled their colors and rejoined their families. Now, officially, the Confederate Reunion was opened.

Our families went back to the farmhouse, Grandpa hitched up teams of mules to two wagons, and the immense picnic dinner, packed in a small trunk, was loaded into one. Grandma would never sit on the wagon seat with Grandpa. She always took a comfortable old hickory-bottomed chair. She sat in it during the ride to the picnic grounds, then it was placed under the shade of an immense oak tree, the same tree every year. She sat all day there, never intrigued by the carnival, never wandering around to see who was there —

for everybody came to her. There was always a cluster of people visiting Mary Tolleson Holt in her chair under the oak tree. But she laughed a lot at the antics of the children and the fun we had.

Hucksters sold balloons, canes, small rubber balls with a long rubber string attached. I hated those rubber balls, for the boys had much fun snapping them against the girls' fannies. Even the uncles couldn't resist making us jump. A group of girl cousins would be walking around happily sucking on candy canes, when wham! a rubber ball would sting one's behind.

It always hurt and it always made us jump and scream and it always made me angry. I would whirl around. "You stop that! It hurts!"

"Aw," the boy cousins would say, "it can't hurt much. It's just a little old rubber ball."

But rubber or not, loosed with enough strength it could raise a welt.

Dad gave each of us a quarter to spend — for the entire day — which was literally all he could spare. Mama would admonish us, "Don't ask for more. And don't ask any of your uncles for more, either."

But we didn't have to ask. Aunt Emma's husband, Clifford Hartzell, and Aunt Billie's husband, Elisha Cannon, were generous with us to a fault. A dozen times a day they would slip each of us an extra quarter, and since everything was only five cents, we drank enough soda pop to drown us, we had balloons, the canes, the rubber balls by the dozens, and until we got seasick from the merry-go-round we were its best customers.

I would have loved the balloons if the boy cousins had let

us alone with them. But they loved to sneak up behind us and stick a pin in them and of course they popped with a loud and unexpected bang, which always made us jump. Thank heaven, there were no firecrackers at the Reunion. The boys would have made us miserable. We had no fire- works on the Fourth of July, either. Fireworks were for Christmas. I suppose this was a carry-over from the old Mis- sissippi days — but, no, it could not have been, for it was general in our entire section. It must have been a carry-over from the days of the Civil War when the Fourth of July ceased to be a holiday to celebrate.

We brought everything for Grandma to see. She would smile and say, "Isn't that balloon pretty," or "My, isn't the merry-go-round nice!"

We would bring her a strawberry pop, but she would only shake her head. "No. I don't like soda pop. When I'm thirsty I want water."

We always had a great jug of cold water from the well so she always had a good supply on hand.

At noon, a big white tablecloth was spread in the shade near Grandma and all the food the aunts had been preparing for days was spread on it. We children seemed to have bot- tomless stomachs, for no matter how much pop and candy we had eaten, the fried chicken, the slices of cold mutton, the potato salad, the pickles and cole slaw, the pies and cakes always tasted good and disappeared like magic. Grandma presided like a queen over the table making certain everybody had enough to eat. And there were always several guests, in- vited far ahead of time to have picnic dinner with the Holts.

In the afternoon, about two o'clock, there was a "speak- ing." Some fairly important person, if only the county superintendent of schools, made a speech. To me the speeches were long and dull, and we were required to be polite, to sit still and listen. "Listen," Grandpa would say, "and you'll learn something."

But how could one listen, how could one even sit without wiggling, when a boy cousin dropped a caterpillar in one's lap, or a girl cousin nudged, giggled and whispered. Nearly all of us came in for a good scolding, but that was all, when the speaking was over.

Then the town band played for about thirty minutes. Nobody had to tell us to be quiet for that. We always loved it — but we were always a little impatient, for the big event of the afternoon followed the band concert — the baseball game.

Grandpa was the most partial and loudest rooter of us all. All his dignity was forgotten at the baseball game. He whooped and yelled, waved his hat and bawled at the umpire like the best Brooklyn Dodger fan that ever lived. There was only one umpire and he stood behind the pitcher. Inevitably he missed a few balls and strikes, and inevitably he called a few men safe or out wrongly, especially at first base. One man simply cannot umpire a ball game, but that was all the Reunion funds could afford.

If Charleston lost, Grandpa was always disgusted. He never felt they had really lost the game — it had been stolen from them! Rarely — I think I could even make that never — would he give the other team credit for outplaying them. Naturally we echoed him.

Mama and Dad, often knowing better, would tell us, "You must not say that!"

"Grandpa does!"

"Well, Grandpa is an old man and he can say what he

pleases. But today the other team was simply better than the Charleston team and you must learn to be fair and give credit where credit is due."

"But, Mama, we *can't* say the Charleston team isn't the best."

"You can keep your mouths shut," she would snap at us.

We never did. She couldn't actually punish us for echoing Grandpa. "Damned umpire," he would say, "just *gave* that game away to Paris!" Or Lavaca, or Ratcliff. We didn't dare say "damned." Our mouths would have been washed out with strong lye soap. But we could and did say, "The umpire just *gave* that game to Paris." Or Lavaca, or Ratcliff.

The parade was not repeated on the second day. It was held only to open, officially, the Reunion. Nor was there a speaking on the second day, much to our relief. There was a longer band concert and another baseball game and more soda pop, balloons, candy canes and rubber balls.

The two days of the Reunion were never long enough for us, but I am sure it was more than long enough for the adults. After that there seemed to be a sort of letdown, but usually the big families stayed on for a few days, some for the rest of the week, some even longer. Grandpa never wanted any of us to go home. I know we usually stayed a week, but one or two of the families living farther away left the next day.

One of the things I most enjoyed about the Reunion was not having any chores to do. There were so many aunts that I never even had to wipe a dish, much less wash any. Mama tried, though. She would say, "Janice, go help Aunt Belle with the dishes."

Dutifully I would go to the big kitchen, where half a dozen aunts were already in charge. "Can I help?" I would ask.

Aunt Belle, who was usually in charge, would look at me

gently and smile sweetly. "No, honey. You run along and play. There are plenty of us grown-ups to do the work. You children have a good time while you can."

Aunt Belle had three sons and no daughters. I have often wondered if she had had a daughter if she might not have been badly spoiled by that tall, slender, dear woman, who always worked so hard herself. She died too young — I think in her fifties — of that dread disease which seemed inherent in the Holt genes, tuberculosis.

Slowly, over the years, the gray ranks thinned until finally only a dozen or so could march in the parade and they were beginning to be pretty old and feeble. They still tried to step out smartly, but it could no longer be done. Some of them almost shuffled.

*

During the years of the Reunion we only missed one or two. Either Dad was teaching a summer school and could not find a substitute or he was attending summer school in refresher work and could not spare the week away from classes. For whatever reason, it was heartbreaking for us children. Dad said, "We have to miss the Reunion, but I promise you we will visit Charleston this fall."

By this time, through some quarrel between Dad and the Kinta school board, Dad was no longer principal at the Kinta school. He was principal and one of two teachers at what had been one of the Choctaw schools, Edmonds Chapel.

I have never known what the quarrel with the school board was about, but at this late date I have a theory. I think probably it was because we went fishing on weekends too often, instead of staying at home and attending Sunday School and church. This would have been Dad's fault, because while

Mama liked to fish she felt a duty to her children to bring them up in the church.

I think, too, it may also have been because they played cards. This would have been Lucy's fault, because Dad never cared much for any kind of card game.

Very much in what is now called the "Bible Belt," either of these offenses would have been enough to get my father into trouble. This is simply my own theory, however. I have nothing to go on except my theory because Mama and Dad never discussed it with us children. And once I was grown myself it never occurred to me to ask.

Edmonds Chapel was a school with a divided term. It had three months of summer school and about five or six months beginning at the end of October, continuing until spring. It was out near Sans Bois within daily driving distance for Dad so that we continued to live in Kinta, and Mary C. and I continued to go to the Kinta school. I was in about the fifth grade by this time, Mary C. in the third. John must have been about four years old.

The second year Dad taught at Edmonds Chapel Mama became the second teacher, taking John with her to the schoolroom. Between them they more than made up Dad's salary as principal of the Kinta school.

When the summer school was out at Edmonds Chapel, our school had already begun in Kinta. It was late in September, or early in October, when Dad said, at supper one night, "We're going to Charleston, children."

We were beside ourselves with joy. This was a summer when we had had to miss the Confederate Reunion. "When? When?" we cried.

"Pretty soon now."

"But we're in school!" I suddenly remembered.

"You can easily make up the work you'll miss when we get back," he said. We accepted that and began to jabber among ourselves.

"Aren't you going to ask how we're going?" Dad said.

Mary C. looked as puzzled as I felt. We always went to Charleston the same way. We took the Fort Smith & Western to Fort Smith, changed there to the Arkansas Central, the short dinky which made one trip down to Paris, Arkansas — the coal-mining town where Mary C. had been born — each morning, and came back to Fort Smith each evening. It went through Charleston.

"Well, how *are* we going?" I finally said.

"By covered wagon!" Dad said, triumphantly.

"But we don't have a covered wagon," I protested.

"Oh, that." Dad dismissed it easily. "I've already rented a team and wagon and the wagon has a canvas top that can be rolled back or up, depending on the weather, and we are going to drive to Charleston and back."

This announcement was cause for new joy. "Just like the pioneers," I said, "going to California or bust!"

"Just like the pioneers," Dad agreed.

"Yes," Mama said, "and just about as slow."

"Oh, no," Dad said. "It seems a long way to Charleston when we go by train, but it actually isn't much more than fifty miles by road. I think we can easily make ten or fifteen miles a day. We'll camp out every night and . . . "

"And," Mama put in, "if you find a good place to fish or hunt some game we might camp out two or three days in one place!"

Dad grinned. "What's wrong with that?"

"Nothing," she replied, laughing. "Not one thing. I shall love every minute of it. But we can't keep the children out of school *too* long."

"I'll keep that in mind," Dad promised.

We knew we would love every minute of it, too. "How did you ever come to think of it?" we wanted to know.

"Oh, it just came to me. We had to miss the Reunion this summer and I thought we all deserved a vacation."

Dad and Mama certainly deserved a vacation, but naturally the reason he had thought of the covered wagon trip was because that was the only way they could afford to give us the vacation in Charleston.

*

We were so excited about this covered wagon trip and talked about it so incessantly that every child in Kinta envied us and said so, or made fun of us, and said so. We didn't mind either way. It was precisely the kind of thing Dad liked to do. Get out into the country, travel slowly, see the country, stop and fish when he wanted to and camp out every night. He was an environmentalist long before the term was ever used. His idea of education was way ahead of its time, too. He strongly believed that experiences were as educational, sometimes more so, than the classroom. One did not bring home report cards from camping trips, but one learned much. And he made good campers of all of us. "A poor sport as well as a poor camper," he used to tell us, "is one who doesn't pull his weight. In camp, *everybody* falls to and pulls his weight."

Not even Little John was excluded. He could gather the light wood which served to start a fire. Mary C. and I could gather the heavier wood and bring pails of water from a stream, to wash our hands with, to make coffee with and to heat for dishwater. Our camp dishes were not china, of course. They were granite ware (that beautiful blue and white spattered ware that is called agate today), tin and iron. Dad did the heaviest chores and Mama did the cooking. Not until the camp was tidy and shipshape were hooks baited and the fun began.

Mama entered into the plans with as much enthusiasm as Dad. In October it was cool, but not yet cold. Dad took along the bedrolls. "We'll sleep in the open," he said, when we called attention to the fact he wasn't taking the big tent. "We'll sleep under the stars except on rainy nights, then we can all sleep in the wagon. It will be a little crowded but we'll manage. You children would be too crowded riding with *all* the camping equipment. We don't need the tent this time."

He bedded the wagon with a good thick layer of hay and Mama took the feather bed to further pad the hay. Then many quilts went on top the feather bed. As a matter of fact, I think we children slept in the wagon most nights anyhow, we loved it so.

The usual grub box was packed, our clothing was packed and very, very early one morning in the covered wagon, the tarpaulin cover in place to please us children, we rolled slowly out of Kinta toward Lequire and McCurtain. At McCurtain we left the road that went on to Fort Smith and turned due east for the little towns of Shady Point and Panama. Shortly we crossed the Oklahoma line and were in Arkansas headed for Charleston.

Once the thrill of leaving town with the wagon sheet in

place wore off, we children, who rode in the back of the wagon, grew tired of not being able to see except through the hole in the back, and from then on the tarp was rolled back when the weather was good. When it was bad we gathered at the little puckered hole at the rear and could at least see where we had been.

We had a good trotting team of horses and the wagon wasn't heavily loaded so we made good time. Some of the new wore off, and we were sometimes too hot and at all times too dusty, but Dad and Mama always picked a good camping place for the night, beside some nice stream where the horses could be watered and where we could all have a good wash-up, where water was easily available for cooking and drinking, and where, hopefully, Dad could catch a nice string of fish for supper.

We finally reached Charleston, spent our week, a blissfully happy one, then it was time to start home again. The trip home was not nearly so exciting as the trip over had been because we knew what lay ahead of us.

One night, unable to find a stream to camp by, we came across a schoolhouse. Dad found a home nearby and asked the owner if he thought it would be all right if we stopped in the school yard and used the water from the school well. The man was sure it would be, so there we camped. Dad always took his violin everywhere with him and that night, sitting around our campfire, Dad was fiddling away when the owner of the farm came to visit.

"Go ahead with your fiddlin', sir," the man said, "I always did enjoy good fiddlin' and you're a master fiddler."

"Why, thank you," Dad said.

I glowed with pleasure for I agreed with the farmer. I thought my dad was the best fiddler in the world. When

I heard other men fiddling "Soldier's Joy" or "Devil's Horn-pipe," I always compared them with him and they came in a mighty poor second. For one thing they always seemed off-key, or they hit sour notes. Dad never did. His fingers were so nimble that one could barely see them move on the strings on a really fast piece and he never sawed with the bow — except to joke with us when he ended a piece. He bowed clearly and the notes were always distinct, even when fast, and he bowed sweetly and beautifully.

Dad fiddled a while longer, for the man's benefit, then the farmer said, "I guess I better get on back up to the house. My old woman'll be wonderin' if I'm going to spend the night down here. But I'd like to buy a bushel of apples from you," and he brought out a big tow sack.

Dad stared at the sack a moment then he began laughing. "You've made a mistake," he said, "we're not apple peddlers. We don't have anything to sell."

"Oh," the man said, "well, excuse me then. I knowed you wasn't gypsies so I figgered you was driving across the country selling apples and I like to lay in a bushel or two every fall for the winter."

"So do I," Dad said. "And I'm sorry I can't oblige you. We're just traveling. We've been on a visit and are returning home now."

"I see."

But I don't think the farmer did see. He looked puzzled as if people who drove across the country in covered wagon and camped out at night were more than a little out of their heads. But he apologized again and left us.

The mistake was a natural one for the man to make. In those days people with more apples than they needed often filled their wagons with them, stuck a branched stick in the whip socket with apples stuck on the branches to show they were selling apples and went out across the country peddling them. We depended on apple peddlers ourselves for our apples each winter. Dad always bought a barrelful which, when packed in straw as he knew how to pack them, generally lasted us all winter.

By the end of October, as we were returning, the nights were more than cool, they were just plain cold. "It's going to be an early and hard winter," Dad prophesied, and he was very good at such prophesying. He was an excellent amateur weatherman. He had grown up on a farm, remember, and nearly all farmers, in those days, were good weathermen. I think they mostly knew from the behavior of their animals when bad weather was brewing. We already knew it was going to be an early winter, for it was too cold for October. How hard it would be, we would simply have to wait and learn.

On one of the last nights before we reached Kinta ice had formed along the edges of the little stream beside which we camped and Dad built up an immense fire after supper.

Then occurred an event I have never forgotten and which I used in my book *Hannah Fowler*. Suddenly we could see points of light reflected in eyes which ringed our camp. It was terrifying to see all those eyes all around the camp. "What are they, Daddy?" I said. "Why are those little lights all around our camp?"

Dad, who never lied to us, did lie that night. "Just some small animals that are cold and want to come near the fire."

He knew they were prairie wolves, however, and after a few more minutes, when more tiny pinpoints of lights entirely encircled us, he said quietly, "Lucy, take the children and get in the wagon. We'll sleep in there tonight."

Mama also knew what they were, but she said nothing either except "Yes, John." She hurried us into the wagon. We were scared, but as long as Mama and Dad were with us, nothing very terrible could happen to us.

They *were* wolves. The fire and the smell of the horses had attracted them and they had encircled the camp. Neither of our parents slept a wink that night. Dad had a gun with him, but had he fired it, it would only have brought the whole pack down on us eventually. Mama wouldn't stay in the wagon once she had her children bedded down. She went out to join Dad.

Quietly, going not very far from the fire, they gathered up all the wood they could. Dad brought the horses and tethered them to the wagon. He did not try to keep a big fire going all night, but he did keep a good one going, and there was always a knot of wood burning with its handle near his hand, or Mama's. When the circle of eyes started to close in, Dad would say, "Lucy, throw yours to that side, I'll take the other."

These clubs of burning wood would scare the wolves very far back. With horrifying yelps as the burning wood hit, they would flee. But within an hour they would be creeping back.

This went on all night. Not until nearly daylight did the silent but dangerous circle of wolves leave, not to return. Dad had been afraid of two things, naturally. He feared first for his family. But he feared almost as much for the horses, for if the circle of wolves had ever grown bold enough to attack the horses, the horses could not have stood a chance.

Mary C., John and I slept fitfully, but we slept, secure in the knowledge that our parents were on guard and that everything would finally be all right.

I am certain that never was dawn more welcome to two

people than it was to our father and mother that morning. Dad made haste to hitch up, Lucy gave us a cold breakfast and we put that place behind us in a hurry.

I think we reached home the next day. I am not sure that the tale Mary C. and I had to tell to all our friends of being attacked by wolves on the prairie was believed. Children do love to exaggerate danger. But there could not possibly have been any exaggeration of our danger that night. And had Dad not known that faggots of burning wood would keep wolves at bay, none of us might have reached Kinta alive.

The prairies wolves used to come up near enough to the town on cold winter nights and howl. I never heard them after that without a chill of fear. Their howls are chilling enough without having gone through that silent, deadly dangerous night we had known as a family.

*

Just when the final Confederate Reunion was held I have forgotten, but I imagine it was in 1917, the year Grandpa Holt died. He had tuberculosis but he died of pneumonia.

The entire family was gathered there already for the Reunion. I shall never forget that as he lay dying, Grandma went to the bed in which they had slept together almost all their lives, slipped her hand under the cover, felt of his feet, and they were already cold. She quietly said, "Goodbye, Jim," and left the room. Five minutes later he was gone.

Why I was in the room at the time I can't imagine, but I was and I could not understand how Grandma knew he was dying. I was in the room when he died, but it was somehow not horrible to me at all. It seemed natural instead, for he had been sick a long time and I had heard my father say, "Grandpa can't last much longer."

All the younger children had been sent to Uncle Jim Holt's, partly to keep them from being in the way but mostly, I suspect, to keep them from witnessing the grief and tragedy. I was sent to bring them home and to warn them Grandpa was dead.

Grandpa had asked to be buried in his old gray uniform and for his casket to be draped with his old Confederate flag. I cannot swear to it, but I am sure his wishes were carried out. The funeral was held in the parlor in the home. I suppose there were no funeral homes then. There certainly was no law requiring embalming. Grandpa lay in state, therefore, in the parlor, his casket open while people from miles around came, only the one day, and then he was buried.

The cemetery in Charleston was very near the Confederate Park and picnic ground. It did seem very strange to be driving in a funeral procession past that place which had always held so much life for him and in which he had taken so much pleasure.

*

For years I missed those summers and I never pass through Charleston now that I don't look at the school and yard that stand on the site and wish it had not been necessary just there, and that the old farmhouse still stood, even if somebody else lived in it. The only thing left that was there when we were children is an immense oak tree which had been in the front yard.

13

NOT SO MY ALTUS

✻

WHEN WE VISITED the McGraw grandparents in the summer, our father usually did not go. Generally we spent a month at Mama's parents', and Dad could not take that much time off.

To get to Altus we took the Fort Smith & Western to Fort Smith, then there was a layover of several hours before we could take the Iron Mountain (Missouri Pacific) for the forty-five-mile journey to Altus.

We usually spent this layover in the parlor of the old Main Hotel, right in downtown Fort Smith. To me it was an imposing place, and very elegant, two or three stories high. Perhaps even four. The parlor was an immense room, with old-fashioned Victorian furniture.

For some reason I had a propensity for getting locked into rooms. I suppose doors and locks and keys fascinated me and at first it never occurred to me I might not be able to unlock the door and get out.

The first time this happened to me was in that parlor at the Main Hotel. Mama had taken John and gone out to do a little shopping. Mary C. and I did not want to stay in the parlor at the hotel. "Why can't we go with you?" Mary C. asked.

"Because I can't keep my eyes on three children and concentrate on my shopping. John is enough for me to handle, also because I say you can't go. I won't be long," she said.

I felt like telling her she always said that and she was always gone longer than she thought she would be. But I had sense enough not to. Right there in the Main Hotel parlor I would have gotten a spanking!

She *was* gone longer than she thought she would be and when she came back it was to great excitement. A porter on a stepladder was trying to crawl through the transom over the big double doors to unlock them and free two badly frightened little girls.

Why I shut those huge double doors and turned the key, I'll never know. Boredom, perhaps. Just something to do. Or curiosity, maybe. Just to see if they *would* shut. Anyhow, I did shut them, then far worse, I locked them. But much to my surprise, when I tried to unlock the doors the key was so big and clumsy to operate — it probaly wasn't used more than once or twice a year and may have been rusty — that I couldn't turn it. I tried and tried and tried, but it wouldn't budge in any direction.

At first this didn't bother me. I was a strong child for my age and I thought if I just kept on trying the key would finally turn. Mary C. lent her strength, which was puny beside mine, but the key still wouldn't budge. We couldn't even get it out by now. What we had done, of course, was get it firmly wedged crookedly.

I became badly frightened and Mary C. started crying and we both began pounding on the double doors and screaming our heads off. "Help! Help! Somebody come unlock this door!"

The porter arrived and through the doors tried to tell me

how to turn the key. "Press down on the key real hard and turn," he said. "It's and old key and a little rusty. Now, try again. Press down hard on it and turn."

I did my best, but nothing at all happened.

"Try again," the porter said, "keep trying."

I kept trying. I know I exerted every ounce of strength I had because I was frantic with fear. I could imagine that Mary C. and I were going to be locked up in that parlor for the rest of our lives. But all my strength wouldn't work. The key would *not* turn and I could not unlock the doors.

Finally, when Mary C. and I started crying again, the porter said, "Now, you all just be quiet. There's a big transom over this door. You got no cause to be afraid. I'll just go get my stepladder and I'll crawl through that transom and let you out."

We looked up and he was right. There *was* a big transom over the door, exactly the width of the two doors, and about twice as high as most transoms. We calmed down then, knowing we would be saved. But it seemed hours before we heard the porter's voice again and the noise he made setting up his stepladder. "You been real good little girls," he said. "I'll have that door open for you in no time at all now."

About that time Mama got back. The porter was just in the process of crawling through the transom, having shoved it open from his side. "What's going on here?" Mama wanted to know, naturally.

"Your little girls got theirselves locked in the parlor," the porter told her, "and they ain't strong enough to turn the key and open the doors. I'm gonna get 'em out."

Through the door Mama's calm voice called to me. "Janice, did you lock these doors?"

There was nothing to do but confess. "Yes, ma'am."

By this time the porter had swung himself lightly through the transom and onto the floor and was working at the key. He had a hard time himself. It took him about ten minutes to get that key unwedged and get the doors open. But he didn't scold us. "No wonder you couldn't turn that key," he said, "this ole key is rusty. We got to oil it."

Mama marched in, John clinging to her hand. Her displeasure was measured by the sternness of her "Why?"

"I don't know."

"You *must* know."

"But I don't."

"People don't shut doors and lock them without a reason."

"I guess I just wanted to see if they would shut. They never *are* shut."

"They aren't supposed to be shut except by the hotel people. You are *far* too meddlesome, Janice. Now, let this be a lesson to you. You see what kind of trouble you can get into, and how much trouble you can cause others when you do things you aren't supposed to."

"Yes, ma'am."

"What on earth did you make such a fuss about it for? Nothing could happen to you."

"We were scared."

"Scared of what?"

She threw up her hands helplessly. There was no point going on with it. Janice was a meddlesome troublemaker. The truth is, and she admitted it many, many years later, that she should not have left us alone in the parlor. I could not have been more than six or seven, Mary C. two years younger. We were not old enough to be left alone in the very safest place in a strange city. Mama had a little shopping to do, she didn't, truly did not, mean to be gone more than ten or fifteen minutes. She couldn't imagine anything happening to us. But a part of her anger at me was, she later told me (and I had a daughter of my own before she confessed this) her own sense of guilt. Perhaps oftener than parents realize, anger at their children is at least partly mixed with a sense of guilt.

The next time I locked myself into a room was truly frightening to me. The Main Hotel parlor experience paled beside it.

We were on the way to Charleston on the little, dinky Arkansas Central. As with nearly all children, one or the other of us had to go to the toilet every hour or so, wherever we were. (Mama had to keep a weather eye out for a place for us, no matter where we were or under what conditions.)

The rest rooms in the day coaches we rode were little cubicles, a tight fit for even a child. Mama usually took us, made certain we did not actually sit on the toilet seat. "You might get germs. All sorts of people use these public rest rooms," and cramped herself into the corner until we were finished.

About halfway to Charleston I nudged Mama. "I have to go to the toilet."

"Oh, Janice!"

She had already taken Mary C. and John once or twice.

"Yes, ma'am. If I don't I'll wet my pants."

By this time I was about seven or eight. Mama decided I could go alone. "You're big enough to go by yourself," she said. "And you know what to do. But don't lock the door. Nobody but another woman might try to come in."

But I had seen the conductor open that little door and peek inside. I didn't know why he did it and for once in my life didn't ask why. I didn't realize he only did it after we had stopped at a way station. I didn't notice that he knocked before he opened the door. I didn't know that he was merely checking the rest room for a new passenger who might have gotten on at the way station, and whose ticket needed punching. All I had noticed was that a *man*, the conductor, *did* open that door sometimes and peek inside.

As I have said, we were reared with such modesty it amounted to prudery, and the idea of the conductor opening that door with me squatted over the toilet bowl was a horror I could not face. So, in spite of Mama's warning, I locked the door.

Then I couldn't get *that* door unlocked! I didn't panic immediately. I doggedly kept trying to turn the key and get out. I *felt* panicky enough inside, but I had disobeyed Mama and I was more afraid of her anger than I was scared of being locked in.

I did cry, but quietly, as I kept on trying to unlock the door. Finally enough time had gone by that Mama herself came to see what was keeping me. Naturally she couldn't open the door. She rattled the handle. "Janice, let me in."

"I can't," I said, in a very small voice.

"Janice, you *didn't* lock the door!"

"Yes, ma'am, I did."

"I told you not to!"

"But Mama, the conductor comes in here!"

"Oh, for heaven's sake! Not between stations."

"I didn't know."

"Well, you could at least have obeyed me."

It was a little late to remind me of that. Mama gave advice, the best she could. I pressed down, I pressed up, I used all my strength to turn the key while pressing in either direction.

Then Dad came, several passengers gathered about, everybody giving me advice. Nothing worked. The key would not turn. Unlike the big one in the Main Hotel parlor it was not wedged in crookedly. It just wouldn't turn.

Dad even looked to see if there was room enough for me to slide the key under the door so he could unlock it from the outside. But the door fit tightly against the floor, it even dragged a little when being opened or shut.

I don't understand now why my parents went through all this rigmarole, allowing me to become more and more frightened as time went by. It would have been so much simpler to find the conductor, who had a key himself, and who in no time could have gotten me out.

I think it was Dad who finally thought of this simple solution to the problem. Where he had to go to find the conductor I don't know. And nobody thought to explain to me what he was doing. All I knew was that everything got very quiet outside all at once, and stayed quiet so long I really did panic and begin crying noisily. Then Mama called through the door and said, "Stop that crying, Janice. Dad has gone to get the conductor. He'll have the door unlocked pretty soon."

It seemed forever, but finally there came a new and unfamiliar voice. "Little girl. Take your key out of the door, so I can get mine in."

I was afraid to try taking the key out of the door, although I knew it would come out. I had taken it out half a dozen times already, but suppose it wouldn't come out this time, when it was so important for it to. I stood there a second or two trying to get up the courage to do it again. The conductor became impatient and rattled the doorknob. "Take the key out! Right now, little girl. Or I won't be able to get you out."

I could see myself riding on the Arkansas Central forever,

locked in that tiny cubicle, so in desperation I yanked the key out. "It's out," I called.

In two shakes of a lamb's tail, as Dad had a way of saying of a fast movement, the conductor had inserted his key, easily turned the lock and I was free.

Mama escorted me to our seats, her hand so tight on my arm it hurt, and I knew she was very angry with me. When we had reached our seats I looked at her, sneaked a look in fact. Her face was very red, with both embarrassment and anger. She gave me a hard spank on the thigh nearest her (she was never undignified enough to punish us in public, or even to scold in a loud voice in public. She thought women who did that were ill-bred) and then sighed. "I declare, Janice, you can get into more trouble than any child I ever saw."

Dad intervened. "You should have gone with her, Lucy."

Mama snapped at him in a low voice, "And she could have obeyed!"

"She's too little yet to be sent to the rest room alone."

"Well," Mama ended their little spat, "you go with her next time!"

I looked at Dad horrified. Never in my memory had I been to the toilet in front of a boy or man, even my father. And I thought Mama meant it. Dad chuckled quietly, and that was that. I caught on that it was just a joke. Although I was afraid Mama would punish me when we reached Charleston, she was so good at remembering offenses. But apparently she thought I had had enough punishment, through my fright, and she *did* go with me to train rest rooms until I was ten or eleven years old.

*

In no sense was there ever a family reunion at the Mc-
Graws'. In fact, the first and only time the entire family, the
father and mother and the ten children who survived to adult-
hood, ever sat down to a meal together was on Grandmother
and Grandfather McGraw's fiftieth wedding anniversary.

This was not because they would not have wished to get
together before then, but by the time the last of the children,
Babb, was born, two of the eldest children had married and
no longer lived in Altus, and as the other older children married and also moved away, the occasion for them all to get
together never came. There would always be one or two who
lived too far away, or for whom the time was never convenient.

But when we went for our visit — not every summer by any
manner of means, but four or five times when I was a child —
there was nearly always a sister of Mama's, with her two or
three children, visiting also, and the big house on the hill was
pretty full.

Summer visits to Altus were great fun, but they lacked the
excitement of the Reunion at Charleston, and they lacked the
freedom we had at our Holt grandparents'.

I must admit that I never loved my Grandfather McGraw.
I was much too afraid of him to love him.

Mama and his other children loved him, although I think
as children they had been afraid of him, too. He had been
a very stern father. He was a stern grandfather. He must
have been in his middle fifties when I first remember him,
perhaps a little younger. He was as slender as any young man
— no paunch, not an ounce of extra flesh on him. He
was clean-shaven except for a very distinguished, exquisitely
trimmed, short Van Dyke beard. He still had a full head of
iron gray hair. I hardly ever heard him laugh, and then it
would be only a snort or two. He smiled oftener than he

laughed. He was a very silent man except when annoyed, then his annoyance made him speak gruffly. He was nervous, high-strung and restless. Grandmother adored him, and she wasn't afraid to quarrel with him on occasion.

Meals in their home terrified me. The dining room was a little formal with a square oak table, a sideboard and a set of six or eight chairs with red plush seats. The family always ate in the dining room, even breakfast. There was always a spotless white tablecloth and while the beautiful Haviland china was not used daily, the regular china was too fine to suit me, for I was always afraid I would break a piece of it. The white tablecloth scared me because I was always afraid I would spill something on it. When that happened to any grandchild, or even to the adults, Grandfather never scolded. He simply looked a hole through you which showed his dis-approval and frowned.

But what most frightened me about meals was that we were compelled by him to eat every bite on our plates. In our own home this was not a rule and if we asked for second helpings and then couldn't quite eat all of the food, nothing was said. There were chickens who would eat scraps, or the dog, or even, occasionally when Dad was raising a pig or two, the scraps went into the pig slops.

But I learned the rule at the McGraw grandparents' the hard way. Nearly all the children like to eat. Grandmother and the aunts were excellent cooks. The food was wonderful. I think I must have been about six or seven when, not quite full enough to stop, I asked for second helpings of fried chicken and mashed potatoes. Grandfather said, "Are you sure you can eat second helpings?"

I was so certain I did not hesitate at all. "Oh, yes, sir," I replied.

But I could not. I could not get more than halfway through that plate that now looked so full of food I did not want. "Mama," Grandfather said to Grandmother, "put Janice's plate in the pantry. She must eat that plate of food for her supper tonight."

And eat it for my supper I did, although I was allowed, once I had eaten it, to have some hot food also. I was almost afraid to take it. After that, I stuffed myself more than once to get down every bite of food on my plate, or left the table still a little bit hungry rather than risk his disapproval again.

To me, it was one of the great and fortunate things about our visits to Altus that Grandfather had not yet retired. As superintendent of Western Coal and Mining Company his work hours were long — or else he so loved the work he made them long. He left home, in his horse and buggy, shortly after a very early breakfast, came home briefly for what we called dinner, at noon, then was gone again in about fifteen minutes, and he did not return until suppertime, about dusk. So we had a very long, and for the most part, happy day in which to play.

I had another humiliating experience, this time with Aunt Babb. She was getting ready to take a bath. As I have said, she was badly spoiled and she was inclined to be lazy and let people wait on her. She let me hang around and do a lot of the chore work of getting her bath ready. Then, when she was partially undressed, she suddenly said to me, "Oh, durn. I forgot my teddy-bears. Janice, run upstairs and look in the bottom bureau drawer and get them for me."

It was the first time I had ever heard the term "teddy-bears." I had no idea it was an undergarment, made tight around the top to serve as a brassiere, then loose and divided into panties. Mama didn't wear them. She still wore a padded camisole (she had small breasts, thus the padding), knee-length, home-made drawers and skirt petticoats which tied about the waist on a gathered string which she tied in the back.

I looked and looked for a real teddy bear. I even summoned up the courage to look in *all* the bureau drawers, thinking Babb might have been mistaken about the bottom drawer. I couldn't imagine what she wanted with a teddy bear, but if she wanted one or two, she should have them if I could find them.

I finally had to admit defeat. I went back to the bathroom, where the door was now closed and Babb was sloshing about in the tub. Through the door I called, "I can't find any teddy bear, Aunt Babb."

There was a long silence as Babb thought through my predicament, then came a gleeful peal of laughter as she realized I had no idea what I had been sent to look for. "Oh, Janice, I didn't mean a real teddy bear. Teddy-bears are underwear. They're in the bottom drawer of my bureau and just pick up the first one you find and bring it to me."

"You mean your panties?" I asked.

"Yes, that's what I mean."

I was the butt of *that* joke for days, too. I seemed never to be able to do anything right with the McGraws.

*

The house was large, as I have said, something like ten rooms of which five or six were bedrooms. I recall at least one summer visit when there was room enough for Mary C. and me to have a bedroom of our own.

The house was built with a porch on three sides of the entrance hall and parlor. In my earliest memories the porch was squared off at the corners, so that it had a pentagonal shape and there was fancy scrollwork and a banister all around it. Grandmother loved geraniums and she must have had dozens. of big pots of red and pink and white geraniums set all along this banister. Between the pots the grandchildren often rode horseback on the flat railing, but the big pots of geraniums made walking it, which we would have dearly loved to do, impossible. We were too afraid of breaking off even one leaf of those beloved geraniums.

The porch was always kept painted a fresh white. Finally the awkward pentagonal porch with all its scrollwork was torn down and the rounded one of the picture my grandson took in 1970 was built.

One entered the house by the front door which led into a long and sufficiently wide hall so that the stairway going up to the second floor left plenty of room for passage alongside. This stairway was carpeted, but what made it especially attractive to us was that the banister curved at the top and formed the railing for a narrow hall which led to a bedroom built over the parlor. We were allowed to slide down this banister. We usually shoved off slightly in the curve at the top of the stairs, sailed like the wind down the mahogany banister and were stopped by the round newel post at the bottom.

In May of 1970 I visited this home again and was kindly received by the present owner, a Mr. Richmond, and allowed to go through it and over the grounds. In that front hall I put my hand on the newel post of the stairway and thought how often I had had to sit very gingerly because of having hit it too hard too many times sliding down that mahogany banister!

The door into the parlor opened to the right off the front

hall. But the hall continued and led into the dining room. To the right of the dining room, and behind the parlor, was what we called the sitting room, for as with most families the parlor was not constantly used. Big double doors that slid back into the wall opened from the sitting room into the parlor and were usually closed. The sitting room had an enormous coal-burning stove, several comfortable chairs and a tufted leather couch — the kind that had no back but a sloped headrest. This was the room used most by the family.

An open hall, or breezeway, behind the dining room led to the kitchen and at one end of this open hall, not built into it, but built onto it, was the bathroom. It was a bathroom only in the sense that it had a porcelain tub with a drain. Water was not piped into the house, nor was there a hot water tank. The water for a bath was heated on the kitchen stove and pored into the tub. But it was great fun when we had our baths to slither around in that big tub, then slide down its sloped, soapy back and make a great splash. We were allowed to do this on pain of cleaning up the mess we made, which we always faithfully did for fear of losing the privilege.

The kitchen was quite ordinary. I don't remember much about it except that it had a sink which also drained. I am almost certain because of the ease with which coal was obtained (it may have cost Grandfather nothing) that the kitchen range, big and black, was coal-burning.

At first there were four bedrooms upstairs. But Grandmother had loved an open fireplace all her life. She kept nagging at "Dan" to build another room onto the sitting room and build her a fireplace. He kept saying he would, but as men have a way of doing he kept putting it off.

Catherine McGraw was not one to sit down and accept

being put off forever. I am certain that one of my mother's favorite clichés, "Where there's a will, there's a way," came from her mother.

She had the will for a fireplace, so she made the way to get it. She always wrote, or "scribbled," as she called it. Essays, poems, articles, little stories. She wrote constantly and sold many of these pieces to various small magazines, mostly the church periodicals, and she must have squirreled away every dime she made from her writings.

Recall that she also taught school when she was between babies or a school came to her seeking a teacher. She taught more frequently now than she had been in the habit of doing. She even took an agency for selling corsets! How many corsets she sold nobody ever knew, but she was faithful in her efforts, and very persuasive, and it is likely that a considerable number of uncorseted women in Franklin County suddenly found themselves the owner of an excruciating instrument of torture — the whalebone corset.

At any rate she finally found herself with something over three hundred dollars saved. And for that amount of money, in 1912 or 1913, you could easily build a room with a fireplace. Grandmother learned that she need not stop with one room on the ground floor, but that she could also add another bedroom on the second floor by just going on up one more level. That second floor room, however, did not have a fireplace. She must have been the happiest woman in Altus when her building project was finished and she finally had her fireplace.

The fifth bedroom upstairs became a sort of children's dormitory in the summer. There were many windows in it. In fact it was a sort of closed-in sleeping porch. I don't recall ever being in Altus in the winter, so I don't know how comfortable it was in that season, but it was a delightful summer bedroom, open, airy and light, and half a dozen grandchildren could easily be accommodated in three beds in it.

I saw my first lawn mower at the Altus home and considered it a privilege to be allowed to help mow the lawn. There was an iron picket fence around the lawn, with an iron gate, and a slatestone walk up to the front porch. I'm not certain but I think only the front and side lawns were kept mowed. This is because I remember high grass in the backyard. As at the Holt grandparents', it was wonderful to roll in, hide in and slide down the cellar roof into.

We had all the freedom in the world outside. It was only inside the house we had to be careful. Since our visits were always in the summer, this was precisely what we wanted anyway — to be outside. I don't understand today's children who hang around inside a house, wanting their parents to do things with them. We wanted away — outside — free from do's and don'ts. Our parents never played with us. We didn't want them to, and they were delighted to have us out from underfoot. The last thing we ever wanted was to stick around our parents. They only thought up work for one to do. We wanted *out*, free of them!

The water supply for the house came from an immense cistern situated some twenty or thirty feet behind the house. A raised wooden walk led to it and it was housed in a hexagonal-shaped house roofed over, but sided with lattice work which was kept painted white.

The water was raised with a windlass, but instead of a bucket there was a sort of paddle wheel affair, like a water mill, and the full cups emptied down a spout into the bucket. We were allowed to play in the cistern house because the cistern was cemented over and it was perfectly safe. We were not allowed, however, to touch the water wheel. The first time I was allowed to operate this apparatus and bring a bucket, about half full, to the house I felt as big as an adult.

There was an exciting incident involving me and the cistern one summer. High grass grew all around the latticed building which was lovely and cool to roll and play in on a hot day.

Several grandchildren, including Mary C. and me, were doing just that one day. Just rolling and tumbling around, yelling and screeching. Suddenly I saw something gleaming in the grass. I picked it up and it was a bright, shiny new penny. Saying nothing to the others I looked around further and found four more. I kept looking, still selfishly saying nothing, but five was all I could find. Then I dashed to the house with them. "Look, Mama, look what I found out by the cistern house! Look! Five new pennies! Can I keep them, Mama? Can I? I found them, and you know finders keepers! Please? Mama, please can I keep them?"

Mama held out her hand. "Let me see the pennies, Janice."

She looked at them carefully, then drew in her breath sharply. She then turned to Grandmother and said, "Mama, you won't believe it, but look here. Janice has found those five five-dollar gold pieces Papa lost the other day."

She handed them to Grandmother who exclaimed, "I can't believe it! Papa has looked everywhere for those gold pieces. Where did you say you found them, Janice?"

"In the grass behind the cistern."

Both women looked at each, snickered, then laughed heartily. "No wonder he couldn't find them!"

They knew, as I did not, that Grandfather had lost the gold pieces when, like most rural men, he had stepped outside the cistern house a night or two before, probably after he had drawn up a bucket of water for the night, to relieve himself. In managing his trousers he had somehow managed to lose the five gold pieces in the tall grass. No amount of searching could ever have found them, for Grandfather had no idea of where or how he had lost them. Only a child, playing carelessly in the tall grass, rolling about in it, had by sheer accident seen the sun sparkling on something shiny and picked it up, then, feeling rich at finding even one penny, had looked eagerly for more.

The good news that the gold pieces had been found could not wait until Grandfather came home. He was telephoned. When he got home from the office that night he was pleased and happy to have the money back and for once did something for which I loved him.

"Janice," he said, "because of your good, sharp eyes, and your honesty in coming straight to tell your mother you had found these 'pennies' I am going to give you one of them. I was very worried about losing twenty-five dollars. But you deserve one of these five-dollar gold pieces and you may have it." And he placed one of the small gold coins in my hand.

I clutched it tightly, not forgetting to say, "Thank you," however. And for safekeeping I put it in my own small purse.

Shortly after, however, Mama said, "I'm afraid you'll lose that gold piece, Janice. You might lose your little purse, so perhaps you'd better let me keep it for you."

I turned it over to her readily. The last thing I wanted to have happen was to lose that precious gold coin.

But the gold coin was only kept several months. One day that fall Mama said to me, a little sadly, "Janice, we're going to have to spend your five-dollar gold piece."

"Oh, Mama, no! Why?"

"We'll have to buy your winter shoes with it," she said.

"I'll wear my old ones," I said quickly. "Daddy can half-sole them for me."

He was very good at such chores and kept our shoes in good shape for us long after other parents had to buy new shoes for their children.

Mama showed me my old shoes. They had been half-soled over half-soles, not once, but two or three times. "The leather is so perished," she explained to me, "they won't hold another half-sole."

I never liked the shoes that five-dollar gold piece bought and all my life I wished it had not been necessary. To tell the truth I wish I had it still. It was one of the few beautiful memories I had of my Grandfather McGraw.

*

The cellar was immediately behind the house and wooden steps led from the cistern walk down into it. It was merely a dug cellar, with wooden braces for the roof which was of sod. The cellar was not floored. It had a cool, dusty odor which was very pleasant. We were allowed to play in the cellar so long as we did not touch Grandmother's shelves of canned vegetables, fruits, jellies and jams. You may be sure we never did. The cellar door slanted back and was always left open except in the winter. It had no lock of any kind on it, and while a high wind *could* blow it shut, it could not lock us in. A good hard shove would open it.

"P'like we're digging coal," we said.

We knew nothing about mining, for Grandfather would not allow any of us to visit the mine. In my entire life I never saw one of the mines over which my grandfather was superintendent. But we knew they were underground.

On windy, rainy days we sometimes closed the door ourselves and pretended we were in a storm cellar, that a tornado was raging outside.

The best game of all with the cellar was outside where we used its sod and well-grassed roof as a slide. If we couldn't actually slide down it onto the grass below, with a nice soft thump, we could roll down it. We played on the cellar roof a dozen times a day.

There were some trees around the house but not many, not nearly as many as at the Holt grandparents' in Charleston. Grandfather planted two young ash saplings on the west side of the house. I recall them as quite young trees giving very little shade, but in May of 1970, when I visited the place again, they were enormous, giving a generous shade to the west side of the house. I think touching those trees moved me more than anything else during that brief visit. Here was something of my grandparents, living yet, in the old home.

One of the most exciting things that the McGraw grandparents had was a lawn swing. The kind that had a slatted floor, was built on a framework with seats facing each other. The framework of the swing was red, but the slatted floor and the facing seats were simply varnished with a natural oak finish.

We could play in the lawn swing all we liked and nearly always it became a train for us, with a conductor and engineer. One made it swing by pushing hard with one's feet on the slatted floor. Occasionally we got it going too high and fast, then an aunt or Grandmother would stick her head out a window and yell at us, "You children are swinging too high! You'll break the swing. If you can't swing gently, you'll have to stop."

Somebody among us would mutter, "Oh, shucks. Now we'll have to swing like old folks."

But we always obeyed. Even swinging gently like old folks

was better than not swinging at all. But we wanted our train to go fast, as fast as it could, and it was disappointing to slow it down to the speed of a freight train.

We didn't know many cities for our train, just the places we lived, and Fort Smith, of course. "P'like we're going to Little Rock."

But the Little Rock cousins would object. "No. We don't want to p'like we're going home."

"P'like we're going to Kinta."

Then Mary C. would object. "No, we don't want to go home."

We had heard of St. Louis — the Iron Mountain came from St. Louis — so that usually suited everybody. No one we even knew lived in St. Louis. We had heard of New York City and, similarly, nobody we knew had ever even been there, much less lived there. Both those cities were acceptable. But mostly we liked distant places and it didn't matter to us if they were states instead of cities. "P'like we're going to California!"

We knew it was a long, long way to California, so it was a long, long swing — and if nobody had yet caught us, the fastest, highest swing we could manage. Finally when the conductor yelled, "All out for California!" we slowed the swing and *somebody* had to get off. I needn't say, I'm sure, it was usually one of the younger children.

But the stay in California was always the briefest time possible. Not more than a minute or two. Nobody was willing to stay out of the swing longer than that. The first thing we knew we had our California passenger back aboard and he was heading for Arkansas!

We also went to Mississippi a lot, about which we had heard so much, but which none of us at that time had ever visited. It wasn't so far away, we knew, so the fast, high swing was shorter. The passenger for Mississippi never stayed long either. We knew we had relatives living there — second and third cousins. They would have been disappointed at the few seconds their visitor stayed with them.

Late in the evening, when the house shaded it, the swing belonged to the adults and we were told, "Go somewhere else and play."

We *were* noisy and when told to go somewhere else and play we knew it meant the other side of the house, the barn lot, or the cellar roof.

A lot of courting went on in that swing at night. There were two unmarried aunts, a wide difference in their ages, for Aunt Ophelia must have been nearly thirty (she was only four years younger than Mama) and Babb was seventeen or eighteen. But both had "beaux" and Babb had so many one never knew which young man would be calling on any given night.

When young men came to see either aunt, we children were carefully kept on the other side of the lawn, or in the house, because the lawn swing was definitely reserved for whichever aunt had company that evening and wanted privacy.

I don't recall there ever being a conflict because naturally Aunt Phele had fewer beaux than Babb. Had there ever been, I'm afraid Aunt Phele would have had to entertain her young man in the parlor.

*

One summer there was quite a collection of McGraw daughters and their children visiting, at least three, with two or three children each.

We were always allowed to stay up much later when visiting either set of grandparents, I suppose because it was vacation time and we didn't have to get up and go to school, therefore we needn't go to bed so early.

It could not have been later than ten o'clock, however, when Grandmother decided Babb's young man was overstaying his time. She had very strict ideas about curfew for this baby daughter of hers, and Babb *was* still quite young.

She drew her married daughters into a plan which would embarrass the young man into leaving, therefore. Aunt Leita (Uncle Grover's wife), whose voice was quite resonant and *could* be, when she wanted it to be, quite loud, was to stand at the west upstairs bedroom window, overlooking that part of the lawn on which the swing was placed. She was to call very loudly, in fact she was to shout as if to somebody downstairs or at least half the house away, "What time is it?"

And somebody, it may have been Mama, stationed at the front door downstairs was to scream up the stairway, "It's after ten o'clock. Growing *quite* late!"

The plan was put into effect, but it didn't work. We children were convulsed with laughter, not only at the plan but also at the fact that it didn't work. We thought the plan was hilarious enough, but when we heard Babb giggling out on the lawn and heard the young man's nice laugh, we had to hold our hands over our mouths to keep from disgracing ourselves by whooping out loud.

Grandmother muttered, "No young man ought to stay later than ten o'clock. I've a good notion to march out there and tell him so!"

But she would never have done it. She would never have done anything so embarrassing to her daughter. She only muttered and retired to her room, as did the rest of us to ours. I don't know what time Babb's young man left, but I presume he did take the obvious hint and leave shortly enough afterward to show that he was not intimidated, but that he was courteous.

Babb came in for a scolding the following morning and a threat that she could not have any more young men callers if they didn't have the sense or good manners to know when to go home. *That* wasn't put into effect either. Several more times that summer Grandmother fussed about how late Babb's young men stayed. But Babb was never really denied anything she wanted and the young men continued to come, to stay as late as Babb herself wanted them to stay. And all Grandmother did was mutter and fuss.

*

A paling fence divided the house yard from the barn lot on the west side. This fence continued all around the barn lot to enclose the chickens, the cow and the horse. There was a big, wide gate at the entrance from the road and we considered it a great compliment to be allowed to open this gate for Grandfather when he came home from the office at noon and in the evening. It swung easily and widely and he turned through it with a flourish.

We were not allowed to swing on the gate, which I learned the hard way, as usual. In a summer when we were the only grandchildren visiting, Mary C., John and I were playing in the barn lot. I saw Grandfather's buggy turn the corner into the home stretch and ran to open the gate for him. As it swung wide, I hopped on and rode back with it.

Grandfather immediately hauled up on the reins and stopped. "Janice," he said sternly, "don't ever do that again."

"Don't ever open the gate for you again?" I asked.

"No. You may open the gate as often as you please, but never, never let me see you swing on it again."

"No, sir, I won't swing on it again."

"You'll be punished if you do," he said. Then without further ado he drove on to the barn.

Later I asked Mama why Grandfather didn't want us to swing on the gate.

"Have you been swinging on it?"

I didn't dare tell her how often all of us had swung on the gate that summer. Every time we went in or out to the roadside to play, in fact. And all three of us thought it was such great fun that many times we made the gate swing us back and forth a dozen times before tiring of it.

"Yes, ma'am," I said.

"When?"

"When I went to open it for Pappy tonight."

"Well, don't do it anymore. That gate is his pride. It is so perfectly balanced it swings with the touch of a finger and he keeps the hinges oiled so it will stay that way."

"How can swinging on it get it out of balance?" I wanted to know.

"Your weight, child, your weight! In time it would make the gate sag."

"He said he would punish me if I swung on it anymore. What would he do?"

"I have no idea," Mama said, turning back to her ironing, "but you don't need to worry about punishment because you aren't going to do it again."

"No, *ma'am!*"

And I certainly meant it. To have incurred Grandfather's anger was all the punishment I needed and I steered clear of him for several days. I'm afraid I mostly steered clear of him anyway, for I feared him even when he was in a good mood.

I feel no guilt about not loving my grandfather, for when a child does not love an adult relative it is because that adult relative does not really love him. I think Grandfather would have done anything he could for any of us, materially, but I do not for one moment believe he truly loved any of his grandchildren. He sort of tolerated us, was occasionally affectionate with a pat on the head, but I think he was simply so high-strung and tense and engrossed with his work that we were mostly a noisy annoyance to him.

I have only to remember the widespread, open arms, the loving, happy laugh, the big bear hug swinging me off the ground and snuggling me close, the bearded face smothering me with kisses, of Grandpa Holt to feel that upswing of joy and love I felt for him. Never in my life did I feel it for Grandfather McGraw and I shrank from the little peck on the cheek which his bristly Van Dyke spoiled by scratching.

Grandpa Holt's full beard was soft and silky, and he even let us braid it sometimes, sitting under the shade of the big mulberry tree, laughing as heartily as anybody at the ridiculous figure he cut with a braided beard. Oh, he was a lovely, lovely human being.

He never played with us. In those days parents and grandparents did not try to be pals and playmates with their children. And we liked it that way. We knew the limits of our freedom and I think we felt far more security that way than today's children who have been reared so permissively. You knew perfectly where you fitted in, not only in the family but in the larger family of aunts, uncles and grandparents. But Grandpa Holt was always interested in what we had done during the day. "What did you do that was fun to-day?" And a dozen voices would clamor to answer him, be-cause everything at Charleston was fun.

*

One reason we went in and out of the barn-lot gate at the McGraw grandparents' so often was because outside the barn lot, between the fence and the road, was an immense oak tree. It was so old that most of the roots were exposed and they, too, were huge.

One game of ours was to try to walk around the tree, jump-ing from root to root without touching the ground. It was almost impossible to do because of one or two very wide spaces between the roots, but occasionally some long-legged grandchild or neighbor did it. And the first time I did it — I felt as if I had conquered time and space. "I did it! I did it! You saw me!" For hawk eyes were always on the child trying it and even a bare toe touching the ground counted against one.

I should add that one could not touch the tree trunk for a handhold, either. But I had learned, suddenly, that if you hugged as near as possible to the trunk without touching, the almost impossible stunt could be done.

That oak tree and its roots caused Mary C. a lot of tears before she grew big enough to accomplish the feat. It never bothered John. He just ignored all rules and jumped down on the ground between the roots, laughing, and jumped back up when he got to the next one. Because he was the baby and such a joyous one, mostly, we praised him and let him get by with it.

There is no way of knowing how many hours were spent under that old oak tree playing in the moist sand. The next door neighbors were a family named Morgan, whose adopted daughter, Eugenia, spent most of those hours with us. We did not often go to the Morgan house because for the most part we saw enough of Eugenia under the old oak tree. Then, too, there were so many of us that such a horde of children would have been a bother to Mrs. Morgan, accustomed as she was to her one well-behaved child.

Eugenia was the first adopted child I had ever known, and this fact fascinated me. "Don't you know who your own mother and father were?" I asked, rather impolitely.

"No," she said, "Mama and Papa never talk about it, and I don't care."

Eugenia was well-mannered and well-behaved (we would not have been allowed to play with her had she not been!), but there *was* a streak of recklessness and carelessness in her. I thought that she probably *did* care who her real parents were but would not admit it.

I would have cared. I wouldn't have wanted to be anybody else's child at all but Lucy and John Holt's. And I had been through some anguish over the fear that perhaps I *had* been adopted. Perhaps all children wonder a little about this, at some time or other, and especially if they come into contact with an adopted child during the impressionable years. But I had wondered even before I knew Eugenia.

On both sides of the family, the Holts and the McGraws, the aunts, uncles, even the grandparents said so often, in the presence of us children, "Mary C. is a McGraw out and out. She looks enough like Lucy to be Lucy herself. And Little John is a Holt in every way." Grandma Holt even used to cuddle him and say, "You look just like your daddy did when he was a little boy."

Then they would look at me and shake their heads.

"Janice? She doesn't look like anybody on either side of the family."

And I didn't. I would examine myself carefully in the mirror and even I could tell that I didn't look like any of the aunts or uncles or the grandparents. The horrible thought would cross my mind, "Maybe I'm adopted. Maybe I don't really belong to Mama and Dad."

This finally became so unbearable to me that I had to go to Mama with it. "Mama, are you sure I'm yours? Everybody says I don't look like *anybody* in the family. And I don't. I can tell I don't. Did you and Dad adopt me?"

For once Mama was all love and understanding. She gathered me into her arms and said, "I am *sure* you are my and Daddy's child, Janice. And I promise you I would tell you if we had adopted you. It wouldn't be fair not to. But you *are* our very own, very dear little girl. You just got a good mixture of both sides of the family and turned out to be especially yourself, Janice Meredith Holt."

"Does that mean I'm all mixed up inside?"

"No, it doesn't mean that at all. It means you got about equal parts of Holt and McGraw and that makes you look like neither side particularly. You are just yourself, but you most certainly are my daughter and you are Daddy's daughter."

"Cross your heart?"

"Cross my heart! But I'll tell you something else. When we are at Charleston, all of us for the Reunion, and you are in another room and laugh, I can't tell whether it's you or Aunt Emma. Your voice and your laugh are exactly like hers!"

How wonderful! There *was* something tangible in me like somebody in the family. Of course I would have believed

Mama, especially after she crossed her heart, but it was a lovely thing to know I really was like somebody in the family, and I took special pride that it was Aunt Emma. She had always been one of my favorite aunts.

All my apprehension and anguish ended. In fact, I became a little proud of not particularly looking like either a McGraw or Holt. I felt it made me a little special, in some way.

Pride goeth before a fall. Because by the time I entered my early teens and began to slim up and grow taller, I slowly took on the look of the Holt women — rather plain, lean, raw-boned and tall. But I realized about that same time that while I looked like the Holt women I was almost all McGraw in temperament, characteristics and nerves. Now, *that* was a real mixture to face! I wished many times if I were going to look like a Holt I had been given the Holt easiness of temper and quietness of ways. I could even have done without the driving energy and ambition which went with the McGraw temperament. But genes have their own way of mixing and there was nothing I could do about it.

However much fun we had at the McGraw grandparents', I was always happy to see Daddy come, for that meant we were going home and a month away from him could sometimes seem a year.

He was always with us at Charleston and I never grew homesick there. But at night, in Altus, when all the lights were out, when the entire household had gone to bed I sometimes lay and listened to the katydids and crickets and felt very lonely — not only for my father, but for the Moore children, who, after all, were the best playmates in the world. We had fun with Eugenia Morgan and the Pendergrass children, but they were just summer children. Corinne, Inez and, when he was old enough to tag around with us, H.M., were our very own, part of our family the year round. I think I missed them almost as much as I missed our father. They, and they only, knew our favorite games. They, and they only, fitted into our normal life. I was always glad to go home from Altus.

14

A SEED IS PLANTED

*

I WAS SEVEN years old now, and in the second grade.

One day at noon Mama handed Dad a letter and said, "Verna isn't very happy at home these days."

Verna was Verna Darr, my father's eldest niece. Because she was some twenty years older than I, even eight years older than her own youngest aunt, we had been taught to call her Aunt Verna. Her mother, our Aunt Lizzie, had died when Aunt Verna was a child. Her father had remarried and her stepmother reared her and was a good mother to her. But Aunt Verna was now approaching her thirties and felt unhappy and restless at home.

Dad read the letter and handed it back to Mama. "Would you mind if we asked her to come here for a few months? Maybe a change of scene would be helpful to her and I might be able to find some kind of work for her to do."

Mama didn't even hesitate. "You know I wouldn't mind. I've always enjoyed Verna and I'd love to have her here. She would be good company for me."

There were only a few things a lady could do in the field of earning money. Highest on the rung was teaching, but apparently Aunt Verna was not qualified to teach. She could become a seamstress or milliner. She could clerk in the dry-goods section of a general store. Most often she would clerk in a post office, which, then, did not require a Civil Service examination.

In those days a spinster sister, aunt or cousin often went to live with a relative for a year or two for various reasons, but mostly I think because a new town often yielded fresh opportunities to catch a husband, when the old town, where one's entire family was so well known and perhaps one's own self a little stale, had nobody left to offer.

So a letter was sent to Aunt Verna asking her to come stay with us awhile. We children were delighted. From what little we knew of her, we liked her. I can't say we loved her, for we didn't know her that well. But it was exciting to think of a new member in the family.

"If I can't help her find work to do," Dad said, "Verna can help you with the housework for her room and board."

I whispered to Mary C., "I hope she does the dishes sometimes, don't you?"

Afraid to whisper back, Mary C. nodded. By now she was having to take her turn doing dishes. We alternated breakfast and supper dishes. Mama still did the noon dishes. To both of us, washing dishes was the most tedious chore we had to do. Even to get out of having to wash them after one mere meal a day would have been heavenly to us.

There finally came Aunt Verna's reply. Yes, she would be happy to come. "She'll get here on the night train Sunday," Mama announced to us.

A great upheaval in the arrangement of the house began. "Where is she going to sleep?" I wanted to know.

"We're going to move the couch into the sitting room," Mama said, "and she can sleep on it."

Mary C. and I had been sleeping on the couch in the

dining room for some time and I, at any rate, was reluctant to see the couch go. It was not only comfortable for sleeping, opened out full, but with the sides let down in the daytime it was so nice to loll around on and to lie on and read. "Why can't we buy a bed for her?" I asked. "We could put it up in the sitting room."

"For one thing," Mama said, "we can't afford it. For another, Verna will probably have young men calling on her. And you don't entertain guests in a room with a bed in it."

I didn't see the sense in that, for I didn't see why she couldn't have her young men call and sit with us in the nice warm dining room. "It sure will be cold for them to sit in there," I said. "There's no stove."

"Dad is going to buy a little kerosene stove," Mama said.

These were contraptions made on the order of an enormous lantern. They even had handles that made them portable. A little like an electric heater today, they could be moved from room to room. Many families had them for small rooms that were rarely used. They didn't put out much heat, but they did take the worst of the chill off. "Well," I said, "they won't be very warm in there with a coal oil stove!"

Mama laughed. "Maybe they'll have something else to keep them warm."

Not having the slightest idea what Mama meant, my comment was, "Yes, they can keep their coats on."

Even Dad laughed at that.

*

We were all excited about her coming, and all of us wanted to meet the train. Mama said, "All right, but don't complain if the train is late and you get cold."

"We won't," we promised.

Dad hitched up the horse and buckboard and we all went to the depot. The train was on time and Aunt Verna was the only passenger to get off. A gust of wind caught her long skirt as she stepped down onto the platform and blew it up immodestly. With one hand clutching her hat and the other trying to control her skirt, she laughed as we greeted her and surrounded her with our warm welcome.

Dad took her large suitcase (called a grip, then) and checked to see if her trunk had come with her on the same train. But it hadn't. It was sometimes two to three days after one arrived at one's destination before a checked trunk or other luggage arrived. Aunt Verna would have packed all her necessities, however, in her grip.

She was not really pretty. Few of the Holt women were. They had a certain gaiety and in the case of one or two of the aunts they were handsome, in a tall, big-boned way. But pretty — no.

Aunt Verna had bushy black eyebrows and unfortunately a rather dark growth of hair on her upper lip, which she did nothing about. Bleaching or plucking were unknown in those days. But she was graceful, she had pretty white teeth and a nice mouth. The nicest things about her, however, were her voice and her laugh. Her voice was low and pleasant and she had a grand sense of humor and a husky, throaty, happy laugh.

She fitted well into the family, helping Mama, for about a month, with the work to pay for her room and board. I am afraid she was allowed to do more than her share, for as I have said Mama was a lazy housekeeper and she was willing to let anybody at all take over any chore which freed her for a book or magazine.

But within three or four weeks Dad had managed to find

the ideal job for Aunt Verna. The Kinta postmaster needed a clerk. As I have said, one did not need to take a Civil Service examination for a clerkship in those days. All a clerk did was sort the mail and put it in the boxes, hand it out to those who called for it and sell stamps. She could not make out a money order, nor could she weigh and estimate the postage on Parcel Post packages. It was light, simple work, easy to do and perfectly in accord with the etiquette of the times. In fact, such a job carried a little prestige with it.

The eligible young men of the town rallied around, too. Rather often Mama would say, "You children must go to bed by the back door tonight. Aunt Vera is having company."

This meant we could not go through the sitting room to bed, but must run as fast as we could down the icy back porch, in our bare feet, and into the crowded bedroom by the door which opened onto the back porch.

But often Verna would bring her young man into the dining room and the entire family sat around the big stove with them eating popcorn, nuts and apples. Occasionally a whole crowd of young men and women came and there was a taffy pulling. We were allowed to stay up quite late on these occasions. Neither Mama nor Dad had the heart to make us miss the fun *or* the taffy.

By the time these things began to happen, however, Aunt Verna had settled on her young man. She had a steady beau and she didn't mind sharing him with the family. He was Will England, the son of the president of the Kinta bank.

"Why does Mr. Will come so often?" I asked one day. "He comes three or four nights a week, and nobody else comes anymore."

"Because he is Aunt Verna's steady beau now," Mama said.

"Oh. Does that mean she can't have any other beaux at all?"

"Sometimes having a steady beau means that."

"When?" I persisted.

Mama looked at me, half provoked, half amused. "Janice, you ask more questions than any child I *ever* saw. When a young man and a young woman fall in love they don't *want* to have any other beaux or girls. They just want to be together."

"Are Aunt Verna and Mr. Will in love?"

"I think so."

"You *know* so," I accused, taking more liberty than I normally would have, because I could tell Mama was in a good mood.

"All right, then, I *know* so. Can you keep a secret?"

"Not even tell Mary C.?"

"Not even tell Mary C. Not for a while yet. She's too little yet to keep secrets."

"All right. *I* can keep a secret."

"Cross your heart?" Mama laughed.

Solemnly I crossed my heart. This was like swearing on the Bible. When you crossed your heart you were committed. You didn't dare break your promise or something terrible would happen to you.

Mama lowered her voice. "Aunt Verna and Mr. Will are going to be married."

I was delighted. "When? When?"

"Don't jump around like that and shout so loud! Not for quite a while yet."

"Why not?"

"Well, they have to save some money first. Aunt Verna has to have some nice clothes and Mr. Will has to have enough money to build a house or buy one and they must have some money for furniture."

"Oh," I said, losing a considerable amount of interest, "that'll probably take forever."

"No, it won't," Mama said. "Mr. Will is a good, hard-working man and I imagine they will be able to get married in about a year."

I kept *my* secret, but that spring the entire town knew the secret. It couldn't be kept once Mr. Will began driving Aunt Verna about in his beautiful buggy. Everybody in Kinta noticed that Verna Darr saw nobody but Will England and he was the only man she ever went out driving with. This meant an engagement. It was never formally announced. It didn't have to be. Their constancy to each other was the only announcement necessary.

Aunt Verna, considered the ugly duckling of the family, destined to be an old maid forever, had actually succeeded in making one of the best matches ever made in the family, for in her long marriage to Mr. Will she never lacked for anything she needed or wanted and their home was always lovely.

*

The summer after I was eight in March, Aunt Verna had a month's vacation. She was going to Charleston to spend it with her family. "Why don't you let me take Janice with me, Lucy? Let her have a nice long visit in Charleston."

I held my breath almost, I wanted to go so badly. But Mama never liked any of us children to be separated from her. She rarely allowed us even the privilege of "spending the night" with a school friend. "She wouldn't be too much bother?" she asked, now.

"No, she wouldn't," Aunt Verna said. "She can spend part of the time with us and part of the time with Grandpa and Grandma. It would be good for her, and you could use a rest from her energy." Aunt Verna laughed.

"We-e-ell," Mama said, "we'll think about it."

My heart sank. When Mama said, "I'll think about it," she usually meant, no. I felt certain she wasn't going to let me go.

Knowing better than to beg, I let matters drag along for a few days. Aunt Verna's vacation would end immediately after the Confederate Reunion. Not only were my parents, and of course Mary C. and John, coming for the Reunion, but Mr. Will was coming. Aunt Verna wanted everybody in her family to meet him, and he was eager to meet his future in-laws. We would all return to Kinta again together.

After several days of silent longing I could keep quiet no longer. "Mama, please let me go to Charleston with Aunt Verna."

"A month is a long time, Janice. You might get home-sick," she said.

"No, I won't. Not in Charleston."

"Yes, even in Charleston you might. And if you did, you'd just have to tough it out. We couldn't come get you and you couldn't come home alone."

"Well, then," I said, "if I *do* get homesick I *will* tough it out."

Dad and Mama must have talked it over several times and I don't know what finally decided them, but one day Mama said, "Dad and I have decided you may go to Charleston with Aunt Verna."

Overjoyed is too mild a word for what I felt. I was almost delirious with happiness. "I'll have to get busy and make you a few new dresses," Mama continued. But she was an excellent seamstress and could have made a new dress a day for me for a week and had me ready.

The day to leave finally came and the family took us to the depot to catch the early morning train to Fort Smith. I had a funny feeling in my stomach as the train pulled in and I looked at my dear Mama and Dad, at Mary C. and John, and felt a strange reluctance to leave them. When Mama kissed me goodbye she didn't linger over it. It was a quick hug and kiss and a final, "Be a good girl. Mind Aunt Verna and Grandpa and Grandma. And don't forget whose child you are."

This last was said out of sheer habit. Even if we just went over to the Moores' to play she said those words to us. For a long time, until I was in my teens, in fact, I thought it meant I mustn't forget I was Lucy and John Holt's child. What she actually meant, I finally learned, was that I must *not* forget that I was the professor's daughter. Like Caesar's wife, the professor's children must be above reproach. They weren't. Not by a long shot — but Mama tried. She really tried.

We climbed up on the little stool, onto the train, went inside and found a cindery, red plush seat. Aunt Verna let me sit by the window and I looked and waved as long as I could see the dear people I was leaving behind. By now I had a chunk in my throat and tears in my eyes and I was sorry I was going. I suddenly didn't want to go to Charleston with Aunt Verna at all. But it was too late. Willy-nilly, I was on my way.

Understandingly, Aunt Verna put an arm about me, hugged me close to her and said, "You'll have so much fun this summer you'll be glad you came. Right now you're just feeling sad over saying goodbye. But a month isn't long at all and the first thing you know they'll all be coming to Charleston for the Reunion and we'll be going home with them."

I wanted to be going home with them right that moment, but I swallowed the chunk and wiped my eyes and settled myself to tough it out.

More than once during that month I had to tough it out. The days were great fun, for Aunt Verna let me spend most of them and many of the nights at Grandpa and Grandma's. Uncle Jim Holt lived in Charleston and his youngest child, a daughter named Jessie K., came every day to play with me, and when I spent nights at the grandparents, usually Jessie K. was allowed to spend the night with me. (The K. in Jessie K.'s name was for Knox, after Grandpa Holt.)

Nights at Aunt Verna's home, down in a sort of valley from Grandpa's, with nobody but adults in the family, just Aunt Verna, Aunt Martha and Uncle John Darr, were my most homesick times. But Aunt Verna let me sleep with her and although I was often so homesick that I cried a little, silently so she wouldn't know, I had, for the most part a marvelous and wonderful summer.

I am sure it was that summer, playing alone with Jessie K. so much in the plum thicket, that it was impressed on me to such an extent that it remained to haunt my subconscious and come out years later in the book, *The Plum Thicket*, for we played there, in the dimness and coolness, almost constantly that summer. And after that book was published Jessie K. wrote me that the plum thicket and the tiny little grave had always haunted her, too.

In spite of the happy times, however, when we went to meet the dinky and my family and Mr. Will England, I was glad that the month was over. Aunt Verna held my hand and said, "Now, wait until they all get off before you go rushing over to hug and kiss them."

I did as I was told, hanging tightly to her hand. Dad got off first, tall, thin, his eyes instinctively finding me immediately in the little group of people who were meeting the train. As in Kinta, and Altus, for that matter, there were men who went to the depot for every train "to let the train go through," they said. It was all I could do to restrain myself when I saw that dear, gentle face as it broke into a wide smile at the sight of me.

He helped John down next, then Mary C. I felt as if I hardly knew them! I thought, "John has grown at least an inch and Mary C. is getting to be a *big girl!*" It didn't seem possible they were the same brother and sister I had left in Kinta a month before! Partly, perhaps, it was their new clothes, unfamiliar to me. But mostly it was seeing them with new eyes, not having been with them daily for a month.

Then came Mama. I had forgotten how pretty she was, how white her skin was and how blue her eyes were. And I had forgotten how trimly her clothes always fitted her. A perky new hat, straw for summer, almost hid her piled-up chestnut brown hair. Her eyes flew to find me, too, and she laughed aloud at seeing me, so solid and chunky, standing so obediently beside Aunt Verna. Aunt Verna had taken great pains to see that I was dressed in my Sunday best for the occasion, even making me wear my wide-brimmed sailor straw hat, with the elastic under the chin. I loathed the thing, because the elastic cut into my fat neck, but I had worn it without protest for this very special occasion.

As Mama stepped down, Mr. Will came into view. Aunt Verna turned loose of my hand and said, "Now!" And I flew to hug and kiss and be hugged and kissed a dozen times over. It wouldn't be two hours until Mary C. and I were squabbling and Mama was scolding, but for the moment I felt as if I would never find fault with any of them again. My family! My own dear mother and father and little sister and brother!

Finally Dad put a stop to all the exclamations and hugs and kisses by saying, "Let's let Aunt Verna greet Mr. Will."

But if he thought they had been waiting patiently, closed off from each other by us, he was mistaken. Mr. Will had found his way around us to the woman he loved. It would not have been thought appropriate for him to kiss her in public, engaged though they were, but their hands were clasped, tightly, and their faces reflected their happiness. They had to wrench their eyes and hands from each other to pay attention to the mundane business of getting all the luggage together.

It dawned on me, for the first time, that the month's vacation had not been *all* happiness for Aunt Verna, either. She had been separated a long, long time from her beloved.

Every day brought more relatives, then, until finally they were all there and the summer was normal again, a big, happy Holt tribe, with the Confederate Reunion only a day or two away.

We stayed a week after the Reunion, as usual, but it was a restless week for me. I had had all of Charleston I wanted for a while and I was eager to get back to Kinta and Corinne and Inez.

15

AUTOMOBILES

*

THE FIRST AUTOMOBILE I ever saw, much less rode in, was the Ford "touring" car which Mr. Moore bought. I must have been around nine at that time. Like all those early Fords it sat very high off the ground, it had a canvas top and side curtains to put up when it rained. There were wooden-spoke wheels with small rubber tires. When one had a flat tire there was no taking the wheel off, one pried the tire off, took out the inner tube, patched it, put it back in, pumped the tire back up by hand after somehow, with immense labor, getting the tire back on the wheel.

The car had a lot of brass work on it, the horn was a klaxon which was sounded by squeezing a huge bulb. The driver's door, on the left, did not open. The fenders were wide and the tool chest was welded to the left fender. The seats were brown, buttoned leather and the headlights were brass and had to be lit by hand because they burned carbide. Rarely, however, was the car out after dark. The car would be a classic now, of course. This was status upon status, to own an automobile when the two doctors in town were still driving a horse and buggy.

Nearly every evening after our early suppers, Mr. Moore would yell, "Come on, kids! Let's go for a spin!"

And six deliriously happy kids would pile into the car and take off. The prairie roads were flat and while there were oc-casional rough ruts, for the most part they were dusty but fairly good automobile roads. Compared to the very best speed of a horse and buggy, we felt as if we were flying at twenty-five or thirty miles an hour!

When occasionally we met a farm wagon and team, which was not often at that time of day, Mr. Moore courteously pulled as far off the road as possible and stopped. "Why do we pull clear off the road and stop when we meet somebody?" I asked one day.

"Haven't you noticed how scared most of the horses are?" Mr. Moore said. "The sound of the engine scares them and if I didn't pull out of their way and stop the car the team might run away."

"But you don't stop the engine," I said.

"No. But I do throttle down as much as possible without stopping. It would be too much trouble to have to get out and crank again."

I had thought nothing of the fact that when we met a team and wagon, or even horse and buggy, the owner would get out and lead his team or horse by us. It was merely a pe-culiarity of automobiling, as far as I was concerned. But now I began to notice that the team did usually rear up and act frightened of this strange, noisy contraption. But because of Mr. Moore's courtesy I do not recall a single runaway team. The driver would lead his mules or horses past the car, then get back in his vehicle and go peacefully on his way into town.

If we met cowboys coming into town they simply gave the road a wide berth and while a few of their horses flattened their ears and sunfished and pranced around a little, for the most part they were too far from the car to be very badly scared of it.

The Green McCurtain house and the Wesley Anderson house were on top of what we called a hill. It was actually more of a knoll, merely a slight rise in the road. The ambition of Mr. Moore's life must have been to make that hill in high, for inevitably we would end the ride with his intense effort to reach the McCurtain house without having to go into low gear.

He would get up as much speed as possible on the narrow, dusty road and say, "Now, this time we'll make it! Just watch her go!"

But we never did. Always as we neared the top he would have to push in the pedal that put the car in low gear and we labored very slowly on up the hill. He was always so disappointed that I felt sorry for him and would practically hold my breath and pray that *this* time he would make it. I would have got out and pushed if it would have done any good. Whether he ever did make it in that particular car I don't know, for when we left Kinta he was still driving that Ford.

With the Moores owning a car, naturally the Holt children wanted one to. "Why *can't* we buy a car, too?" we asked.

"We can't afford one," Mama said, "they cost a lot of money."

"We'll have one when our ship comes in," Dad said. He said that every time we wanted something we could not afford and when I was a very small child I actually envisioned a ship coming sailing right across the prairie to our house.

Dad's ship was a bone of contention between Mama and Dad. Mama was of the firm conviction that Dad's ship was well anchored in safe waters. She was the one who was always ready to take it out into the storm and see what it could weather. Dad was always happy just rocking gently along.

"Well, anyway," he reminded us, "we have a new horse."

We did indeed have a new horse and that had given us a lot of pride until Mr. Moore bought his Ford.

The horse's name was Bob and we did not change it when he became ours. He stayed Bob all his life. He was what was called in that country a cow pony, although pony he most certainly was not. He was a big, fine horse. The term meant simply that he had been trained as a cowboy horse — trained to cut out cows and calves on a roundup and to herd cattle on the trail.

This meant his reflexes to his rider's actions were almost instinctive in him. He had grown a little old for cowboying, so Dad was able to buy him. By this time he had also been broken to a buckboard, though he still danced a little when being backed into the shafts. But he had been so well broken and treated that he was a beautifully gentle horse. While we were not allowed to ride him, we played fearlessly all around him in the barn lot and I have seen my little brother swing on his tail. Bob would simply turn his head and look, and one could almost swear that he would grin at the little boy making a swing of his nice long tail.

Our parents' decision not to let me or Mary C. ride him yet was made the very day he was delivered to us. Dad couldn't wait to try him out. He saddled him immediately and went for a gallop out across the prairie. He came home an hour later with all the skin off his nose and most of it off one cheek!

"John!" Mama screamed. "What happened? Does he buck? Did he throw you off?"

Dad grinned crookedly. "No, he doesn't buck. And he didn't throw me off. It was my own fault. I had him on the dead run and simply forgot his training, happened to touch his neck with my knee and he turned left on a dime. I kept going straight ahead and just plowed up half the prairie with my nose and face. Don't forget that, Lucy, when you ride him. Keep your reins tight and don't knee him, whatever you do. He is still a cowboy horse. Probably always will be."

Mama put some kind of soothing salve on his skinned nose and cheek. They could both laugh about it now, although for several weeks Dad's laugh was rather wry and he took a lot of joking from the men in the town. "Well," his answer would always be, "the horse is a cowboy horse, but I'm just no cowboy!"

Bob had another bad habit. He had been trained to run with the herd. Cattle will stampede occasionally and a horse that won't run when he hears stampeding hoves isn't worth a nickel to a cowboy. We had no stampeding cattle to make Bob run away with the buckboard, so we never once thought about his training along that line.

One Saturday, however, we had been out to Sans Bois when a bunch of cowboys came thundering up the road behind us on their way to town. They split and passed us on each side. That is, they tried to pass us, but Bob wasn't having any of this passing business. He joined the thundering herd and, almost jerking our necks off, took off at a dead run himself.

Dad yelled at us, "Hang on!" — which we were already doing for dear life — and wrapped the reins around his hands to hang on himself. There was no stopping Bob. He was running with the herd. Delighted, the cowboys made it worse by whooping and yelling and urging him on, while we bounced around like peas in a pot of boiling water.

Mama lost her hat but hung onto John and screamed at us over her shoulder, "Lie down, girls! Lie down!"

I don't remember whether Mary C. did or not, but I wasn't the least bit frightened and wouldn't have missed seeing what was happening for anything in the world. So I just hung on, as Dad had said.

Eventually, having to pull a truly bucking buckboard behind him, Bob tired and with last whoops and waves of their hats the cowboys began to put distance between us and them. It was to their credit that they had not pulled a mean trick on us and left the road to cut across the prairie. Bob would have been unmanageable and would have followed them. But remember they were on their way *to* town and were sober. Had they been going home *from* town, with too much to drink under their belts, there is no telling what might have happened to us and the buckboard.

When Bob finally tired and slowed down and began to answer to the reins again, Mama said, "John, this horse is dangerous. You'll have to sell him. We can't risk our lives every time we drive some place."

"Nonsense," Dad said. "He's got spirit and life. I wouldn't take twice what I paid for him. Wouldn't think of selling him."

"What if this should happen when I'm driving with the children alone?"

"It won't, because you never drive with the children alone except around town."

Mama's dander was up, though. "Maybe I would *like* to take them for a drive sometime. What then?"

"Just hang onto the reins until he runs himself out," Dad said.

"Or one of the children is killed!" Mama said.

But she had lost the battle and she knew it. As long as we lived in Kinta, Bob never lost his cowboy training and he reacted instinctively. Mama was a good horsewoman and she wasn't at all afraid to ride him. But she was always a little apprehensive when we went out for a drive, especially on Saturday afternoon or Sundays when the cowboys were free to come into town. There *were* several more runaways, but by now we knew what would inevitably happen and as far as we children were concerned, we just hung on, thrilled and excited at the speed to which Bob could stretch his legs on such occasions, and adding our own whoops and shouts to egg him on. It was almost as good as riding in the Moores' automobile!

When we moved from Kinta, out of cattle country, Bob slowly lost his cattle training until finally he was perfectly safe for any of us children to ride. The only trouble we ever had with him was that he had what Dad called a hard mouth. He would amble along, answering to the rein beautifully, as long as we were headed *away* from home on him. But once we turned him to head *toward* home, there was no handling him. He was headed for home, he knew it and there would be no foolishness from that child astride his back. Willy-nilly, he took us home!

If we had several errands to do on him, we learned to route ourselves so that his head wasn't turned toward home until they were finished.

Bob stayed with us until after we moved to the city, for we first moved to a suburb of Fort Smith where cows and horses were commonly kept. We did not buy our first car until six months later. Then, sadly, we had to see Old Bob, as we now called him, go out of our lives.

*

The second automobile we ever saw gave us at least the status of having it in the family. It was not ours, but much to the surprise of everybody Grandfather McGraw bought an Allen coupe. He learned to drive it, after a fashion, but Grandmother hated it and continued to drive herself wherever she wanted to go with the horse and buggy.

Watching Grandfather drive through the barn-lot gate became a little breathtaking. Sometimes he made it without scraping a post, but more often than not he took a little more paint off the right side of the Allen.

Over the years Grandfather owned some of the strangest cars ever made. He ran to off-brand makes. He never owned a Ford or Chevrolet, an Overland or Maxwell — the name brands of those days. He had an Oakland once, a Reo, he even had a Franklin. And after the first one-seated car, he always bought sedans. In his latter years he preferred an Essex to any other make of car. Dad always said that the first salesman who got to Grandfather made a sale.

Once Grandfather graduated from the Allen, however, into the touring car class, Grandmother gave up and began riding with him. "I might as well," she said, "he's going to sell the horse and buggy."

She, herself, never learned to drive a car, and she would *not* ride in the front seat. I have never known why she did not like the front seat of a car. Perhaps the instrument panel scared her, or Grandfather's erratic driving habits. Perhaps it was the way the road seemed to be tearing up to meet one. My private opinion, however, is that by this time, as she was only five feet one inch tall and weighed nearly two hundred pounds, she was simply more comfortable in the back seat, where she could more comfortably spread out all that poundage.

Occasionally Grandfather and Grandmother had to go to

Ozark, the county-seat town, on business and they would let as many grandchildren as could pile into the car go with them.

It was only five miles to Ozark, but the last mile was down a pretty steep, winding hill, called the Ozark Hill. Grandmother hated this hill. Going down was bad enough and from her place in the right-hand corner of the back seat she would admonish Grandfather, "Now, Dan, don't go too fast."

Grandfather, even as men today, loved speed in a car. The last quarter of a mile or so of the hill was straight and not so steep. He dearly loved to let in the clutch and let the car coast into whatever speed it would attain. Grandmother let in her own clutch, with a gasping breath and a wild hanging on to her hat, and scolded. "Dan! I told you not to go too fast!"

"I'm not going fast, Mama," he would say, "just thirty-five miles an hour."

"That's too fast! Slow down! Slow down, Dan!"

The car slowed of its own momentum then; inevitably when letting out the clutch, Grandfather would stall the engine. By this time, however, there were self-starters on cars. It sometimes took a lot of grinding away on the starter, but they usually worked, given enough time and grinding. If not, one could still get the crank out of the tool kit and hand-crank the engine.

If Grandmother dreaded going *down* the Ozark Hill, going up it practically paralyzed her. Grandfather would get up as much speed as he could, trying to make the hill in high gear, but it was an impossibility. About two thirds of the way up, on the steepest, most winding part of the road, he always had to shift gears. And the same thing happened every time. He shifted gears so awkwardly that the engine always stalled. Half the time he would forget to put on the brake, much less pull up the emergency. Then the car would start slowly rolling back down the hill.

This was when Grandmother deserted him. She just opened the car door and out she got, dragged her grandchildren out behind her, and nothing would persuade her to get back into that car again until it reached the top of the hill. Grandfather would finally get the car started again, into low gear, and crawl on up. At the top he would stop to wait for the rest of us.

But *we* walked. However hot the day, however dusty the road, with Grandmother marching in the lead, puffing and panting like a small steam engine, the sweat running down her face in rivers, we trudged up that long winding hill. And then, and not until then, could we thankfully ride again.

"That hill," she said, every time, "is going to be the death of me yet."

"It will," Grandfather snapped at her, "if you don't quit walking up it. I always get the car into low gear in time, Kate."

"You always roll a long way back down the hill before you get it in gear, too," she said. "And someday you might not make it. Then you and this car will go off into the hollow!"

He never did. He always managed to start the engine and engage the gears, and at least as the car slowly rolled backward he never dangerously veered from the road. But one never knew. Like Grandmother, when he stalled the motor on the Ozark Hill, I wanted to get out and walk also.

Eventually Grandmother came to love riding in a car. She thoroughly enjoyed going all over the United States "to visit the children" in the car. But undoubtedly they were the most unique touring couple the United States ever saw until hippie buses came into style. Grandfather, very erect, at the wheel, with Grandmother in her favorite place, the right-hand corner of the back seat. She was *chauffeured* everywhere she went, but not by a paid chauffeur.

I have no idea how often they argued over this, or whether they ever did. Grandfather knew when he was licked, anyway. He had a way of saying, "When Kate sets her foot down, it's set, and only the Lord Himself could get her to unset it."

Kate had set her foot down about riding in the front seat. Grandfather may have known her reason, but certainly her grandchildren, at least this one, could only surmise.

16

PAPERDOLLS

*

WHEN DID WE BEGIN to play paperdolls with such obsession? And why was it such an obsession with us?

First — when? Corinne and I had to be seven and eight at least, perhaps eight and nine. We had to be old enough to be allowed the use of our mothers' sewing scissors, because we did use them, while Mary C. and Inez were still restricted to the small, blunt-nosed kind that were used in school and which, almost since babyhood, we had been allowed at home. As a result Corinne and I had to cut out almost all the paperdolls for the four of us.

"Cut mine for me, Janice, please," Mary C. would beg. "Please?"

I didn't mind because I had a finicky thing about any white showing around the edges of the figures and Mary C.'s club-footed and club-handed dolls irritated and frustrated me.

This was before the day of paperdoll books with dresses with shoulder tabs to change the dolls' clothing. We cut our paperdolls out of the mail order catalogs. Fortunately our parents got the same catalogs or I'm afraid fur would have flown. They both got the ubiquitous Sear, Roebuck catalog, and catalogs from two companies which must long since have gone out of business or merged with some other business, the National Cloak and Suit Company and Bellas, Hess Company.

Both Mrs. Moore and Mama made most of our clothes, but they ordered our winter coats, sometimes our shoes, their own suits and coats and certainly their hats, from these mail order catalogs. We were never allowed to have the new catalogs. Each spring and each fall a new catalog came from each company. But not until that new catalog arrived were we given the old ones. We had, however, long since picked out our paperdolls. It didn't matter to us at all that we sometimes duplicated the dolls.

This was also long before the day of colored or photographed illustrations. The clothing was on a full-length sketched figure. The women's faces were always the same, although some had light hair, meant to be blond, others had dark hair. One of the most crucial decisions we had to make in choosing our dolls was whether to have a yellow-haired mother or grown daughter this season or a dark-haired one. As far as the children were concerned, we could have both, just so we stuck to the same hair for each child. There were men, little boys, little girls, babies, and of course hundreds of women and men. Sometimes we added another adult to our family of paperdolls, say an aunt or cousin, so that we could have both light- and dark-haired women.

We cut out the entire figures and we had huge families, a husband and wife, a beau for a grown daughter, five or six children and always a baby. There were babies in carriages, in baths, and babies in cribs.

Our women had every variety of clothing imaginable — tailored suits and coats, with which they always wore hats; housedresses, tea gowns, evening gowns, negligees, night dresses, and our men had work clothing, business suits, overcoats (they, too, wore hats when suited or overcoated) nightshirts and pajamas, bathrobes and evening suits.

We had to be old enough also for Corinne and me, at least, to have some knowledge of geography, which did not begin for us in school until the fourth grade, for we knew about distant, romantic places. We sometimes squabbled over where our families should live, for naturally they must all live in the same city, and it had to be a city because only in cities were there theaters, the opera, big teas, receptions and social affairs. Our favorite city was New York. We thought it was the largest city in the world and I, at least, had seen stereopticon views of it and knew it had tall buildings and busy streets and many wealthy families. We sometimes settled for Chicago or St. Louis and, occasionally, even for Fort Smith or Little Rock. All of these cities had opera houses, then, and theaters, big restaurants, zoos, and many, many activities went on in them about which we knew only vaguely.

Naming our families was an agonizing affair, but in a delightful sort of way. It usually took days and much changing of minds, for once we had made up our minds and begun to call our people by their names, naturally we could not then change them, any more than one could change the name of a child in a real family.

I still go through this same kind of anguish naming characters in a book, and once they *are* named, do not try to change them, or if it is absolutely necessary, I do so with great reluctance for book characters are now my people as paperdolls once were.

And that, of course, is the answer to *why* playing paperdolls became such an obsession with us. It was the only activity in which we engaged in which we got totally out of ourselves. In every other game we played, no matter how much fun it was, no matter how boisterous or active or imaginative, we were still Janice and Corinne, Mary C. and Inez, playing at games.

But with paperdolls we got outside our own skins. We kept our paperdolls in shoe boxes and the moment we took those tops off the shoe boxes we walked straight through the looking-glass into Wonderland. We *created* people, who became very real to us. We were all-powerful with them. We could make them do and say what we pleased. They had nothing to do with us, ourselves. They caused us to use total imagination. We became, in other words, young novelists, or perhaps a better term is, we became playwrights, creating drama. Plots and counterplots were developed and played to their end. Our people were busy all day long, as characters in a book or on the stage must constantly be. Our grown daughters had beaux and love affairs which ended either in broken hearts or weddings, and if they ended in weddings we could add grand-children to the families. There was no end to the drama we could create, even though our people were the same people for a full season — until the next catalogs became available, and then we had the same agonizing, anguishing business of creating new families to go through with. Just as a novelist feels when he begins a new book, it was at once total happi-ness mixed with total indecision until the new familes were settled in their new roles.

We ran to odd, fanciful names. There were no Nancys or Sallys or Marys or Janes or Johns or Williams or Roberts for us. I remember naming a husband Lancelot one time, and his wife was named Elaine. I must have been reading *Idylls of the King* at the time and simply took a fancy to the two names. As a child, Tennyson was my favorite poet. I remem-ber giving a family the name of St. John, too. But it was an era of fancy names in novels, too, at least in what we would now call the "trashy" novels of Mrs. E.D.E.N. Southworth, Mary J. Holmes and Bertha M. Clay.

Strangely enough we never made doll furniture or houses for our families. It took an entire room for the four of us to play paperdolls because we simply blocked off rooms for our houses with box tops. Thus each of us had to have a corner of a room.

There was a constant hum of conversation as each of us individually took our people through their day, from rising in the morning to going to the opera or a play at night. We had all been to a few movies in Fort Smith, and we knew about the theater or opera only through those movies and from the magazines our families took which at least Corinne and I were old enough to read. We did know that women must wear full evening dress with long white gloves, and our men must wear white tie and tails. The shoe-box lids became limousines on nights when our people went to the theater or opera.

Each of the four of us played separately, but talked aloud as we made our families dress and undress and go through the activities of their day. From Mary C.'s corner would come, "Now, Clarence, you must take your nap. Mama has to make a new dress for Rosemary."

From Inez' corner would come, "Now, Suzanne, if you get into mischief again, Mama will have to punish you!"

From Corinne's corner came, "Cecile, *don't* wear that dress to school today! It's much too fancy for school."

And from my own corner, "Elaine, Papa doesn't approve of that young man. He *drinks!* You mustn't see him again."

Heartbroken weeping would follow, but nobody even looked up from the total engrossment with her own people. My

Elaine or Rebecca or Eulalie could boohoo all day and it was entirely her own affair (and mine). The other girls were having their own problems with their people.

Always, however, at some point in the various dramas we created, there would be a party, the theater, the opera, a Sunday drive in the chauffeur-driven limousines, in which all our people participated.

One of us, usually Corinne or I, would interrupt the intensity of our people's daily living and say, "P'like my lady is going to have a tea party this afternoon for her sister. You must all come."

We all went.

Or I would say, "P'like we're going to the opera tonight!"

We all went to the opera. We dearly loved these events which we had personally never experienced, because we could dress our people to the gills and make stilted, unrealistic conversation between them all.

Sometimes we had our people do such mundane things as we knew about from personal experience. Somebody would suggest a revival was going on. All our people must certainly go. We chose the appropriate clothing, got them to the church, ranged them in rows and sang the dolorous hymns of the day. Occasionally a teen-age girl or boy would be baptized. Corinne usually suggested this. She was fascinated with baptism and since we were prohibited from real baptizing, baptizing paperdolls had to make do. We did not really baptize our people, naturally. Dunking a paperdoll in real water would have ruined it. We used a matchbox for a baptistry, or we marked out a creek with paper strips and a man paperdoll (not one of our own men) would be the preacher.

The mothers of our families went shopping and bought

new clothing for themselves and their children. This was when we would thumb back through the mutilated catalogs for some attractive figure we had missed. They kept their homes, they cooked and washed dishes, they bathed their children and dressed them frequently, the children went to school, to Sunday School and to church.

Once in a great, great while a member of a family was ill. Sometimes we had a death. We could never bear for this to happen to the actual members of our family, so it was usually a visiting relative or the child of a visiting relative. By this time we had all been to enough funerals that we could go through the entire procedure letter perfect. And our mourning was so real that often we actually wept ourselves. We did not particularly enjoy funerals, however, so they rarely occurred. They occurred all too often in real life and were much too sad.

Inez and Corinne were allowed to have cats and Inez remembers a cat funeral we had when one of them died, at which she wept inconsolably. I probably felt no great grief, for I do not remember that event at all.

Inez and Mary C.'s families did things together more often than not, while mine and Corinne's were thrown together more frequently. They went fishing, they went on picnics, they went for long rides in their automobiles. All our families were rich, naturally, and sometimes they even had maids, for maids' uniforms were included in some of the catalogs. Our people became so real to us that we could hardly bear it when told finally we must put them away for the day.

The little brothers and the Oklahoma wind were the natural enemies of our paperdolls. The little boys weren't included in the game and when they grew bored, or lonely, they would invade the room in which we had all our people set out and frequently scattered them and mixed them up, deliberately or because they let in the wind. We were reduced to tears as we painfully sorted them all out again, and at such times we thought little brothers the biggest nuisances in the world.

The wind, which seemed to blow constantly, could also play havoc with our sets. Therefore we closed all the windows and doors, even on the hottest days. In much sweat, but absolutely no discomfort, we were safe from the wind. Occasionally Mrs. Moore or Mama would worry about our being closed up so tightly all day and would break up the game (no game to us — total reality) and tell us, "Put up your paperdolls now and go outside and play."

We hated such interruptions, and as now with me when the people in my books are so real to me it sometimes takes me an hour or so to get back inside my own skin, so real were our paperdoll people that we were a little dazed at coming out of that world and could frequently think of nothing we wanted to play outside. But there was never any argument about it. Both mothers, or either, had to be obeyed.

The best place to play paperdolls was the "side-room" in the Moore house. It was off to itself, it had only one entering door from the rest of the house and no outside door. It had only two windows. Since it was what was called a lean-to room, the roof was rather low and, closed airtight as we required it to be, it must have been like playing in an oven after an hour or two. I must ask you to believe that we never noticed the heat at all, such was our absorption.

When we played at our house we had to use the sitting room, and we rarely got to play as long as we wanted to because Mama objected to having the air shut out of the adjoining rooms. Besides, each room in our house had an outside door and at least one inner door and windows in each

wall. Sometimes, when Mama made us open the doors we
would move our sets behind the doors to keep the wind from
blowing the dolls, and behind a door on a hot day could be
almost as torrid as the Moores' side-room.

We rarely played with real dolls after we discovered the
joys of paperdolls. We never had many real dolls to begin
with and they were always little girls or babies and we had to
be real mothers. Our sense of drama was too heightened for
such childish nonsense. We did not enjoy having to be
mothers and playing house and actually having tea parties,
washing up dishes, cooking, bathing and dressing real dolls.
With Mary C. and me, at least, we had entirely too much of
that sort of thing in real life. It was no fun "p'liking" any
more of it.

Occasionally Corinne would balk at one of my suggestions.
She wasn't in any mood to have her family go on a picnic.
She wanted, perhaps, instead to have them go to a party. Or
I would balk at one of her ideas. But rarely did we quarrel
over such things. To quarrel when playing paperdolls would
have meant gathering them all up and going home. We so
enjoyed this game that this was unthinkable, so we usually
came to some sort of compromise. I'm afraid Corinne and I
did not often consult the wishes of Inez and Mary C., and
I don't really know why, but they usually went along with
whatever we suggested. It may have been, to our shame, that
both Corinne and I were pretty bossy older sisters and the
little sisters were simply used to it.

One of the great beauties of paperdolls was that it was a
year-round game. It was perfect on a rainy Saturday during
the school term, or on a cold, windy Saturday, and as we
grew older it became so much our favorite p'like game that

outdoor games slowly took second place and we had to be forced to put the doll people up and go outside.

I suppose I was becoming a writer even that early, for it was never any trouble for me to think of the next exciting thing that should happen to our paperdoll families.

*

As John and H.M. grew older they tagged after us girls less and less. They had their own boys' activities, with their wagons, their tricycles and H.M.'s Irish Mail cart. This was a low-built wagon which propelled itself by pulling the handle back and forth. John never had one and I think he never ceased envying H.M.'s. H.M. was pretty generous with his, however, and the cart would hold two.

The envied position with two in it was the front position, where the guiding and propelling were done. Why, with two husky little boys in the cart, either should ever have wanted the hard work of propelling the thing I can't imagine. I suppose it was a little like being the engineer of our play trains. You were the boss.

It must be an instinct in every human being to want to be the boss of something or somebody. It is the instinct for power, I suppose. I know I was a bossy and dogmatic big sister to Mary C. and John. I was the biggest and I could enforce my will by sheer physical strength if necessary.

Mary C. had her own way of getting what she wanted from me or forcing me to do her will. It was a sort of blackmail. "I'll tell Mama! I'll tell Mama!"

If I had done something I was afraid I would be punished for, this was always effective. However, it didn't always work. Mama didn't have too much patience with tattletales and it had to be something really dangerous or wrong for me to get punished. Even so, Mary C., to her surprise was often punished equally as much for telling. "Don't be a tattletale," Mama would say, as she grabbed up Mary C. and switched her legs, too.

We never had roller skates or bicycles in Kinta. What few sidewalks there were, were too rough for skating on. Purposely they had been rolled while the cement was wet with a roller with shallow spikes in it. These spikes made small, regular pits in the walks. They were thus considered safer for walking in snowy, icy weather. And perhaps they were. But they wouldn't do for roller skating.

The Moore children may have had bicycles after we left Kinta, perhaps when they moved to Stigler, but we had none in Kinta. Nobody had bicycles in Kinta. They were not considered toys and as a means of locomotion, in cow country where everybody had horses, if one had to go any distance at all naturally one rode a horse or drove a team.

*

The earth must have been going through a fairly warm cycle during the years of our childhood. I don't remember many snows in the winters. When, on the rare occasions it did snow, our greatest joy was snow ice cream. Both Mrs. Moore and Mama made delicious snow ice cream. I suppose every child in America, even today, knows what it is. Clean snow was dished up, sugar, cream and vanilla were added to make it the consistency of ice cream, then we ate it by huge bowlsful. We never tired of it and as long as we could find a clean patch of snow, we kept bringing in the big bowls of it for more.

We were allowed to play hide-and-seek in the house in the winter, in both homes, in certain restricted rooms. We could not hide in the parlor at the Moores', and Mama would not have us underfoot in the kitchen in our home.

The biggest problem with hide-and-seek in both the houses and outside in the summer was that when the little brothers were still very small they had to be hidden before we could hide ourselves. Once, on a cold winter day, I had a very bad fright.

Our piano sat cater-cornered in the sitting room. Desperate for a place to hide John quickly, I was just able to slide him, by much pushing and shoving, behind the piano. But then we couldn't get him out! It was one thing to push him through that narrow opening, it was something different to pull him out. It scared all of us half out of our wits, especially since Mama was out somewhere, probably over at Mrs. Moore's.

Finally I had the sense to crawl up over the piano. There were lifting bars across the back of the piano and by hoisting him up onto them, I could barely shove him high enough for Corinne to get hold of his hands and pull while I shoved harder. We skinned him up considerably, but we finally got him safely back onto the right side of the piano. He was howling bloody murder all the time, of course, and both he and Mary C. were threatening, "I'll tell Mama!"

She had to be told because we had skinned John's nose and one of his arms — not badly, but enough to bleed. Fortunately Mama was in a good humor when she came in, a little later, and there was no punishment. Instead she laughed about the whole affair, since no harm had come of it.

She solaced John by putting a bandage on his arm. He was fascinated by bandages, as some children are by Band-Aids today, and the slightest hurt had to be bandaged immediately and he would insist on wearing the bandage until it was so dirty Mama would make him take it off. Since he was so accident prone there was usually a bandage on a leg or arm, finger or toe.

We all went barefoot all summer long. We wore shoes only to Sunday School and church, and to parties. Somebody always had a stumped toe, or a stone-bruise on a heel, or a cut on the foot, or a splinter, and we all had briar scratches on our legs.

Occasionally we were stung by the big red ants which had a giant hill in the corner of our yard. The ants fascinated us and in spite of warnings we *would* creep up close enough to watch the huge things as they worked endlessly day after day, building their hill higher and higher until sometimes it would reach a height of three feet or more.

Occasionally, when the hill got too high, Dad would burn them out by pouring kerosene down the hole and setting it afire. He did not like to do this, and the ants did no harm to anybody as long as they were let alone. But Mama was afraid of them and when the hill got too high she would begin nagging at Dad to burn the ants out. I think she was afraid they might finally get bold enough to invade the house.

I don't remember ever seeing a snake in Kinta, nor do I recall ever being warned against them, even when we played on the prairie. Undoubtedly there were rattlesnakes in the mountains, but we were too far from the mountains for them to migrate to our town. Farther west, on the plains prairies they nested as thick as gophers and prairie dogs, but we were not that far west.

I do remember being warned against water moccasins in the sluggish little creeks around Charleston, but then we were rarely allowed to fish or wade in those creeks without an adult along.

And I remember watching Grandmother McGraw chop a

small snake to pieces with a garden hoe once at Altus. It was probably only a small green snake, what was called a garden snake, but she had such a horror of all snakes she chopped it into a dozen little pieces. Each time the hoe came down she went "*Eeeeek!*" But then Altus was in the foothills of the Ozarks and there were apt to be more snakes than in our prairie town. I am sure, also, she had seen and perhaps worried about them, in the log cabin homestead up in the mountains, and these would have been the poisonous rattlesnakes. So her horror of all snakes was probably well founded.

There were, however, scorpions in Kinta, and I think I remember a few centipedes. None of us children was ever stung by a scorpion, but if we lifted a piece of planking or big rock which had been lying in one place a long time on the ground a nest of scorpions could nearly always be found. We smashed them with other pieces of lumber or big heavy clods of dirt or stones.

An indication of Mama's kind of housekeeping is that she was stung by a scorpion one night as she was going to bed. He was in a curl of dust just under the edge of the bed and her big toe brushed against the dust curl. The entire household was upset for an hour or more, because a scorpion sting was certainly the most painful sting one could ever be called on to bear. I think it must have been slightly poisonous, too, because Mama's toe swelled to twice its normal size and it was several days before she could wear a shoe.

She swept under the beds more faithfully for a month or so, then scorpions in the house were forgotten again and dust curls were just dust curls, something unavoidable if one preferred reading to sweeping.

Except for paperdolls and the inevitable other indoor activities on rainy or extremely cold winter days, we were outdoor children, and there were never six more strenuous ones (my daughter's three sons were more strenuous than all six of us put together, but that was still a long way in the future). We p'liked so hard at everything we did that bedtime was always welcome. We would be worn out.

However, one of my dearest memories of Kinta is of the long summer twilights. Kinta was almost in the exact center of the central time zone and in the summer dark did not come until about eight o'clock (and this before daylight saving time had ever been heard of). After supper, which was always early, the children for several blocks around us would gather at our corner and we would play until called in at dark by our parents.

I think Shiloh was our favorite late evening game. There would be enough children to form two groups of five or six and at that time of day the streets were empty of traffic (not that there was ever enough to endanger a child) and we roamed a block in each direction for good hiding places.

Even the older boys and girls joined in our twilight games. Sometimes we played baseball, or Run, Sheep, Run, or just plain old hide-and-seek. The heat of the day would be over, the last lingering rays of the gorgeous prairie sunset would be gone, it was still light enough to see, but dusky enough to give one a sort of shivery, mysterious feeling, a little fearful, but exciting because of that. Then, as the dark grew there would come the calls from the various mothers and lingeringly, a little sadly, we would part and go home.

There was the inevitable washing up so as to be clean for bed, the putting on of light cotton nightgowns, then the good-night hug and kiss for each child. As we hugged each parent we had a ritual saying, "I love you a bushel and a peck and a hug around the neck!" The hug around the neck was so tight it's a wonder we didn't choke our parents to death. But they never complained.

Then to bed and to our nightly concert when Mama played the piano and Dad played the violin so long as a single child was awake. The music would begin with whatever they thought of, but as we grew sleepy it softened into dream music. I think no children ever had happier bedtimes than we did. There was never that fear of the dark, nor that long silence until one went to sleep. We went to sleep with a light streaming from the next room and the lovely sound of music lulling us, like a mother singing and rocking her baby to sleep, into the deep unconsciousness of the night.

The next thing we knew it would be morning and Dad would be rousing us. He used an old slave saying, from Mississippi: "Wake up, Jacob, day's a-breakin', peas' in the pot and the hoe cakes a-bakin'!"

Then, solemnly, he would say good morning in the Choctaw way. The Choctaw greeting, at any time of the day, was *chukma*. It was, however, pronounced *chickama*, with the accent on the first syllable. It meant not only good morning, but was a general greeting which meant literally good health and good fortune to you, but which was used as we use "hello" today.

We began and ended our days beautifully, with good cheer and a blessing in the morning, and love and music at night. No children were ever more fortunate than we.

17

A BIG GIRL NOW

✳

THE BOTTOM dropped out of my world when I was ten years old. And yet the year began as normally as any other.

John was five years old on January 11. Mama always made a big thing of our birthdays. We did not have birthday parties, but within the family each child's birthday was very specially his day.

There was always a cake, with candles. The candles were lit and we sang "Happy Birthday," then the candles had to be blown out. All in one breath or one's special birthday wish would not come true. I think, when we were very small, Dad always cheated a little and surreptitiously added his breath to ours, although we never saw him do it or suspected that he did it.

But it could not have been borne to have one's birthday wish fail to come true! They were always selfish wishes, I'm sure — a wish for a special present, or for some special event or happiness. At any rate, every candle was *always* blown out. Then the gifts were opened and there was always that special gift that we had not been at all silent about wanting.

These birthday events always occurred as soon as the entire family was awake and up in the morning. With John's birthday and mine, it would be dark and the candles would glow in the early morning darkness. It would be daylight on Mary C.'s birthday, in July, but neither she nor any of the rest of us minded that. The birthday cake was always the special dessert for a day or two.

John had become accustomed to being told, so often, that he could not do something "because he was too little" that he had grown very persistent about knowing when he would be big enough to do certain things. I think it was Mama who first told him that when he was five he would be a big boy and he could then begin to do those special things he so badly wanted to do — such as being sent to town on errands alone, or shooting off his own Roman candle at Christmas without Dad holding his hand, or riding the horse without Dad leading him, or being allowed to hammer and saw and make things without somebody supervising him.

At any rate he looked forward intensely to his fifth birthday because then he would be a "big boy." He awakened early on that morning, too excited to sleep longer, and the first thing he did was to run to the long beveled mirror in the sitting room to look at himself. He began to cry — squawl is a better word for it because it was so loud it wakened us all and brought us running.

The entire family gathered around him, alarmed. "What's the matter, Son?" Dad kept asking, as Mama gathered him into her arms. "Have you hurt yourself? Why, today is your birthday! You should be a happy boy today!"

"But I'm not a bit bigger!" John sobbed. "I'm just exactly the same size I was yesterday. I thought I would be a lot taller and fatter!"

It took a long time to convince him that one could be bigger mentally, more mature, have better judgment without being bigger in size.

The school year moved along and I was doing well in the fifth grade under Miss Ada. I had also begun to grow taller and wasn't so short and tubby as formerly. And because we were a family of talkers, and I was accustomed to being allowed to have my say, I had learned to hold my own with older and larger girls who tried to harass me.

It may have been because Mama grew up in a big family who were all good conversationalists that within our own family we were encouraged to have our say — on any subject that came up. I can remember sitting around the supper table, when we were a little older, talking and arguing for an hour or two before we did the dishes. But we soon learned, even as children, that if we argued a point we had better be able to prove it, for both Mama and Dad were merciless on this point. "How do you know?" was frequently asked.

It wasn't enough to say, "Miss Ada said so," or anybody else said so. We had to be able to go to a history, geography, dictionary or the encyclopedia and prove the point. Of course sometimes a point could be proved by logic. This, too, was recognized.

It made great arguers out of all three of us, it may even have made us rather belligerent in argument, but our parents thought it was good for us to think for ourselves and they encouraged these long supper conversations and arguments, taking part themselves as much as we did.

This was not just chitchat, it wasn't just talk for the sake of talking — this was conversation, the subject matter was interesting to all of us, the arguments were often heated. It was truly part of our education and I agree with my parents that it was good for us and that it stimulated our thinking. If the argumentation grew too heated, if somebody showed signs of temper (and that happened, too), we were made to be quiet until we cooled off. Arguments were fine — quarrels were not.

My birthday was in March and by the time I was ten the most welcome gift was always a book. I think perhaps Mary C. and John gave me small material things, such as new hair ribbons, some small trinket or such, but the gift from my parents was my *own* copy of *Rebecca of Sunnybrook Farm*. I devoured it in two days, but it was reread so often it became soiled and dog-eared. I also had *Little Women* and *Little Men* at about this same time. Perhaps on this same birthday, from grandparents.

I don't know what became of all my childhood books. When the Five Civilized Tribes Museum in Muskogee, Oklahoma, asked me some years back for some personal memento for their files, I found two books in an old chest which has long been set aside for personal things of mine, my daughter's and my husband's — things going back to childhood and even babyhood. I could find only two books which had been mine as a child, *The Sunbonnet Babes* (with which I would not part for anything because it was my first book) and *Black Beauty*. I sent the museum the copy of *Black Beauty* which had been a Christmas gift from my father in 1916.

Incidentally, I am not included in those honored by the Five Civilized Tribes Museum because I grew up in Oklahoma and the state has some small claim on me as an Oklahoma author. I am included because I am a part-blood Indian, as must be all those honored by this museum. Only those writers, artists, craftsmen who are at least part-blood Indian of the Five Civilized Tribes, Cherokee, Choctaw, Chickasaw, Creek and Seminole, are honored by having their works in the museum. For such a museum, this is the way it should be, and whether my part-blood is Cherokee or Choctaw, I feel it a great honor for my books to be on sale in their gift shop along with the wood sculptures of the great Cherokee sculptor, Willard Stone, the paintings of Jerome Tiger and the artistry of other great part-blood Indians of those tribes.

*

Easter must have come late that year. A traveling photographer was drumming up business in Kinta around that time or shortly after, and Mama had the last childhood photograph of the three of us made by him. We are all wearing our Easter clothes. Mama had made them herself and her good taste in dressing her children is evident in the clothing.

Easter was almost as exciting to us as Christmas. By now, Mary C. and I knew there was no Easter bunny who laid colored eggs in tin cans, under weed piles, in crevices of lumber stacks and other odd and strange places for us to find, but John did not. Nor would Mary C. and I have enlightened and disillusioned him for the world. It was such fun for us to know and for him not to know. He would talk for hours about where he was going to look Easter morning for eggs. I had no mercy on Mary C. I thought she was old enough to find her own eggs, but many times I passed up an egg and hinted to John where it was, or even led him near enough for him to spy it out for himself. After all, he *was* the baby.

Mama must have stayed up and dyed three dozen eggs every Easter eve, until even John was too old to enjoy the hunts anymore. The eggs were exquisitely and perfectly dyed — no splotches or blots and they were every color — pink, red, yellow, orange, blue, green, purple. I always was partial to the purple eggs. They looked so royal somehow. I was even more partial to the one duck or goose egg which was dyed a gorgeous gold. To find that particular egg was really a feather in one's cap and not even for John would I give that one up if I spied

it. And it was always hidden in the hardest place. I truly believe, however, that it was found about equally among us. If
I found it one year, Mama or Dad would see to it that Mary
C. or John, somehow, found it the next year. I do not recall
that any one of us ever found it two years straight.

New Easter clothing continued until we were well up in our
teens, however. Everything we wore to Sunday School and
church on that morning was new — hats, dresses, socks or
stockings, shoes, and we two girls carried new handbags. Why
this was a necessity in American life for so many years I do
not understand, but it was, and Mama would not have broken
with it for anything. Particularly if it meant hurting her children.

John's Easter suit that year our last childhood picture was
made was white and red. The little white shirt had red trim-
ming on it and the pants were striped red and white. After
Easter it continued to be his "new" suit and his best suit,
worn only on special occasions.

We must have gone somewhere one night — to church
probably — and been late enough getting home that John was
sound asleep. Mama didn't wake him to undress him. She
just put him to bed in his clothes. The next morning he came
into the kitchen, rubbing his eyes open and laughing. "I *knew*
I slept in my new suit last night," he said, "I could feel the
stripes in my pants!"

Occasionally one of the churches had a huge Easter egg hunt
for all the children of the community. One that we participated in was held on the Watkins property, west of town, on
a woodsy hillside. There were limits roped off, for the hiding
places of the eggs, hundreds of them, and we were warned well
ahead that no eggs were hidden beyond those limits.

All the children lined up and when the whistle blew the

dozens of us participating scattered in all directions. There were so many good places to hide the eggs in the woods — under stones, or in their crevices, under piles of leaves, in the shrubs and bushes, among the tree roots, that sometimes not all the eggs were ever found. But no child ever left one of those community Easter egg affairs without a good share of the lovely dyed eggs.

I don't recall that we participated in but one of these hunts. Just as at Christmas none of our gifts were ever put on the community tree, usually put up in the Methodist Church, Mama and Dad felt that our own Easter egg hunt at home was all the Easter egg hunt we needed.

The one year we were allowed to participate, the Christian Church must have sponsored the community hunt. I do most certainly remember that while I found plenty of eggs I did *not* find the golden goose egg. Like our parents, we felt our own egg hunt was best and we were never disappointed when we didn't go to this big community affair. I'm sure we knew that it was held largely for the benefit of those children whose parents paid no attention to Easter and held no Easter egg hunts for their children at home.

*

When school ended that year those of us in Miss Ada's room had a party, of sorts, for her. Each child brought something, an apple, an orange, a little box of cookies, some home-made candy or bought candy, whatever he pleased or whatever his mother sent, and while Miss Ada was out on the school ground during the afternoon recess we piled all these small gifts on her desk. No names or cards were attached. They were not gift-wrapped. They were just piled as high as possible all over the top of her desk.

Miss Ada reacted precisely as we had hoped she would. Undoubtedly she knew something of the sort was happening. We were all much too excited all afternoon, but she acted surprised and her gratitude was so sweetly expressed that we all but burst with love and happiness. She was most dearly loved by all of us.

It was in August that the blow fell.

I had noticed an unusual collection of barrels and wooden crates accumulating on the back porch. "Why are all those boxes and barrels out there?" I asked Mama one day.

"We are going to move," she said.

"Move to another house?" I asked, my heart sinking at the very thought of not living next door to Corinne and Inez.

"No, we are moving to another town. We are moving away from Kinta."

"Moving away! Leaving Kinta? But we can't *do* that!" I wailed. "We can't leave Kinta. This is where we live!"

"It isn't where we're going to live but one more week," Mama said, "then we are moving to Cowlington and we will be living there."

"Cowlington?" I had never heard of such a place. Quinton, yes, or Bokoshe or Spiro. Those were familiar names. But Cowlington? "Is it very far away?"

"Not really, as miles go. About thirty or forty miles from here."

"But that's too far! We can't play with Corinne and Inez anymore." I was so heartsick I was nauseated.

Mama was so busy that she had no idea how deep my feelings went. She didn't stop what she was doing to comfort me. "No," she said, "you'll make new friends there to play with. Friends you'll think just as much of."

I knew better than that, but I didn't say so. There was no

going against one's parents. "Why must we move?" I asked. "Why do we have to go to this new town?"

"Because the school pays well," Mama said. "Dad's salary there will be one hundred and twenty-five dollars a month and I will also teach and my salary will be fifty dollars a month. We can't turn such a good opportunity down."

I had sense enough to know that this was riches compared to what the two of them had been earning at Edmonds Chapel, but it didn't begin to console me for leaving the Moores.

"What kind of a town is it?" I asked. "Does the railroad go there? Is it bigger than Kinta?"

"No," she said, "it's a farm and ranch town. The nearest the railroad comes is Bokoshe. We'll have to drive to Bokoshe to catch the train and do most of our shopping. It is a smaller town than Kinta. But Dad must go where his opportunities are best and there are no longer any opportunities for him here. You're a big girl, now, you must know that."

I did not know, then, that Mama had been nagging at Dad for at least two years to leave Kinta. She wanted him to get into the Fort Smith public school system and she knew it could never be accomplished as long as he was teaching in a little two-teacher country school. She truly felt that we children would have a better education in the city school system. At least there would be a full four years of high school for us when we finished the elementary schools.

No matter how badly Dad might have preferred to continue to teach in small towns, and I am sure he would much have preferred it — he felt far more at home in them and he loathed the city — when Lucy MacGraw Holt set her head and began to shove him from behind, to nag at him and scold, she usually got what she wanted from him. He was too gentle to keep his will set against hers for very long. And even he could see that the Edmonds Chapel school had no future in it for him or for her.

I understood this only dimly. Looking backward through the years, I know she was right about moving to the city where our high school education was concerned, but she was wrong about what it did to our family life. I am not at all sure that the four years of high school education was worth breaking up that close unity of the family. I suppose when we reached our teens it would have broken up to some extent anyway. But surely it would not have been done as badly as it was done in the city where we all went to different schools and after the first two years Mama and Dad did not even teach in the same school. We seemed to scatter in every direction, with different interests, and none of us was too much concerned with any but his own special interests. Small towns are beautiful places for families and Kinta did eventually have a four-year high school.

But evidently that was so far in the future Mama could not foresee it. So we had to move. In this game of chess she was playing with Dad, the next move would be from Cowlington to Fort Smith, and that's the way it turned out.

"Is Cowlington in Haskell County?" I wanted to know. Besides being loyal to the Moores, to Kinta, I was loyal to Haskell County.

"No," Mama said, "it's in Leflore County. Dad will have his old county superintendent again. The one he had in Howe. He's happy about that."

Well — that was something. Somebody in the family was happy, but it certainly wasn't Janice.

"When are we going to move?" I asked.

"Next week."

The Moore children had been told about the same time we had been told, presumably, and that last week we couldn't even play together happily for knowing it was the last week. It was more like one long funeral than anything else, with first the Moores, then the little Holts weeping over the move.

The packing proceeded at Mama's rapid and efficient rate until finally everything was ready and we were just camping out. Finally, "We'll start early in the morning," Mama said.

Of course the move was made by wagons. I think it took three to haul our household effects, since we now had a piano. Dad must have hired them.

We said goodbye to the Moore children that night, but my heart was so broken that as we started to get into the wagons the next morning, I said, "Can I go tell them goodbye one more time?"

"All right," Mama said, sensing, perhaps for the first time, what the move meant to me, the eldest child, whose total remembered life had been centered here. "But hurry. Don't stay long."

I went flying across the street to hug and kiss Corinne and Inez one more time — to hug and kiss Mrs. Moore one more time. It was Corinne I specially wanted to see once more. By age, sex, positions in the families we had been best friends, Inez and Mary C. had paired off naturally and the two little boys had been most together. But Corinne had been very special to me.

She was stoical and I'm not sure she cried, but I did. I wept inconsolably. I knew, in my heart, that there would never again be anybody who meant as much to me as a friend, with whom I would share so much, who would know so instinctively from such long association what I was thinking, feeling and knowing, for she had thought and felt and known with me for so long. I knew I would never find anybody else who knew just how to play as we did; sometimes without even having to say words, the same idea would come to us. And I knew I would never love another friend as much again.

And I never did — not in my childhood, for Mama was right. I was a big girl now and in a very real sense I left my childhood behind me with those precious Kinta years.